An ALMOST ATHEIST WALKS *with* CHRIST

Hope you enjoy reading.

Roy
17 June 2023

JAMES ROY

All the best for your future.

Wasteland Press
www.wastelandpress.net
Shelbyville, KY USA

An Almost Atheist Walks with Christ
by James Roy

Copyright © 2017 James Roy
ALL RIGHTS RESERVED

First Printing – March 2017
ISBN: 978-1-68111-165-0

Scripture quotations taken from the HOLY BIBLE,
NEW INTERNATIONAL VERSION®, NIV®.
Copyright © 1973, 1978, 1984, 2011 by Biblica, Inc.®
Used by the permission. All rights reserved worldwide.

NO PART OF THIS BOOK MAY BE REPRODUCED IN ANY
FORM, BY PHOTOCOPYING OR BY ANY ELECTRONIC OR
MECHANICAL MEANS, INCLUDING INFORMATION
STORAGE OR RETRIEVAL SYSTEMS, WITHOUT PERMISSION
IN WRITING FROM THE COPYRIGHT OWNER/AUTHOR

Printed in the U.S.A.

0 1 2 3 4 5 6 7

ACKNOWLEDGEMENTS

This book would not have been possible without the directions of Lord through the Holy Spirit. I owe it to the Lord for giving me a second chance in life and in being there for me in this entire journey of writing the book.

This book is dedicated to my family, my late father Shri Kamal Vinod Roy; my mother Shrimati Maya Roy; my sisters Madhu and Mamta di and my younger brother Khrist. They have been a great strength and have uplifted me in my life. I cherish them and love them. God bless them. I am blessed to be born in this family. My wife Tripta, sons Fazal and Rahul for being patient with me while I was writing this book. They did a lot of work at home so that the book could be written. I am blessed to be a part of their life. God bless them and protect them. I am blessed to be married in Tripta's family. Blessings of Dillu uncle and Sannu aunty have always been there for us.

My special thanks to Pastor Mahender Chawla who has been with us in our walk with the Lord. Pastor Bob Greene who guided me to learn from the Holy Spirit and Vic who made me stronger in the Word of the Lord and has guided me a lot in worldly matters too. During the time of my small scale persecution and in good times, Gerry was always there motivating me to be serious towards our Lord's calling, I am grateful to him too.

I am grateful to many people who helped me in editing this book right from the beginning stage. My mother being the foremost one who edited during her holidays, Madhu di, Mamta di, Khrist, Tripta, Anita Threlfall, Kenny Jones, and my colleague Chuck Simms. Merwyn Pereira for creating the website and Fazal for my twitter account, Facebook link and initiating the setting up of the YouTube channel. Thanks to Rahul for helping me to finish the setting up of YouTube channel. I am grateful to my publisher who went out of his way to help me publish this book. God bless him, his near and dear ones, business and use him to glorify the Lord.

My special thanks to those who contributed financially to help this book publish.

PREFACE

I believe the Lord wanted me to write this book. I do not have a definite answer as to why He wanted me to do so. There could be varied reasons in different permutations and combinations or it could be only of the few that I have written.

Perhaps our Lord thought I might become like the Israelites, who forgot their blessings during the Exodus as recorded in the Bible and run away from God's calling in my life. Therefore, the Lord drew me to this humble work so that while writing this book, I would recall His goodness and remember His countless blessings and not forget them.

Probably the Lord wanted me to provide documentary evidence for my children and for my children's children that they may read and know how good our Heavenly Father has been to us. How He blessed us, so that they may never forget His benevolence and mercies.

It is quite possible He wanted to remind me even when everything was not going the way I wanted, that the Lord led me and my family to green pastures and running waters. My ever-wavering faith has been uplifted again.

It might even be possible that the Lord wanted me to stand in support of the people who have just come to the Lord, and are not strong in the Scripture, or are illiterate though strong in faith and deeds.

All these are mere possibilities.

What I do know with certainty is that the Lord prompted me to write this book, not just once, but multiple times. On 1st April, 2009; 24th April, 2009; and then again on 28th November, 2011, when He gently whispered in my ears: *This is what the LORD, the God of Israel, says: 'Write in a book all the words I have spoken to you.'* (Jeremiah 30:2)

I interpreted this as a directive to write as a witness to the works the Lord has performed in my life, and to reveal how God used me as an instrument for His glory, and I am happy about it. These true instances of God working in my life cover a period of around six years in this book, though the book itself begins with information from my childhood. This does not mean that the Lord stopped working in my life after six years of my submitting to Him; it just means that there were so many instances that I had to force myself to a cut-off timeline, otherwise the book would never end.

I know God has His plans for this book, and they will be perfect. English is my second language. But who am I to tell that to my Lord? He knows it. To me right now, it is enough to know that my Lord wants my obedience, and that is what I have attempted. My work is to do my best and leave the rest to Him. The incidences written in the book are of small magnitude and intensity, but my walk has been directed by Him.

My prayer is that this book will be read by people with an open mind. My intent is not to convince anybody of anything. I strongly believe that it is the Spirit of the Lord who transforms a person. Neither the greatest orator nor human intelligence can bring anybody to the Lord, but the Holy Spirit.

THE NAMES OF THE HOLY SPIRIT USED IN THE BOOK

The Holy Spirit Luke 11:13
The Spirit John 3:6
The Spirit of The Lord Isaiah 11:2
The Spirit of Truth John 16:13
The Spirit of The Sovereign Lord Isaiah 61:1
The Spirit of Holiness Romans 1:4
The Spirit of the Living God 2 Corinthians 3:3
The Spirit of Christ Romans 8:9
The Spirit of His Son Galatians 4:6
The Spirit of Jesus Christ Philippians 1:19
The Spirit of Grace Hebrews 10:29
The Eternal Spirit Hebrews 9:14
The Spirit of Glory 1 Peter 4:14
The Spirit of Wisdom and of Understanding Isaiah 11:2
The Spirit of Counsel and of Might Isaiah 11:2
The Spirit of the Knowledge Isaiah 11:2
The Advocate John 14:26

Kindly Note:
- Since I have tried to go back in time and write, I might be slightly off in time line and details.
- Names of characters with $^{\alpha}$ as a superscript means the names have been changed due to privacy reasons or because I was not able to contact them.
- Words with an asterisk suggest consult the glossary.

TABLE OF CONTENTS

PREFACE v
THE NAMES OF THE HOLY SPIRIT USED IN THE BOOK vii
CHAPTER ONE: *Polytheism and Multicultural Society* 1
CHAPTER TWO: *Galloping Towards Becoming "An Almost Atheist"* 11
CHAPTER THREE: *Detestable Practices Versus God's Grace* 25
CHAPTER FOUR: *Meandering* 32
CHAPTER FIVE: *The Lord Makes His Move* 42
CHAPTER SIX: *Rendezvous with Lord's Servants* 54
CHAPTER SEVEN: *A Glimpse in the Spiritual Realm* 76
CHAPTER EIGHT: *Jehovah Elohay – The Lord my God* 83
CHAPTER NINE: *Doubts, Directions and Some Clarity* 95
CHAPTER TEN: *Jehovah Jireh – The Provider* 100
CHAPTER ELEVEN: *Jehovah Rapha – The Healer* 113
CHAPTER TWELVE: *Our Lord is Omnipresent* 134
CHAPTER THIRTEEN: *He Loves, He Cares* 138
CHAPTER FOURTEEN: *Jehovah Shammah – The Lord is Present* 142
CHAPTER FIFTEEN: *My Lord, My Guide* 146
CHAPTER SIXTEEN: *The Lord My Protector* 157
CHAPTER SEVENTEEN: *Our Home Group* 174
CHAPTER EIGHTEEN: *Testimonies of Blessings and Israel Trip* 181
CHAPTER NINETEEN: *Community Involvement* 197
CHAPTER TWENTY: *Obedience is What The Lord Desires* 202
CHAPTER TWENTY-ONE: *In God's Rest* 215
GLOSSARY 225
FOR THE ALBUM 231
SOME IMPORTANT EMAILS 241

Isaiah 41:20

So that people may [read] see and know, may consider and understand, that the hand of the LORD has done this…

CHAPTER ONE:
Polytheism and Multicultural Society

⁂

The LORD is my shepherd, I lack nothing.
Psalm 23:1

How wonderful to have been born in the city of the romantic Taj Mahal–Agra, in India. Yes, I am a romantic being. The Taj Mahal, built by the Mughal Emperor Shah Jahan, in the sweet memory of his beloved queen Mumtaz Mahal, is considered a great achievement in Mughal architecture. It is rightly one of the seven wonders of the world situated on the plains of river Yamuna at an approximate elevation of 171 meters above sea level and 262 kilometres southeast of Delhi. If my life is compared to a river then romance was its first tributary.

While this romantic saga is engraved in the history of Agra, it was often absent in one local dwelling: our own home. Where romance blooms, tender loving hearts co-exists; where love is, God is. Unfortunately, this very basic principle of love in the Bible paid fleeting, quiet, unannounced, infrequent visits to our home, especially between our parents. These visits were rarer than the rain in hot desert, yet we were proud of our Christian heritage! Today when I reflect, four lotuses blossomed from the cauldron of nuptial vows, even if it was a decadent one. The facade of my parents' marriage formed the second tributary of my life.

My parents went to separate churches. We siblings went to the Methodist Church of India (MCI) with our mother, while my father went to the Church of North India (CNI). We never questioned our parents regarding this mutual odd arrangement. Even though I was embarrassed by it, I did not try to reason why and simply accepted it. Was I being too naive to think that there was anything strange about it?

While they may not have attended services together, going to church was a must for our parents. I am pretty sure of one thing: even if the world was coming to an end, in the midst of chaos they could still navigate blindfolded to their respective churches! This would be by no means a small feat considering the high density of population in old Agra city, both of humans and animals.

The Methodist church was about 5 kilometres away from our home. Our mother was the Superintendent of Methodist Sunday School and we attended Sunday school. After a good scrubbing, clipping of nails and shoe-shining session on Sunday mornings, we would ride to church with our mother in a cycle rickshaw. Attending Sunday school and church was one of the cornerstones of our upbringing in the Christian faith. It positively impacted and transformed us in many ways. I still remember one particularly surreal incident which I often think about even today in tranquil moments. I had fallen very sick and was in delirium. In my semiconscious state I saw a white shining light next to my bed. I told my parents about what I had seen. I believe they told me "It was Jesus Christ." Was this a precursor of events to follow later in my life? I didn't know, nor did my parents. The ubiquitous presence of Christian faith formed third tributary of my life.

Because of the sacrifices of our parents, the values inculcated in us, and Biblical foundation laid by our parents, we were and still are a close-knit family. I have two older sisters, Madhu di* and Mamta di and a younger brother, Khrist bhula.* The age difference between the eldest and the youngest of the four siblings is just five years. Since we were born so close to each other, the sibling bond has always been strong. We are balanced both in gender and in temperament, and the bonding between us has been another motivating tributary of my life.

Like many sets of siblings, we had beautiful memories of growing up together. What I recall most, with fond nostalgia, are the pillow fights we used to have with each other. At times we would gang up against the winner, and at other times battle lines were delineated by gender. Such sibling fights brought us together rather than suffocated and separated us.

Our parents' patronage also helped us in our blooming years. Each job had its perks. These perks were used by us many times if not by our parents. We used these perks to display our inherited gifts and talents. My father was a Physical Instructor at St. John's Inter College Agra. My father ('Pa' or 'Papa')* was good at football (soccer) and grass/field hockey. He was about 5'5", fair, strong and possessing sharp features. His strength, passion for sports and talents made him an excellent player. I believe Khrist and I have inherited some of his talents and a passion for sports. Once, we organized an athletics championship within our neighborhood. We youngsters pooled together some money to purchase some medals, and I won many of those medals in this athletic championship!

Khrist and I also played cricket and football with our friends in the games field of the college where my father taught. Many years later when Khrist visited our home in Agra while my father was still there, he found our old cricket score notebook, which proved to be a revelation. I had forgotten that in most of the matches that we played, I was the best bowler, the best batsman or the best all-rounder as per the records! I do not know whether my brother still has that score book with him as a cherished souvenir of our boyhood memories.

Whenever I had a chance, I would showcase my soccer talents. The talents displayed may not have made as much of an impression as the 'showing off' the soccer shoes. I remember that I used to wear my father's soccer shoes. How could I have possibly managed with my small feet to fit in my father's shoes? Easy, I stuffed pieces of cloth and cotton in the front, sides and back of his shoes from inside! If necessity is the mother of invention, 'showing off' was the father of our inventions!

As children we really enjoyed two crazy seasonal sports - flying kites and playing marbles. Agra was famous for kite flying and for a child that was the world - a Peter Pan world. It started with Makar Sankranti.* It is a seasonal sport and not one day sport. You could be studying, but your mind would be on kites – they even appeared in your dreams! And flying kites was dangerous too at times. Chasing a kite which was loose and drifting through the air, people ran after them in the hope of winning the prize booty for the day. Some carried long sticks, their eyes glued to the kite that was weaving and dipping through the sky while they ran through infamous, unruly, chaotic, snarling traffic of old Agra. Some jumped the bushes others were seen running, jumping and slipping over thin, slippery, dilapidated old brick boundary walls which would be covered with algae during the rainy season. Yes, it was risky and dangerous, but great fun too.

Amidst all this pandemonium, if you had spotted a thin, runny-nosed boy, four to six years old, running after a loose kite, holding his pants with one hand for fear they would slip down, and a wooden pole in the other hand, in our neighbourhood back then, in all probability it would have been either Khrist or me. The joy which flooded one's heart after claiming a loose kite, I believe would be greater than the feeling a general has after winning a war. To win a kite would at times involve skirmishes. Some claiming that they were the rightful owners of the kite since they got the kite first, while others would claim ownership by virtue of having got the thread first.

Marble rolling was an equally passionate sport during winter months. Oh, man! Most children had different types of marbles of various colors and sizes, and their uses were different. Usually the game would lead to fights. Just as in the western cowboy novels, where the richest guy had the highest number of cattle on his ranch, in the game of marbles the best player would have a huge collection of variety of marbles. He rightfully would display them with glowing pride. In today's world, even Bill Gates would not be able to gloat as much over his wealth as the marble player over his collection of marbles. We had many such Bill Gates - equivalent marble - players in the back alleys of Agra. Their leading positions rose and fell every hour not because of economic boom or recession but because of the prowess of their opponents on the muddy alleys of Agra. Sports is the fountain of overflowing elixir of positivity and high energy and forms yet another tributary of my life.

Out of the several sports, these two stand out in my memory because of the intense interactions they brought with the friends and acquaintances we played with. The camaraderie that was born during those childhood days is the most cherished memory.

Agra is also a potpourri of several faiths and though we were so called 'Christians', we also routinely came in contact with people of other faiths. Both in our school and in our residential colony we were exposed to people who were predominantly Hindus or Muslims. In fact, temples and mosques were quite close to our house. We had first-hand experiences of going to temples and at times to mosques.

The Mughal* muslim emperors had ruled India from about 1526 A.D - 1858 A.D. Agra was ruled by Mughal kings for some generations. Akbar and Shah Jahan were two such rulers who I remember had resided in Agra, and left their legacy too. Agra still has many Muslim inhabitants. They follow Hijri calendar* and that explains as to why their festivals fall on different dates every year. One of the most treasured memories that I have of Agra comes from the celebration of the muslim festival of Eid* – both Bakra (Goat) or Eid ul-Zuha or Eid–al–Adha* and Meethi (Sweet) Eid* also called Eid-al-Fitr. The common factor for every celebration was food.

The muslim students of our parents brought delicious variety of mutton on Bakra Eid. And during Eid- al-Fitr, they would share with us plenty of delicious mouthwatering sweets which we relished during Meethi Eid. We would be ecstatic! Who wouldn't?

If Muslim festivals brought taste buds to the fore in our lives, Hindu festivals brought colour and sweets too! A major Hindu festival Holi* was truly about colours. It is celebrated in the month of March. It is a celebration of colours, and involves people of all ages and gender. The colours are bought from the shops along with "Pichkaari" (water gun), and balloons. As usual the extended shops had mounds of colours in big pans on tables which were on roadsides. Holi celebrations start with a Holika bonfire the night before Holi. The next morning playing with colours would start and finish by noon.

We thoroughly enjoyed Holi. The frolic and fight with colours occurred in the open streets, parks, outside temples and buildings. Colours thrown onto fellow revellers were either wet, colors mixed with water, or dry powder. Balloons and water guns filled with colour were splashed on passersby or people afar. Groups of people carrying drums and musical instruments went from place to place singing and dancing. People visited family, friends and foes first playing colours with each other, laughing and engaging in chit-chat. Later they shared Holi delicacies, food and drinks. Bhang made from cannabis leaves and mixed with seeds was served in some Holi preparations. In the evening, after sobering up, people would dress up visit friends and family. I never enjoyed the bath after Holi, as it required an especially rigorous scrubbing to wash the dyes off bodies and hair. If the colours were permanent, one would go around for couple of days looking like a washed-out colourful multi colored quilt.

The other Hindu festival which we enjoyed as children was Diwali.[*] It is also called the annual Festival of Lights. It is a time for firecrackers and sweets and is celebrated in October.

A couple of days before Diwali, market places would be lined with shopkeepers stretching their stalls of sweets out on the already congested and narrow roads. There would be flies around the sweets, bees and wasps buzzing too! But who cared? The lamp-lit market at nights would be just wonderful. A tsunami of people would come from early evenings to late nights to do their festival shopping. And yes, on Diwali evening, after their worship was over our Hindu family friends would send us those delicious home-made sweets. My mother would put them under lock and key so that we could eat them gradually over time and not get sick by overeating. Unfair practice! But who could challenge her?

Diwali celebrations reach their peak in the night. Firecrackers were such fun, and what a sound they would make! The smoke, parachute bombs, and strings of crackers were fantastic! Almost all young children would go out the next morning in search for crackers that had not exploded the night before and could be used again. Remember, we were children of the age group of six to ten. Searching for unexploded crackers in the early morning hours was like divers diving deep in the ocean searching for the natural precious pearls. These unexploded crackers were our bounty, our precious pearls.

One of the main Hindu festivals which had an impact on me because of its procession was 'Navratri Festival'. The float of fierce-looking Kali Mata idol with several arms carrying a sword in one of them and blood-red tongue sticking out was pulled by her zealous devotees who were probably under the influence of some hallucinogenic substances. They would sing and dance to the loud music played by some of them. The tube lights in a bundle of 3-4 lights stood upright in a bucket supported by bricks. The bucket rested on the shoulder of devotees who walked and formed an edge of the boundary within which many devotees danced. These lights lit the procession and one could hear the generator making "Dhuk" –"Dhuk" sound from behind the float.

Her procession would scare the daylights out of me. I would be frightened of the spectre, wondering if Kali Ma would leap off the float and kill me. I was a child of four or five years, and it frightened and fascinated me, although the fear would go away the very next day. I would often think why couldn't Mother Kali be affable like the Hindu gods Krishna or Rama?

In addition to Muslims and Hindus we met people of Jain faith, and much later came in contact with people who were Sikhs. Although we witnessed harmony and tolerance amongst people of different faiths, it was at times broken in the playgrounds of our neighbourhood though mainly because of our passions and competitive spirit in sports. Such was our upbringing in Agra. We were exposed to different faiths and not just to Christianity at our tender and impressionable age. I believe polytheism and the multiculturalism in the Indian society exposed us to the spectrum of religions which left an indelible impression in our daily lives. This was also a deep and perennial tributary in my life.

Although many memories of childhood are by and large happy ones, this does not mean that life was as sweet as honey all the time. My father was my hero and I did few things which I should not have done. He was fond of local cigarettes called 'bidis'. He would smoke bidis and then throw the butts outside on the porch of our house. When he left the house for some work, I would search among the discarded bidi butts for the ones which were half burnt, and then smoke them. This continued for some time until I was caught. Although I do not recall precisely what followed I can imagine that I must have got a good whacking. Consequently, I decided it was best to forgo smoking discarded bidis.

Amongst these brighter and lighter shades of life lurked a darker side. Agra was infamous for serious fights. Every now and then we would hear about fighting taking place and gang wars on the streets. Stabbings, shootings, and fights with sticks and bicycle chains were common. It was not surprising that we were also affected by it.

Being boys, fighting came naturally to us! I remember one particular fight with one of my neighbours, Kishore. He must have been seven or eight years older than me. The provocation for the fight was related to the ownership of the prized loose kites. It was a hostile takeover bid which we sometime observe in today's business world. He claimed a kite which I had taken possession of and was my trophy. Though the fight left me lacerated and despite being an underdog I gave him a good beating. It was then that I realized that in a fight it is never the size of the dog that matters, but the fighting spirit!

While we were in our Peter Pan world, God had His own plan. He did not, I now believe, want to see us maturing in Agra; a place where we could have been easily scathed, inculcated pungent habits, harmful and decadent beliefs in the very gullible world of childhood fantasy. If we remained, we would be lost in the mire of anti-social behaviour, especially the way the things were going for me. Up to that point of my life, many of my actions and the forces around me had the potential of polluting, clouding and affecting my future. Already some of my youthful aggressions were leading to notoriety in early boyhood.

Meanwhile, the frequent fighting between my parents was increasing in volatility and intensity. Ma was 4'8", slim, fair with long hair, and a round face. Despite her petite frame she was a force to be reckoned with. She knew how to stand her ground and this inner strength made her invincible. I am sure mother wanted to go to a place where her God would take her problems away, even if it meant leaving Agra. Higher education was the vehicle she thought she would use to gain respect, economic freedom and security. Another reason was her desire to make a better and more secure life for us.

Perhaps that is why she first completed her Master's degree from the Agra University so that she could have a better job that paid well. Ma put this feather in her cap against all odds. My mother was a very young bride to a husband who was violent, unsupportive, and suspicious. She was in the family way during the first five years of her marriage, and though she quickly had four children she was not overwhelmed. The births of her children and the prevalent inharmonious conditions strengthened her resolve and desire to give us the best opportunities. Her fortitude did not waver during these insurmountable challenges. She knew in her heart that this decisive endeavour would require considerable effort and encounter opposition and the threat of dire consequences, but her hope and faith in her God prevailed. Ma had a fierce protective love as well as a burning ambition that her children do well in life as witnesses for God.

This certainly speaks of her character; she was a strong woman, and the adverse circumstances only made her more formidable. She was also a clairvoyant. She could see that there was no future for her children in Agra, and that she would have to have a better income and opportunity to raise them. It also meant that she would be a single parent. All these adverse conditions made her a woman of steel, albeit one with a tender heart.

Much later, I came to know that Margret Thatcher too was considered a 'Woman of Steel', but I doubt whether she was half as strong as my mother. With Ma, God was her support. Her faith in her God, instead of diminishing in these difficult times, increased. She took all her problems to God and He gave her the courage to fight, and not spend time wallowing in self-pity. I am also sure that she knew in her heart that God would lead her out of her difficult situation in His own time. I think Ma is a great visionary. She could formulate a goal, plan and act on it. Ma, by God's grace has the spirit to fight for whatever is true and noble. She took a leap of faith that was rather daring from perspective of Eastern world in 1971. She started discreetly applying for better jobs. Did her God take her hand and lead her out of Agra thereby bring her period of wilderness to an end? Did her God take our mother and us to a promised land? Remember Psalm 23?

> *Inscribe it in your soul: The Lord breezes in and brings relief in the overheated, sizzling, enervating, challenging dungeons of our lives if we seek Him will all our heart.*

CHAPTER TWO:
Galloping Towards Becoming "An Almost Atheist"

⁂

Start children off on the way they should go, and even when they are old they will not turn from it.
PROVERBS 22:6

Biblically, the book of Exodus records that our Lord led the oppressed and enslaved Israelites between 1400 -1406 BC to the land He promised to Abraham's descendants- Canaan, modern day Israel. At that time Israel was ruled by the Egyptian Pharaohs. Canaan, the Promised Land, was the land of milk and honey and it signified opportunities, satisfaction, fullness and happiness. While in their case it was an international migration, in Ma's case it was regional.

Ma had prayerfully applied for a job in a school as a teacher, and she got the job in the Haryana Agricultural University (HAU)[*] at Hissar in Haryana province. Hissar is 154 km northwest of Delhi. Within

Haryana, it lies in the northwest of the semi-arid belt of the province. For Ma, Hissar was what Canaan had been for the Israelites after the Exodus - a land of opportunities. Co-incidentally, Hissar is famous for the Murrah Buffalo, a special breed of buffalo which produces quality milk. In addition to quality, the buffalo produces more than 18 liters of milk per day. A peak milk yield of 31.5 liters in a day has also been recorded. A land of plenty milk indeed, if not of honey! Later we came to know that 'Hissar' meant "Fortress". Indeed, Hissar was also a fortress for her. She felt secure in this new place where her Lord had brought her.

By His Sovereign nature God opened a door for Ma where the pinnacle of education is offered - a university. Ma wanted her children to have at least a Bachelor degree. She had wanted education to propel her and us to greater economic opportunities and security. HAU was indeed such a vehicle. It was a great learning center for those who wanted to learn.

Ma now wanted to reach the other side of the door. There was bound to be friction between Pa and his family because of this bold initiative. There would be arguments every day, but Ma stuck to her guns.

In India in the early seventies, divorce was considered a social stigma. It was clear to both Ma and Pa their children would not be spared this stigmatization. Therefore, for the sake of their children, they did not divorce. This meant Ma would be a single parent. The concept of a single parent was virtually unheard of, especially if the spouse was still alive. But they amicably separated; ensuring the bridge of rapprochement was always open.

To my parents it was conspicuous that we would be moving to a land predominantly populated by Hindus. Therefore, as a sense of identity we were given Christian names. 'James' was added to my name.

December 9th was my Pa's birthday. It was decided that December 9th would be our last day in Agra. Our parents wanted to separate with good memories. On 10th December, 1971 we left for Delhi by bus. After reaching Delhi, we boarded a bus for Hissar. It was a 'Khrishna Bus'. Krishna Bus Services, a private limited bus company provided travel and

GALLOPING TOWARDS BECOMING "AN ALMOST ATHEIST"

transportation services. At this stage, we as children were more excited about the journey and unaware of any other consideration.

We took the window seats and the journey proved to be an education by itself. In Haryana we saw vast expanse of farming lands with Rabi (winter) crops standing. Primarily it was wheat and some fields of mustard with their yellow flowers dancing on the commands of the winds. Tube wells were running and drawing water from underground and pouring it in the small field canals. Tall trees were planted as a wind break every 3-5 acres in a single straight line, and big feeder canals with water were flowing in the agricultural lands. Cows and buffalo were the tamed domestic animals and at times we saw the wild blue bulls standing majestically in the farming fields devouring the hard work of the farmers. On the roads we saw camels in herds and sometimes they were pulling carts also. There were tractors too. Women wore colorful clothes with veils to cover their faces. When the bus would come near a village we could see cow dung cakes on the walls. They were round in appearance and were stuck on the walls to dry in the heat of the summer sun. Cow dung cakes are used as fuel by villagers to cook food and warm in winter. Near the villages we saw large ponds in which cows and buffaloes bathed. As we approached Hissar we saw sand dunes too. After about four hours we reached Hissar after a journey of ten hours.

Haryana is a small state and carved out from Punjab on 1st November, 1966. It is largely dominated by Jats - a Hindu community. They are hardworking farmers and are a magnanimous people. During the time of its formation there was a great political initiative to make it a progressive state. With this in mind, and the fact that Haryana was an agrarian state, HAU was established in February 1970 as an autonomous body in Hissar. The University strives for excellence in teaching, research and extension in agriculture and livestock. Talented and highly educated experts from various parts of India were recruited. This opened yet another window for us through which we could see various cultures of provinces amalgamating. It was even more of a 'Melting Pot' than one seen in the western societies.

It is a publically funded Agricultural University and is of one of the biggest in Asia. Spread over an area of 298 hectares, the University has scientifically well planned spacious buildings to accommodate six constituent colleges: College of Agriculture, College of Agricultural Engineering & Technology, College of Veterinary Sciences, College of Animal Sciences, College of Basic Sciences & Humanities and College of Home Science. It also has Sports College, a school, a hospital, and a central library.

The University has well planned residential houses for its employees and hostels for students. We were given a house in the campus. Thanks to the vision of the administration and sprinkle irrigation, HAU was a paradise on earth from a child's point of view. There were lush green expansive playgrounds and lots of open spaces, nice brick built houses, and had underground drainage system, unlike Agra. It was resplendent with Gulmohar, Eucalyptus, Acacia, Neem and few other trees planted along the clean wide brightly lit roads, and even had two lakes. No animals were present and the roads had very little traffic. Coming from old, congested Agra where the animals had more rights to the roads than human this was a pleasant situation. We were also pleased as there were extensive playgrounds.

We were delighted and fortunate to be living within the University campus. It meant that we were in the company of well-educated people who believed strongly in the role of science and in evolution, therefore eschewing creation. Curiously enough, in India religion is taken seriously even if a person is a scientist. Religious tolerance among most Hindus is very high. Because of this, we Christians were easily assimilated in the social fabric of the University society.

If Ma had any doubts about her God's Sovereignty, plan, will and timing in relation to this interstate migration, they were dispelled when we saw two landmarks. These two landmarks were witnessed by all of us and my mother embraced Hissar as a city in which God wanted us to reside. The first landmark was observed as we were about to enter the University campus for the very first time. After alighting from the bus at the bus stand in Hissar, we were picked up by a university car. While entering gates of the University, we saw "Haryana Agricultural

University" (HAU) written on the gate. One of my sisters then excitedly exclaimed, "This University is called HAU!" 'Hau' is the nickname of Khrist. Oh! We all were excited. This was our first emotional connection with Hissar.

We saw the second landmark when we were going to the St. Thomas Methodist Church on the first Sunday of our arrival week. The Church was established in 1860 and was dedicated to one the disciple St. Thomas, who was in India around 52 AD in the province of Kerala in South India. Halfway on the road to the church we saw a park and on the gates of the park a name was written. My sisters pointed out, "The name of the park is Madhuban Park!" Madhu is the name of our eldest sister. This was our second emotional connect with Hissar.

In this world there is only one North Star. In Ma's case, these two emotional connections were her two North Stars. Now it was confirmed that her good Lord was indeed leading her to this land. Ma now surrendered herself completely in her Lord's hand and started settling in. In my case, HAU was a tributary which brought nourishing and plentiful water.

Campus School, where Ma was selected as a teacher, was in the University campus and within walking distance from our house. We joined the school the next day and then time flew, just like the kites in Agra.

Ma was very particular about church attendance and to reinforce that she took all of us to the St. Thomas Methodist Church every Sunday. We just walked to the Church – just walked. It was about two kilometres, one way only! Imagine the four of us walking with our mother and not going to play sports, which interested me far more than attending church. This continued for many years. No matter how hot or cold, we had our marching orders: Left, right, left, right. The scorching hot temperatures in summer would reach 45°C and in winters the temperatures would plummet to 6 °C. But that could not deter Ma. Democracy? Not with my mother. We also attended Sunday school in the morning.

For a boy of 8 years the most important activity is participating in sports, but when that time is snatched and allocated to attend some monotonous sermon on a Sunday evening, there is a sense of loss, disenchantment, frustration, and discontent. I was not yet willing to be molded in a religious frame. Perhaps this was why my heart spouted anger and disillusionment and I revolted against what the church embodied. I wanted to play, but had to go to that dreary church. Inexplicably, this anger was not towards mother, who gave us our marching orders every Sunday, but it was channeled towards God! Was it because we were afraid of Ma, and it was easier to vent against God whom we could not see and who would not give us any immediate punishment, unlike Ma, who could and would?

Eventually, I found a way of staying out of the church service even while attending church with the family. Here's how my scheme worked: when we arrived at the church, I would go to quench my thirst from the water pump located in the church compound; consequently, I arrived a little late for the church service. I would then sit in the last few pews. When the hymns started I would sing aloud in my flat voice, loud enough so that Ma could hear that I was there. Once the listless sermon started, I would sneak out of the church. Later, at the time of the last hymn which would be sung after the sermon and approximately 45 minutes into the service, I would quietly slip back in and sing loudly – again like a croaking frog! In fact, any frog could turn red in embarrassment.

What did I do outside the church? First, I was very happy just to be outside. This happiness was enough reason to go outside. Second, I would meet other boys who also did not like to attend church service. Much later, I got interested in exploring the graveyard within the church complex. It had graves which were 100 to 150 years old – from the time of the Indian mutiny against the British in 1857.

This way, hopefully I was pleasing Ma by attending church service; myself as I was at least not confined within the walls of the Church and listening to the lifeless sermon. And hopefully I was appeasing God too by coming to His sanctuary to worship Him. How foolish can a person get!

But no matter how smart you are, you cannot be smarter than your mother! Soon she detected what was happening. I was then made to sit with the family on the same pew. Well, I found another way to be out of

GALLOPING TOWARDS BECOMING "AN ALMOST ATHEIST"

church: As the church service progressed I would leave the church feigning that my sister had pinched me and it was paining. Nobody likes a crying child! To avoid being caught by Ma, I started going outside the church compound and window shopped in the nearby marketplace.

Despite all this, Ma never stopped loving me. She motivated me to read good books and kept on building my character day by day by telling the Bible stories during 'Relationship Building Time' with the Lord before we went to our respective dreamlands. She never shut the door of communication between us. She now acted as a gardener, who despite the geographical semi-arid location of Hissar and semi-arid conditions of her personal life, wanted to create an Oasis in the lives of her children-her garden. With gentleness and tenderness that only a mother can possess she weeded wasteful habits from her garden; with patience and love she watered it with grace. She applied good habits as fertilizers when needed, and with firmness she applied preventative measures to do combat harmful influences in her garden. She wanted her garden to blossom. Under the protective shade of her wings we all thrived, and her sacrifices did not go waste. Today, we four siblings are closer to the Lord and anchored in Him. In herding us to the Lord her knees got calloused. The day to day grind of life in maintaining her home bruised her hands. Remember there was no washing machine, dish washers and vacuum cleaner at that time in the smaller cities in India. Through it all we could see she was a fighter who thrived and faced the challenges of being a single parent in a traditional society. She did not jettison her precious cargo from her fragile ship even when the tempest of adversity was strong and the waves high. Our values were thus built by the role model that she was and even today she continues as the person we follow and seek to emulate.

Though Ma took us to Hissar, it did not mean that Pa did not visit Hissar. Each visit of his buoyed me as it meant nobody could taunt me of coming from a dysfunctional family. He would visit us on long weekends and holidays. He had to travel 10 hours by bus one way and he did not like travelling by bus! Such is a father's love. He occasionally brought yummy treats for us to eat, which we enjoyed. Once he brought a container of honey. Ma kept it inside the store, saying that we would have it during Christmas time. Eventually, when she decided it was time to savor it, she took the container out. To her utter surprise and disappointment of the siblings it was empty! Khrist had eaten it all, and left a clean and carefully closed container there!

When we arrived in Hissar, we were ranked as outsiders. We now had to make friends. Soon territories had to be marked by sweet talk, manipulation or fight. Role of parents, leadership skills developed in Agra, and sports, helped a lot to create our own circle of friends.

Pa played a vital role in the development of a leadership role and making friends, though neither he nor I realized this. Pa would bring salted meat from Agra. It was the tastiest meat preparation that we ever had and yes, we all enjoyed it. Our friends wanted to partake of it too. To have it you had to be a friend, of course! Our Christmas cake was also rather special. That was a leverage tool which I used unabashedly to make friends. Bribes? Pa also brought an air rifle, catapults, cricket bats and balls, footballs and hockey sticks. We were perhaps the only ones in the neighborhood who had an air rifle. Boys of our age were naturally impressed with it and they also wanted to be allowed to shoot at targets or anything which flew. Now, the only way any boy could use it was if he would first be my friend. I consequently acquired several friends. This helped me to gain recognition as a person of importance. Luring and manipulating is what I did, and I was not apologetic about it.

When manipulation, sweet talks, bribery did not work, it was time for a probable coup. This meant picking fights even when they did not exist and winning them to become a king. You cannot become a king if you cannot fight and defeat the reigning monarch, so fighting was OK by me. The king of one of Agra's small back alley could not remain just an ordinary person in the neighborhood of Hissar. I fought some fights, won some and lost some, but I was able to prove a point: I could fight in a new territory. Pretty soon I had my own friends who would listen and look up to me. It's the law of the jungle in a man's world!

Some favorable genetic traits were also valuable. Sports came naturally to me. Just as there are children who are gifted in academics, there are some children naturally talented in sports. I was good in many sports. Why? Because my father was good at sports - genes!

GALLOPING TOWARDS BECOMING "AN ALMOST ATHEIST"

I was much more enamored by sports than studies – for me it was sports all the way! It gave me power over others and even my peers would listen to me. You name the game I was on the team, be it a club or school team. I represented the District in table tennis. I played football (soccer), cricket, hockey, basketball, table tennis and boxing. I was also a school champion in athletics. There were many times when I captained my school team, and club teams in soccer and cricket.

I had my fan following too. When a person is successful, the accolades honor and recognition insulates a person from God. It is all about the inflated ego. It was apparent that it would happen to me too. Eventually, I was driven far away from God. He was nowhere on my radar. With each goal I scored my rating as a player increased, with each wicket I took numbers of my fans increased. With each basket I netted I was further away from God, and with each medal that I won in athletics, my ego soared like a kite. With every chant of "Go, James! Go!" pride entered and Satan took over. Slowly yet steadily I allowed him to establish a foothold in me.

In my youth, good advice was often ignored or forgotten. I thought I knew the best. When my mentors would tell me to concentrate in any one sport to get to the nationals, I would just brush aside their advice. It proved to be the epicenter of failures. Because I refused to focus on one sport, I could not reach the provincial levels. Pride was the worst diversion of my life. Yes, other factors were also involved, but this was the main one.

Time teaches both good and bad lessons, provided we learn from them. Every ocean wave reaches its high and then crashes low. One such Tsunami of life was about to hit us too. There is no better teacher than life.

It was on the 50th wedding anniversary in 1980 of my paternal grandparents. It was being celebrated at Ranikhet, Uttarakhand, India, and it was when Pa at the insistence of his mother, decided to stop coming to Hissar to meet us. We were the casualties of somebody else's decision. I was distraught but could do nothing to alter his decision. The only way to survive the barbs was to camouflage my hurt. God? It did not help a lot as I withdrew in a protective shell. However, Ma never fed any negative feelings towards Pa. She plainly said that after we complete Bachelor's degree we could go and meet him if we wanted to, and it would be fine by her.

Though our earthly father left us to our fate, Ma's Heavenly Father never abandoned us. Ma's faith in her God did not waver. Though we did not realize it then, today we recognize that it must have been a major proposition for Ma to raise us. This major task was possible because of Ma's Heavenly Father's grace, and Ma's obedience to do His will. Ma's Heavenly Father's Sovereignty and grace soon engulfed Madhu di.

Just as a phoenix rises from the ashes, from this harsh reality of my father's estrangement sprung a life changing event in Madhu di's life. She had gone to a prayer meeting and when she returned home after the meeting she proclaimed with a radiant face and sublime joy, "I am born again".

From my perspective this was weird. I was still not in my teens and she must have been around twelve years. How this could happen was beyond my comprehension. Then the concept of 'The Holy Ghost' was brought in. She told us that The Holy Ghost (the Holy Spirit) had touched her. Now, you do not talk to an eight-year-old boy about 'Ghost' holy or unholy, and think that he would not be afraid and run away! But who could argue with the eldest of the siblings, especially when she was like our mother? I was not willing to bell that cat. She looked after us, cared for us, at times cooked food for us, and protected us. The list could go on and on.

Madhu di had come in contact with a Pentecostal pastor and his wife, Mr. and Mrs. Daniel in Hissar and she accepted Christ as her Lord and Savior. She tried to imbue our lives with a faith akin to hers, but as far as I remember this was the only time she failed. So, instead of changing us she started praying for us. When we would inadvertently commit blasphemy by talking unholy things especially about the Holy Spirit to tease her, she would intercede for us, and pleaded with God on our behalf to forgive our sin!

God bless her, I wish we all have such sisters!

Now, in addition to going to church on Sundays, intermittently we went with her to the Daniels' home for Home Group service. It was

GALLOPING TOWARDS BECOMING "AN ALMOST ATHEIST"

during this time that I gave a Bible each to two of my friends; this was more of an aberration than a rule and it happened when I was 14 years of age.

After passing class ten from the Campus School, I went to the Post Graduate Government College at Hissar. Going to the Government College was logical as the fees were low and my two elder sisters were studying in the same college. Mentorship was therefore available easily at home. In college I had one unwritten rule: "You shall not talk to me and embarrass me in front of my friends." I was diligent that the rule remains intact by changing corridors if I saw them from afar. In case I saw them at a short distance, I would enter a vacant class room if there was any, and if there were no vacant class rooms, I would take off my eye glasses and keep them in my pocket and keep walking, hoping they would not recognize me!

In school many students, academic and non- academic staff knew me, but in the college very few students and fewer staff knew me, and this was a blow to my identity and confidence. I lost my bearings and direction. My life drifted on like a log in the vast expanse of ocean at the mercy of waves and winds. I thus developed a lackadaisical approach towards long term growth; nonetheless, the monotony was sporadically broken.

In the first year of college I made my mark in sports just by participating against stalwarts in athletics and giving them tough competition. In most races that I ran, I got 4th position. An 11th class boy running along grade 16 boys and giving them a good run for their money and reputation fired the imagination of many and also touched emotional chords! Thus I came into limelight. In the last two years of college I started representing the college in Table Tennis and was also the captain of our college team. I won many trophies in paper reading contest and eventually won the college colour in Table Tennis. But something was always missing and I could not put my finger on it.

During the four years that I spent in the college, my circle of friends was limited to friends who mostly resided in the Agricultural University campus only. Therefore, I had just a few friends left. This core group – which is there for each other even today – was a group that was not interested in religion. In fact, some of my closest friends and their families were atheists. Invariably, all of us were great family friends as well. In general, God was not discussed, but whenever the topic arose it was dominated by my atheist friends and their views, and slowly I began to believe that their views were correct.

I was a science student till my Bachelor degree. Science taught us to ask questions, and not to accept any views simply because they were taught to us. As students we would challenge the views expressed in the Bible and the Bible never seemed to give any answers; rather, it expected people just to believe without questioning– only to have FAITH!

A few of the Biblical concepts which were challenged by my group of friends were the creation of the world, Christ's divine birth, Christ's putting the ear of a soldier back when Peter had sliced off the soldier's ear, Christ's resurrection, miraculous healing by apostles, and the concept of heaven and hell. I did not have the maturity of a believer, knowledge of the scriptures, or a nimble tongue to nullify the challenging questions; therefore, I tacitly agreed with my friends or remained silent.

It was therefore paradoxical that my close friends and classmates were instrumental in bringing a drastic change to my life. Even today, I remember vividly how one day I was aggressively challenged by a group of my Hindu classmates of our college. On some pretext they lured me to the boys' hostel. Unlike Canada where many buildings are made of wood, in India most of the hostels are 2-3 level structure and are made of concrete, steel and cement. Partition walls between the rooms are made of bricks which are plastered on both sides. The room size was about 10 feet by 12 feet by 10 feet. In this room they are also given a single bed to sleep, a study table a chair and a ward robe. Diabolically I was ushered and welcomed in a students' cubicle.

They must have been about 8-10 boys sitting around. I was told to stand and then I was interrogated. Question by question they denuded my faith and eroded the foundation of Christianity that our parents had laid. To me they appeared very belligerent, and I was afraid of them. The thought that they had ulterior motives and they might even kill me came to mind. Communal killings, in general, at that time did not occur in Haryana. But that could not be understood by a person who was facing a volatile and confrontational situation. Their questions, as I think about them today, were genuine, but the way they were asking me was somewhat threatening. I was all alone facing those targeted hostile questions in an enclosed room which to me appeared as if it were an incinerator. Nobody in my family knew that I had gone to the hostel! One of the questions they asked me was whether science today (this was 1979) was less developed than the days of Christ.

I tersely replied, "No."

"How could Christ then put the ear of the soldier back in place?" they challenged.

Stuttering, I floundered. "I… I… do not know," I replied timidly. My throat was parched and my voice quivering.

They ridiculed me saying, "James, how could you believe in the theory of Christ's divine origin when you are a science student?"

"I do not know. He was God," I murmured. I cringed and grimaced but there was no reprieve. Fear crippled my thinking.

By now I was sweating and the manipulative setup was nauseating me. My armpits were itchy, my feet trembled, knees knocked and the hairs on the back of my neck stood up bristling. I tried to deflect and circumvent some questions but failed miserably. After a few more questions which must have lasted 10 -15 minutes they let me go. In a second I reached free secular India - outside the hostel. I was unharmed physically, singed psychologically, but my soul was incinerated. God?

After this particular episode I realized if religion threatened to cost my life, I was not going to follow it. It dawned on me that Christianity was not a religion which was taken seriously by others. Moreover, I thought, among the sea of students I could be ostracized and could be lost because of my religion. I did not want that happening to me. Students in the college were tolerant towards, but nothing beyond that. If today (2017) some of them would come to me and say that they did not mingle with me during my college days because of my religion, it would not surprise me.

So, here I was, probably a lost teenager who wanted to make his mark in society, but was unable to do so perhaps because of Christianity. Peter, Christ's disciple, had denied Jesus thrice during Christ's trial. I had an example right in front of me and that too from scriptures! I too followed Peter. I did not want to lose my friends for the sake of my religion. Too much was at stake for a young boy. It appears I must have at a certain period of time blamed my religion for all my problems. So I ditched Christianity and Christ and became an atheist. Today, when I look back I realize that by doing so I had spiritually pushed myself in a dark, deep, cold dungeon. To come out of it I would have to pass through a long dark tunnel with heavy metallic retractable gates. These gates were heavy and had sharp spikes on them.

With this renunciation, the Christian foundation laid by my parents was demolished and put to rest, unknown to anybody. Would it remain in a dormant state or be resurrected after some time?

After I finished my Bachelor's degree, I remember my family advising me, "James, it will be nice to acquire a Master's degree."

"Ok".

Mamta di, who was a college lecturer by then, willingly agreed to pay for my education, lodging and boarding.

In 1982, I took admission in Geography in the Kurukshetra University, Kurukshetra, Haryana. As with the college days in Hissar, I lost my bearing in the University too. How long was I in this self-created desert? Did our God send somebody to take me out?

Inscribe it in your soul: We can run away from God but not from His time and mercy. He waits for our return without holding any grudges.

CHAPTER THREE:
Detestable Practices Versus God's Grace

The mouths of the righteous utters wisdom, and their tongues speak what is just.
PSALM 37:30

India has given birth too many major religions of the world: Hinduism, Buddhism, Jainism and Sikhism all originated there. It has opened its arms to faiths such as Zoroastrianism and Bahai's, etc. It also hosts many famous centers of different religions. Consequently, in India alone, each day billions of prayers go to heaven. One imagines that somewhere up there is the largest postal office busy sorting out which prayer goes to which God. Perhaps on occasion there is a wrong postal delivery and an earnest prayer boomerangs! This religious bent of mind and prayer is not only witnessed amongst Hindus only but most of the followers of all faiths.

One such famous Hindu center is Kurukshetra which has an average height of 252 meters. It is located about 162 kilometres northeast of Hissar. Kurukshetra is an extension of rice and wheat belt

of Haryana. It was here that the famous epic battle of the Mahabharata*
was fought.

When I was considering a move to Kurukshetra to further my studies I was eager to visit the battle ground. Our History teacher in the school had told us that a great number of soldiers died in the battlefield. When quizzed further the teacher said more than a billion. And as if testing our patience she said that this did not include the number of elephants and horses. Therefore, her conclusion was with such a monumental spilling of blood the soil become red! On my arrival in Kurukshetra, I was sorely disappointed since I could not see any red soil anywhere! To dampen my inquisitive mind there were not many historical sites which could tell me more about the Mahabharata.

The Kurukshetra University has a beautiful lush green sprawling campus embedded with Eucalyptus, Acacia, Neem and other trees. It has hostels for students coming from other districts of Haryana. I was there for three years. In those three years, I acquired a Masters' degree in Geography and also Master of Philosophy in Geography. This was the first time I had to live in a hostel that was far away from the prying eyes of my mother and her protective wings.

My enrolment at the Kurukshetra University for my Masters' program was all because of the power of motivation and foresight of Ma. She was constantly worried about my future because of my preoccupation with sports and because I did not live up to the promise and talent I had. I still remember whenever Ma bought new utensils she would inscribe names of her children on them. Intrigued by Ma's act, Khrist inquisitively asked, "Ma, why do you inscribe our names on the utensils?"

"Son, when the time comes each one of you will get the utensil with your name," Ma responded with wisdom.

Sullenly and unprompted, Mamta di spoke: "Ma, why does James' name appear in most? He is the third child so he should not be getting so many utensils. Either all of us should be getting the same number or he should be getting as per his due share based on his being third in the family amongst the children!" Not only is Mamta di is fairest of us all amongst the siblings, she is very pragmatic, and her heart bleeds for her family. She must have been 23 years of age at this time, with slightly brown hair. She was 150 pounds, five feet tall and with a soft round face.

In this case, Mamta di's logic came from her head but Ma was ruling with her heart. This demonstrated the extent to which my mother was concerned about my future and how much she patronized me.

Though Ma was worried about my future she never gave up on me. She wanted me to complete a Masters' degree and I acquiesced.

This time around, my loss of bearings in the University did not last long because of maturity and also because I got an early boost to my ego in the first semester: I was chosen as 'Mr. Previous.'

'Mr. Previous' competition is held every year to welcome new students in each department. The senior students of each department organize this competition and it acts as an ice-breaker. There is some criteria which helps in selecting Mr. and Ms. Previous. I've always felt winning this competition was by default as I am neither handsome nor in possession of great social skills. Superior intellect also kept a safe distance from me. I am just an average in most walks of life. There were many other deserving students; nonetheless, I was happy to win the award and was pleasantly surprised too.

The grind of studies started after this. By the time the first semester was over, an apparent impossibility was achieved: I was among the top four students on the academic merit list! This made me feel that I could leave my mark not just in sports but in academics too. Had the winning ways made a comeback? No, not yet. I had my crests and troughs. It was during this phase of ups and downs in my odyssey at Kurukshetra that I met Mr. S K Narang.

When I had just joined the University as a student, I went to meet Mr. Saxena who had earlier worked in the Campus School, Hissar where I was a student. He was a clerk in the accounts branch in the school and now was a clerk in the accounts branch of the Kurukshetra University. He was delighted to meet me after a gap of approximately eight years and offered me tea. While having tea in the office, Mr. Saxena introduced me to another gentleman and his co-worker: Mr. Narang. The introduction began by stating, "James is a Christian too." The three of us chatted for a little while and then I left.

Probably because of his physical appearance, I did not have a favorable initial impression of Mr. Narang. He was about 48 years old, five feet four inches, had crinkly hair and a bald area at the back of his head. He wore thick eye glasses, had a big pot belly and was unshaven. However, he showed certain warmth towards me. To this date I do not know what aspect of my life impressed him. It might have been out of compassion for a disoriented boy that he opened up to me. Compassion was a trait which Christ displayed in overflowing abundance.

Few days later, I went to meet Mr. Saxena in the office. He had already gone to the office canteen to have tea with someone else. Seeing me, Mr. Narang welcomed me and offered me a chair and started a conversation. This way we came to know each other a little better and over a period of time we were more than just acquaintances.

One day, while visiting Mr Narang over a cup of tea in his office, he completely took me by surprise. "James, come for lunch to my house."

For a student living in a hostel, an invitation to home cooked food is always a heavenly one and that included me too. I hesitatingly responded, "OK, when? And where is your house?" He told me the exact location and we fixed a time and date for the lunch. When I reached their house, I had a good lunch and ate as if there were no tomorrow.

Even after visiting his house, I was not particularly inclined to meet with him again. Reminiscing about it now, I recognized he was a man of God, and I had earlier decided that it was forbidden territory to venture into.

Once while visiting his office as a gesture of reciprocity, I invited Mr. Narang to my hostel for lunch. When he arrived, I took him to my room. And he prayed with me and also for me. Thereafter, we talked for some time before heading to the dining room for lunch. After having lunch, to my relief he went to his house. As I had just reciprocated his gesture of calling me to his house for lunch, I did not visit him again fearing my impenetrable forbidden territory could possibly be breached by getting to know a servant of God!

Nevertheless, we bumped into each other more often than not. Our bonding slowly and steadily increased and so did my dependence for his wise counsel because of his good nature and wisdom which he possessed in abundance. He played a major role in my life just by being there for me, especially at times when I was low in confidence. Was he a part of God's plan in my life? I did not have an answer to that. But definitely it was because of him my sanity was maintained. He was a tributary in my life which brought healthy sustaining waters.

Since I was not yet anchored in the Lord, within me a deep streak of rebellion and superstition was still running in my mind which overplayed its hand time and again and drove me to participate in some detestable practices as recorded in the Bible:

> *Let no one be found among you who ... practices divination or sorcery, interprets omens,.... Anyone who does these things is detestable to the LORD;... You must be blameless before the LORD your God.*
> DEUTERONOMY 18: 10-13

In particular I patronized palm readers and numerologists. I also showed interest in horoscopes, stones and their influence in one's life. It became a fad for me to go to them and ask to unravel what my future held. They were pretty accurate. I was scared of them in the beginning realizing that although I met them for the first time they could predict a lot about me - both my past and my future! Gradually, I started reading books written by palmists and was especially impressed by the experiences of Mr. Cherio, a famous palmist who had written many books on palmistry.

While talking with Mr. Narang, I asked what he thought of astrologers and palmists, and his reply was simple: "People of God do not believe in detestable practices and Karma but in God's grace which is not earned by human efforts but is a gift from God." Was he referring to Ephesians 2:8-9: *For it is by grace you have been saved, through faith--and this is not from yourselves, it is the gift of God--not by works, so that no one can boast.*

Did that open my eyes? Did I stop seeing palmists? No. Much later in life I realized that those who wait upon the Lord need none of these things as 'The Joy of the Lord is our strength'. He wants us to come to

Him, to seek Him. He is always ready to bless us and already has a plan for us.

But Mr. Narang's honest answer and his confident, positive attitude and reliance on his God impressed me. His answer ricocheted in my soul and had a deep and positive resonating impact. Little did I know that sparks of faith were ignited somewhere in my soul.

In the meantime, diligence paid dividends and the winning trajectory continued as I got strong results in academics in subsequent semesters and also in Master of Philosophy in Geography. I won a trophy in a quiz competition held by the Zoology department in the University, and another competition organized by the Regional Engineering College. Accolades and conferring of certificates adorned my bejeweled crown of conceit and I was blinded. I was gratified by people's recognition.

Guess what! I had my first alcoholic drink. This was yet one more undesirable distraction in my life. Fortunately, I never got addicted to it nor misbehaved under its influence. For me it was not easy to start drinking because Ma had laid down a very simple rule: "Do not drink with my hard-earned money; you can drink when you start earning if you want to drink." It was true that for my Masters' program it was not Ma who was financially helping me, rather it was the largesse of Mamta di, and it was also true that I had not started earning. So, I had to continuously marshal my conscience and resources to restrain myself from going overboard. My sister was bearing my expenses, and I had to be judicious about spending. I didn't have a gold mine, and my ego wouldn't allow me to ask for money.

My close friends in the hostel, Girish Kaushal and Ajay Dhul seemed to understand my financial constraints and hence they paid for the tea or coffee in the cafeteria that we often visited. Somehow, whenever I wanted to pay the bill, my wallet would get stuck in my pocket! My friends surmised correctly that although willing, I could not pay. They acted as good Samaritans and bailed me out of such situations a number of times. God bless them.

My monetary position was eased slightly when I got a scholarship from the Methodist Church, Hissar for the Master's degree. Did the scholarship draw me close to God? No. Though the money was His, there was no willingness in me to acknowledge Him as my Lord – Master of my Life.

Was I angry with him at this point in my life? No! Who cared about God? Certainly not me! I could go and play, had my own fan following, friends, food to eat, my new-found liberty and freedom in hostel life, could sleep when wanted to, and do things as and when I liked. I had the freedom of not being answerable nor accountable to anybody; I had few responsibilities. This gave me a sense of new found freedom. It was all that I could ask for, and I got it too – unlike the strict, illogical rules laid down by my mother, such as, "Return home before the sunset." To me at this stage in my life, Ma's rules appeared - illogical!

As the sun of my student's life reached the zenith of its orbit, I completed my Master of Philosophy degree in Geography in 1985. About this time a close friend, Inder Chaudhary[a] showed me the mirror in my life. He had foreseen my obstacles, and warned, "No matter what you do, James, and how much merit you achieve, I will get a job as a lecturer before you." When translated it meant: James you would not be able to get a job as a college or university lecturer in Haryana despite having the credentials and merit. Why? Because I was an outsider in a province where "ism" was the rule and people bowed down to it. It was sheer cronyism and a bitter truth. Had I known Jesus at that time, I would have believed that He would make a way where there is none. I was not aware of this truth. Sadly, I had turned my back on God and was still in the deep, dark, cold dungeon. Did my friend's words come true?

Inscribe it in your soul: Even in our self-created desert our Lord does not forget or abandon us. He cares and sends His people to lead us out of the tempting tempest in our lives.

CHAPTER FOUR:
Meandering

Plans fail for lack of counsel, but with many advisers they succeed.
                PROVERBS 15:22

After I had completed Masters, my mother suggested, "James, you should take a sabbatical. After all God also had taken rest. He made the world in 6 days, and on the 7th day He rested and blessed it."

Her idea of rest was to travel to different parts of India and see her God's varied creation. Logically, she was right. After all, I would be getting a job, hopefully, befitting my credentials sooner than later. Upon intensive reflection she recommended, "Why don't you go and visit your eldest sister Madhu, in Kotagiri?"

I found her proposition quite captivating. Madhu di had recently been married, and they were living in a hill station called Kotagiri in Nilgiri district of the province of Tamil Nadu in South India. To reach Kotagiri, Ma suggested taking Kerala Express train from New Delhi to Coimbatore and from there to board a bus to Ooty. By Train it is approximately 2599 Km from New Delhi. The minimum time a train takes to reach Coimbatore from New Delhi is 42 hours. This was my first major solo outing and that too paid for by Mamta di! Off I started to South India.

I took a bus from Hissar to Delhi and then took Kerala Express train from New Delhi Railway Station to Coimbatore. It was a 24 coach train with 38 scheduled stops. Though seats are reserved, it is a common sight to see day travelers come in hordes in the train and occupy and share the berths. The coaches are interconnected by a vestibule and thus a passenger can literally walk from the first coach to the last. The express goes through approximately 10 provinces.

Travelling by train in India is a unique social skills learning opportunity. In long route trains such as Kerala Express, a traveler can possibly meet persons from practically every state of India. It is delightful to watch the dynamics of how people of diverse cultures mingle and share their food, magazines, papers, and at times toothpaste and soap too. When a train stops at a railway station, men often get off the train to buy food for their family or just stretch their legs or to have a smoke. While the train is at the station, hawkers come in the coaches with their eatables, juices, magazines and in their local language or Hindi try to sell their commodities. "Chai, Chai"- Indian tea, is the most common word spoken that a passenger hears when the tea vendors try to sell their hot tea. Often poor local street singers board the train and sing the latest movie songs to earn money. Usually these singers are marginalized children, old people or people with physical disability. In general they work in pairs. The singers and the vendors board the train at one station and travel for few hours to another station. Later they get off the train to board another homeward bound train and return to their home town. Probably they travel both ways without a ticket courtesy the ticket collectors.

The most envious seat in the coach is the window seat and often there is a quarrel amongst the children of a family as to who would occupy it. I was lucky that I got the window seat. Therefore, I was a spectator watching the marvel of Ma's God's creativity on display. In this entire journey, I saw parts of the plains of the mighty river Ganges, agricultural farms, the famous dry and heavily eroded ravines of Chambal valley notorious for dacoits, the Deccan plateau with its short, dry deciduous natural vegetation (Teak and Sal trees); alluvial, black, red and yellow soils; rivers Narmada, Godavari, Cauvery and Krishan and many more natural beautiful places and also many cities. Dusk and dawn were a treat to the eyes. On this journey for the first time in my life I saw the richness of Indian linguistic heritage. With change of province, I noticed the bill boards were written in the language of the province. I viewed the beautiful creation of our Creator with cool winds blowing on my face and at times when the rain hit the glass panes while the train continued its southward journey.

The train travelled first to central India. When the train reached Nagpur railway station there was distinct change in the environment of the train. All of a sudden, the vendors were also selling South Indian dishes to eat. Other than tea, coffee was also sold. The train then turned towards the eastern coast of India until it reached Nellore, a city in the province of Andhra Pradesh. Then it turned towards southwest of India until it reached Coimbatore. After a journey of 42 hours, I reached Coimbatore.

I was expecting a different culture than those I had previously been exposed to. People had darker complexion, they were short, with dark black hair, and black pupils. People spoke Tamil language and I could not understand a word of it. In small restaurants, food was served on banana leaves instead of plates.

As I moved towards the exit, to my surprise, I saw Madhu di waiting for me at the exit gate. She was about 26 years old, and her hair was short and black, her skin smooth and shining. We hugged each other and came out of the railway station. Outside the station there was a school van. We sat in the van and drove to Kotagiri which is 47 kilometres northwest of Coimbatore. It took about hour and half to reach Kotagiri, and once there I rested for a whole day.

Kotagiri is a small hill station. On the red soil were tea gardens, and some forest area. Nature was pristine and in this beautiful place was one of the schools owned by Madhu di's in-laws. Her husband, Prem worked in the school as a Headmaster. He was thin, about 5 feet 10 inches with short hair and slightly bald and small eyes with black pupils. During the weekend my sister took me to Ooty, a famous tourist spot. It has a beautiful lake, botanical garden, educational institutions and is a favored spot for shooting Indian films.

After some weeks Madhu di and Prem had to go to Kodaikanal to another school owned by Prem's parents. They invited me to come with them in their car. I willingly agreed. Kodaikanal is south east of Kotagiri and by road it is about 230 kilometres. We reached at around midnight after a six hour journey.

I fell in love with Kodaikanal the moment I saw it, and it is rightly called 'The Queen of South India.' It has a high density of tree cover, but low density of human population. Located at the center of the town is a beautiful natural lake at road level. Fog and mist kiss the waters and unveil the beauty of the myriad images of the star shaped lake. Reflections of the sky, sun, moon, and earth, make it seem that they are meeting on the earth. The surrounding Shola forest adds to its natural beauty. No poet can ever write a sonnet, or painter paint, or camera capture the beautiful lake and do justice to Ma's God's work. To me if there ever was a Garden of Eden created by Ma's God, it had to be this one. Ethereal, exotic beauty indeed!

I was offered a job as a teacher in the school owned by Prem's parents. I accepted it. I enjoyed several aspects of teaching in a school, and I was being paid for what I passionately aspired to do: teaching and playing sports. It was a satisfying arrangement and a wonderful experience. After six months of pure joy, I came back to my own nesting ground to try to conquer new territories in North India.

It was sometime during this 'career exploring time' that I decided to compete for the Indian Administrative Service. I studied and studied and I failed! Though I failed the examination, I succeeded in making two great friends in this time period of one year period – Dr. Yogesh Jindal and Dr. Rakesh Seth. God bless both of them and their families. In life, I realized we may fail at certain endeavors, but we gain at others; it's a perfect balance. Even today, they are my great treasures, and we e-mail each other and talk on the phone quite often. They were students at the time we met. My friends taught me to play squash. I got interested in photography because of them, and much later, computers also. We would have long talks about what the future held for us and how we would face the reality of beginning our careers. Tea bills, as usual, were paid by friends. I fondly recall our cups of tea in khokhas-roadside tea shacks while sitting and talking endlessly, at times walking along the farms, and some conversations about girls. No brownie points for guessing that one. Blame it on the hormones! Strangely, we were never that interested in girls. An appreciative and uplifting comment here or there was enough. Occasionally, we would also fall in a hypnotized trance when some ethereal beauty walked by, sharing the same grounds as mere mortals like us. Though hormones raged in our bodies there was a deep fundamental ground rule by our parents laid in our hearts and minds to respect women. These foundations kept the hormones in check just in case they overplayed their hand.

Young men living old people's lives!

I also realized that I would have to come out of the cocoon of comfort and the surreal world that I was living in. Armed with my three degrees I ventured into the endeavor of seeking a dream job for a person of my socio-economic standing. Since I was qualified to teach in a college, I started by applying for postings in various colleges in the province. The process of sifting and sieving by the world was about to begin now. The coin had been flipped and now I had to wait for it to hit the ground. Alas, I found out how true the words of my friend Inder were: "No matter what you do James, no matter how much ahead you are in merit, I will get a job as a lecturer before you." Not only Inder, but many other friends got jobs as lecturers in colleges, even though I had achieved greater merit in university.

Was I being too idealistic and optimistic in applying for postings in colleges? Youth has the inherent right to dream and achieve by stretching boundaries. I did the same but I was rudely awakened. These abrupt shocks melted my idealism and woke me up from the hibernation period of youthful dreams. I understood why Inder had warned about my prospects in securing employment in my chosen profession: I was a Christian in the world of a non-Christian majority! My name was enough for people to reject me. 'James' was a clear signal that I was Christian. It did not matter to anyone that I did not believe in my religion. I was branded. Whether I was practicing Christianity or not was irrelevant. It mattered not that I had ditched Christianity as an undergraduate. The harsh and naked truth was I did not get a teaching job as a college lecturer. I had no political connections and was marked as an outsider.

Also left behind in the job market, despite having high merit, were students who did not have political contacts, financial power, or both. The lens which I was holding was different from the one the hiring authorities were holding-- even the filters were different!

Still, thanks to my friend Inder's comment, though disillusioned, I was somewhat prepared for the reality I encountered and cushioned from the blow of rejections because of his assessment. Nevertheless, I was hoping that it would not prove true because having a job as a lecturer meant a reasonably good salary and some social status as well. Both, however, were not meant for me. Strangely and almost inexplicably, I was not bitter about this.

Did this make me resentful towards God? No. My time for transformation had not yet come. How could it come? He was not yet the Sovereign of my life. I did not accept His Sovereignty, though my family did. There was no shift yet in my paradigm.

Disillusioned by this crash landing, I surrendered to time and circumstances and changed my strategy. I realized I could do nothing to change my fate. I failed in spite of my merit, ignored or rejected for being a Christian! I started applying for postings in schools as a teacher. In India at that time school teaching had a social stigma attached. It meant only those who could not succeed elsewhere became school teachers. It also meant lower socio-economic status. However, I continued to stoke the flames of desire to be a college lecturer burning deep within me.

Though I was not selected to teach in a college, I was relatively easily selected for schools, primarily because there was a shortage of Geography teachers in the school system. At least that is how it appeared to me. My joy knew no bounds when I got my first job purely on my own merit. My compromised professional life had now come to its spring season.

Teaching in the Rotary School in Gurgaon, Haryana was an eye-opener for me. Gurgaon borders Delhi, the capital of India. It is almost a twin city of Delhi and is about 42 kilometres southwest of Delhi. The ancient low and denuded Aravalli Mountains offshoots form a beautiful natural landscape in parts of Delhi and Gurgaon. Since the school was a residential school, boarding and lodging were free. I earned Indian Rupees (IRs) Rs.1,100 per month in 1986. Even though it was not much, I was ecstatic.

My mother, brother, and sisters must have been disappointed and probably were despondent about my incomprehensible decision to teach at the school level. Wise people as they were, they never revealed their disappointment to me.

Within several months I left the school. There was a strike, and several other teachers including myself resigned. Then I applied in another school, Army Public School - Dakshai, Solan, in the province of Himachal Pradesh. It is about 296 kilometres from Delhi to the north of it. I was selected and they offered me a slightly better salary of Rs. 1,600 per month. It was not a lucrative salary but I had never equated happiness with money. The school was again a residential school and was nestled in the hills. After some considerations I joined the school. This time the decision was based on the love that I have for mountains and hills.

My love for the natural beauty of the mountains is perhaps primarily because our family hails from the hills of Uttarakhand in India. The rarefied air, the feeling of being at the top of the world, with all creation under my feet, the vastness of the hills intercepted by rivers flowing, and the beautiful view of the cities in the foothills or valleys in the night with lights glowing… all appealed to my soul.

Again, it was fun time for me. I loved sports, and I played the sport which I always wanted to play: lawn tennis. I had not taken any hard drink in Gurgaon, but I started drinking occasionally during my stint in this new school. At staff parties we were served hard drinks, and we had a good number of parties in the school.

The idea of saving money never occurred to me, so I never saved any. Life was at its peak. I was young, I had good food in the school, played sports and had all the authority a teacher is accorded in the Indian education system. I was content. My life also reflected that I was never a good planner, as my outlook was short-sighted.

Within a year of teaching in the Army Public school, I received an appointment letter from another reputed school- Sports School Rai, Sonepat, Haryana, for the post of a Geography teacher. The school was about 31 kilometres from Delhi and to the northwest of it. Sonepat is in the farm belt of Haryana and is well connected by canals. I had applied for this position a year prior to the present job and had forgotten about it. For some reason I got the appointment letter almost a year later. My mother and sister advised me in a wise manner, "James, this is a government job. You will be paid a pension on retirement and this would be better from a long-term perspective." Hiding a smile, I responded, "Sure, I will join."

The selfish reason of my smile was my very own hidden motive for joining the school: the school was famous for sports! I was happy. I would be able to play with talented, gifted, well coached students who had played in their respective sport at national or international level. Additionally, the school offered me a better salary of about Rs. 2,200 per month, as well as board and lodging. I joined as the Geography teacher in senior school.

Though I was given all I had been promised, my happiness was short-lived. My problems started with the change of the Principal. The new Principal wanted me out to give the position to somebody else. It was all about political connections, caste, and a government job. I was ill-treated and harassed. The Principal had his opinion about whatever I did or didn't do. He was relentless and he hounded me all the time. His intricate system of finding shortcomings enveloped both the academic and non-academic areas. He ridiculed and humiliated me in the classroom questioning my knowledge, teaching methods, lesson delivery, and class management. Ironically, in my entire career as a teacher many of my students got 'A star' and 'A' grades. As I was in my first year and on probation it was easy for the Principal to push me out.

The harassment reached such a height that even the senior students of grade 12 Geography suggested that I should leave the school. One day while I was teaching my Geography class, one of the students got up and in a breaking and choking voice blurted, "Sir, it will be nice if you…uhm,..uhm…, leave the school."

I was stunned. The student's statement came up unexpectedly. Cautiously I asked, "Why do you say so?"

"We cannot stand the way you are being, uhm …uhm …ill-treated by the Principal," another student added.

I could see that their guards were down and they were visibly upset. The frowns, facial expressions; visible agitation, shifting of feet, looking at the floor and the tears in their eyes said it all.

"Why do you think this is happening?" I enquired.

Another student glumly replied. "It's all about politics, sir. He wants to bring his candidate."

Only then I realized that the news of my harassment had become so overt that even the students recognized it! It also dawned on me that in addition to recruitment in college postings, "ism" would rear its ugly head in some government schools. With this understanding and the advice and support of my students, I resigned.

The senior students came up to the school's main gate to see me off, carrying my belongings in their hands – a sight which lingers in my memory even today. Later, when I visited the school after couple of years to meet fellow teachers and friends, I was shocked from a revelation: several senior teachers expressed that they had never seen such a heart wrenching and emotional send-off by the students in the school. Ironically, they also divulged to me that the Principal later regretted the decision in replacing me with another teacher because of undue political pressure. His dissatisfaction was solely based on selfish professional reasons. It was too late, however-- the arrow had left the bow two years ago!

While this venue of teaching was closed, another door opened for me. I could clearly see my life had started meandering. In some schools where I had worked, it was all about inculcation of good moral values in the lives of students. We taught students to honour equality, justice, honesty, punctuality, and demonstrate tolerance towards people of different castes and religions. To value friendship more than money, and few other important values of life. While teaching these values to my students which I had acquired from my parents, I had to reflect them as well. I had to be a role model of the values I was teaching. The new changes which were to come into my life eroded and degraded the values and moral fabric of my existence. The proud heritage was shredded, slowly, by the choices and decisions I made.

This happened in the field of business. By this time Prem was no longer working in his parent's school and he was looking for a reliable partner for his construction business in Kodaikanal. He anticipated that he would be expanding his business and hence needed somebody to look after some aspects of it. Madhu di suggested my name and both of them agreed that I might be the right person. What exactly was 'right' about me, to this day I do not know!

Did I start believing in God's divine providence after this development? No. I was still chained in the dark, deep, cold dungeon and there was no light. To me, the experience in the Sports School at Rai was no more than a lesson in politics. The Principal was a puppet, and that was all I understood.

What were the new values that I imbibed in my new career that eroded my morals?

> *Inscribe it in your soul: We may have degrees as per the standards of the world; still we may not get the jobs offered by the world. In the Kingdom of God, we need no qualification to prove our credentials. Ma's God loved her, accepted her as she was. So was Saul accepted as he was. The Lord met Ma and Saul at the place they were.*

CHAPTER FIVE:
The Lord Makes His Move

⁓≈⁓

Many are the plans in a person's heart, but it is the LORD'S purpose that prevails.
PROVERBS 19:21

My life was constantly taking unexpected, unexplored, unplanned strange new turns. I was just an onlooker in my personal journey of life. Soon I found myself standing on the precipice of the moral foundation laid by our parents in our lives. This rock foundation was based on the Bible.

I found Prem and Madhu di's proposition captivating. So, off I went to South India. I took a bus from Hissar to Delhi and then travelled by Grand Trunk Express (GT) train from Sarai Rohilla, Delhi to Central Railway Station, Chennai in South India. It is one of the oldest trains operated in Indian Railways and stops at 34 stations. Its configuration was almost the same as Kerala Express. It leaves Sarai Rohilla Railway station in the evening and reaches Chennai Central after a journey of two nights and one day.

The express departed from the station on time. While sitting on the window seat I saw vast geographical regions of India with its varied vegetation, the long railway bridges running between ½ to 1 kilometre, depending upon the river. The journey was as captivating as the earlier one when I had gone to Coimbatore just after finishing my Master program. The train moved southwards till it reached Nagpur. After that it went diagonally towards the Eastern Ghats and Coastal Plains till it reached Vijayawada in Andhra Pradesh and then ran southwards along the Coastal Plains till it reached Chennai located on the Bay of Bengal. It was about 35 hours of journeying. Because the station was near to the Bay of Bengal it was hot and humid.

Since there was no train to Kodaikanal in the morning, I stayed in a hotel near to the railway station and wandered in its vicinity. By evening I vacated the hotel and took a taxi to Egmore Railway station. Egmore railway station is an important landmark of Chennai. It is big and built in Gothic style of architecture with imposing domes and corridors. It is predominantly red and interspersed with white. I took Pandian Express from Egmore Railway station to Kodai Road. Kodai Road is in southwest of Madras, about 453 kilometres and it took about nine hours to reach there. From Kodai road I took a private bus to Kodaikanal. It is in the Western Ghats of India and is in the north west of Kodai Road. On the way near Kodaikanal, I saw banana and coffee plantations, Jackfruit trees, and some plants of different spices of India. In about two hours I reached Kodaikanal. After I reached home I was given a warm welcome by my sister and her family.

In business, I saw a different side of life. Profit was very important. For startups and mature business people, the way it was generated could possibly bring with it a person's moral downfall. It could produce a vicious cycle of unethical practices and monetary gains and at times losses. Money becomes religion; nothing else matters.

Fortunately, Prem, as a civil engineer and builder, was on the other side of this wide spectrum. We were not sucked into the vicious cycle – and we paid the price too. To get contracts, competitors would bad-mouth us, but Prem, deeply embedded in ethical values, did not do likewise. Often he was knocked out of contention in the early rounds of tender bidding process to construct buildings! When he got contracts, clients took advantage of him. At times they would not pay him on time, and simultaneously they would bad-mouth him or pay less than agreed. He was thus confined to getting limited contracts. Yet he never allowed his trust in his God to waver.

On the contrary, I learned some bad business practices. Since I was not close to God, going the worldly way was easier for me. So, I learned giving late payments to suppliers, at times gave bribes to get work done and I started bad mouthing other civil construction companies. These newly acquired habits formed the bad and unfortunate passage of my life. Fortunately, these unethical mores never took firm root. The great irony was although I imbibed bad ethics, I was never able to get even a single contract!

Gradually I entered other businesses. I sold readymade garments, opened a restaurant, and also tried my hand at real estate. Although all these were run and managed simultaneously, none was highly successful. Somehow, there was some cash flow which was enough to meet my daily needs.

With passing of a few winter solstices, Prem got a good construction contract in Madras, so he left Kodaikanal with his family. However, we remained partners in the construction business. All of a sudden, I was all alone in Kodaikanal. I withdrew to my shell like a snail. In my personal life, it was ripe time for the cosmic powers to add colour on the dull canvas.

One major turning point in life then occured: I found my missing rib! Rather, my sisters found her. I cannot proceed further without writing about this. My Eve is the most important companion in my life. After Christ, she is the one I love the most. With this development, there was some desire within me to shed off the layers of dirt that my soul had accumulated.

During her children's holidays, Madhu di went to visit our father in Haldwani, in the district of Nainital in the state of Uttarakhand in North India. It is about 270 kilometres northeast of Delhi and is situated in the foot hills of the Kumaon Range of Himalayan Mountains. It is the gateway to Kumaon and parts of Garwhal region.

THE LORD MAKES HIS MOVE

Our father lived in his father's house. Mamta di had already arrived there to meet our father. After spending a few days with him my sisters went to visit our maternal uncle in Kathgodam, a twin city of Haldwani.

Our uncle was around 50 years, 5' 5", was stout, fair with broad round face, slightly bald, had a moustache, and wore thick glasses. Our aunt was about the same height, age and complexion. They had four lovely daughters who were fair and short. Our uncle and aunt were God fearing and they had been on the lookout for a suitable match for Khrist and me. My aunty suggested to my sisters, "Here in Kathgodam lives a suitable match, and it would be nice if she could come into the family through a marriage alliance. Let us go and meet her parents."

My sisters agreed, and they went with my aunt to meet the girl's parents and the girl. My sister's motive was to see if the girl would be a suitable match for me. Later in the evening they telephoned me. There was palpable excitement in their voice as if they were about to shriek "Eureka"! They shouted at the top of their voices. "If you are interested in marriage, we have met a girl who would fit in the family very well," they enthused.

"No. I am not interested in marriage," I refused bluntly. My answer doused their fire of imagination.

My poor sisters! However, their God had some other plan.

After sometime, Madhu di came back to Madras and booked a ticket for me from Madras to Delhi and then from Delhi to Kathgodam. Did I have an option? Ever heard the word 'Bullying'? It worked well for me in this instance even though I was at the receiving end.

I boarded the train and reached Kathgodam. Kodaikanal is in the south of India and Kathgodam is in the north and they are separated by approximately 2688 kilometres. It was a long journey of almost 53 hours, not counting the 12 hour stop in Madras. My arrival took everyone by surprise. In Haldwani, I stayed at our grandfather's house. By this time, Khrist came to know about my arrival and came faster than the speed of light.

The following day the girl's parents were apprised of my presence and they graciously gave their consent to let me meet their daughter. I went with my 'team' to support me. My entourage included my maternal uncle, aunt, and their daughters, my father, Mamta di, Khrist and myself. We went to meet the girl's family at the time given to us.

All of us had an enjoyable time, laughing and talking, especially with the girl's father, who was an entertaining and adept conversationalist. Later on during this meeting, my aunt was called to another room by the girl's mother and sisters. Within few minutes my aunt came out and requested every one of us to leave. All of us got up and moved towards the exit. I too got up. My aunt in a voice full of authority and love commanded me: "You stay back." It wasn't apparent to me, but the threshing and winnowing had been completed!

I did not know why I had been asked to stay back, but I submitted to her instructions. All of my family deserted me. I then understood that everybody does leave a sinking ship!

After several minutes, a short girl in Shalwar Kameez* came into the room. She was 4'8", with long flowing hair and a thin body frame. I started chatting with her. She was listening intently, so I talked more, and more… and even more. Then she introduced herself. "By the way, I am Tripta, whom you have come to meet." Thunderstorm, lightning, stars in the daylight and darkness were everywhere. I perspired; my throat was dry, and my tongue did not respond to my commands. Added to the misery of this new discovery was my support team was not there and the earth was moving like gel. Yet, there was no seismic activity covered by the newspaper or TV the next day!

Well, after I came back to this new strange world I looked at the exit door and considered bolting. But common sense prevailed and I blurted, "Hm…ah…uhm…, let's,… let's go for a walk in the canal, sorry, along the canal." The canal was about 50 meters away from Tripta's home.

"Let me take permission from my parents," Tripta replied meekly, though with a smile on her face.

Within a few minutes she came back smiling and said, "Let's go." We sauntered in awkward silence, hemming and hawing along the canal. The purpose was to know each other and come to decision regarding feasibility of our marriage: yes or no.

We spent about an hour or so looking more at the green mountains, floating clouds and the interplay between clouds and the sun, listening to flowing waters of the canal, observing the farmers ploughing the fields, the cattle bellowing along the road, and the dogs barking rather than getting acquainted with each other. On second thought, perhaps the animals knew and waited for the supernatural power to unravel the plan for these two alien creatures in their world. Perhaps in unison they gave approval to the plan and were playing an orchestra for us? Impeccable timing indeed. Were they rejoicing?

Once we ran out of our respective stockpile of words, questions and clichés, we decided to go back to her house. Before bidding her goodbye, in a gentle tone I said to Tripta, "Please do not feel bad if I say 'no' to you; you are a good girl, and if the answer is 'no' you should not feel bad."

I said this because as a youth I was idealistic and in my solitude would often wonder how crippling it could be for a girl to hear a 'no' and probably it could lead to inferiority complex. I had then decided when my turn comes to see a girl for marriage alliance; I would never put her in such a position. I didn't want Tripta to develop an inferiority complex by thinking that I had rejected her for any reason that diminished her worth.

With wisdom beyond her 27 years, Tripta judiciously responded, "James, you too are good, and if I say 'no', you should not feel bad. Get married to somebody else!" With that answer my image of a meek Indian woman was shattered into zillion pieces. Both my ear drums were scarred too!

Then candidly I disclosed, "I would be leaving in a couple of days, and I need time to decide." I continued further. "You will know about my decision by tomorrow." What about her decision?

I went back to my aunt's house where my entourage, with the exception of my father was waiting in hope of some good news from me. As soon as I entered the house there was a barrage of questions. When my answers to their questions were not to their level of satisfaction they 'took my class,' which means, gave advice and their own opinions about Tripta… which I never asked. As the moon and stars became brighter, my sister, my brother and I went to Haldwani where my father was waiting. I now had 'to bat' for the second time in less than twenty minutes.

With her honey laden voice my ever diplomatic Mamta di asked, "What is holding you back from giving a commitment to Tripta?" I had never anticipated this kind of grilling reception. I did not know what I should look for in a girl to judge if she is suitable to be my life-mate. So I blurted the first thought which came to my mind and mumbled: "She …she, is very shirt. Sorry, short."

My brother, sister and father had drawn the daggers out of their scabbard. With a smile on their faces and their feet dancing they lowered it right in my heart and then gave me a list of couples in this world that had opposite characteristics: tall versus short, and so on. Khrist said, "If you do not say 'Yes' to her, we are going to the girl's house tomorrow and we shall give a commitment on your behalf, saying that the boy has agreed!" Mamta di endorsed it and my father gave his blessings.

They were ready to go to Tripta's house to say 'yes' on my behalf! Somehow I persuaded them to give me more time, and reassured them that I would go to Tripta's house the next day to let her know my decision, and the decision would be a positive one. They relented. It was nice to be out of the furnace they had put me in and I breathed fresh air. I could now understand how Shadrach, Meshach and Abednego felt after they came out of the furnace when King Nebuchadnezzar ordered his men to put them in it. Their hair was not singed, their body and clothes were not scorched and there was no smell of the fire on them! (Daniel: 3). But in my case, I was drenched with perspiration from the tactics of my very own support group!

In hindsight, I wondered why my sister and brother insisted on me to give them a positive reply regarding this episode. Later I understood it was because of the love they had for me. Because I was 32 years of age, if I had said 'no' I would be late for marriage from the Indian perspective. Perhaps, they summarized, I would not be able to discern between a girl who could weave the entire family into one family unit and one who would not be able to do so. In Tripta, they saw a girl who would be able to unite our family and would be complimentary to my nature. Probably other reasons could be that her family was from the same geographical area as our grandparents and they were friends. Bonus was that they were Christians too. I am blessed to have been born in such a good family. From their perspective, our marriage would have all the ingredients of a happy marriage.

The following day I went to Tripta's house and announced my decision: It was "YES." They were happy and relieved by the decision, although, none of them actually said that it was the right decision! In order to spend more time with Tripta and her family I extended my stay in Haldwani by several days and then returned to Kodaikanal.

Later, my mother was informed on the phone of the entire episode by my sister. Ma accepted very sportingly rather than grudgingly which could have been the case, as she had not been involved in this important decision. After a couple of months, my mother went to meet Tripta's parents and they decided on the marriage details. In our family, everybody was happy. After about ten years there would be wedding bells, family get together, good food, Indian sweets, wedding cake, dancing and music.

I had my share of hiccups before the marriage. This was when I first realized that I had an option of marrying either in a civil court or in a church. Being practically an atheist, court was the natural option if I had a choice. But because I was born in the family of believers and marrying into a family of believers, that meant getting married in a church. It was a catch 22 situation for me and also a moment of decision. I could have gone for a civil marriage if Tripta agreed, but I did not want to hurt anybody. I had weak knees too. In India, marriage is more of a family affair and it involves two families, not just two individuals, so it is definitely a major event. Getting married in a court meant missing the blessing of the elders since some might get offended might decide not to attend. Marrying in a church meant receiving the blessing of the pastors, elders of the family and community. If things could be accommodated by going to God, I was willing. For me, it was a matter of convenience. I did not relate to Him, simply that I did not want to break the hearts of so many people. He was to me an unseen, unknown entity. Dealing with him was much easier; I could not see Him cry, pleading or bleeding.

Even now I was not looking towards God, but was bound by circumstances to seek His blessings! Was I using God for my benefit? Yes, I was. I had to pretend that I was a practicing Christian and a member of a church so that I could get married.

I was keen to marry Tripta. Faced with selfish and ulterior motives, I approached my sister Mamta di. She was working as an English lecturer in MP College for Women in Dabwali near Hissar, and was a member of a church in Dabwali, a small town bordering the province of Haryana and Punjab. Due to her tireless efforts, I became a member of her church in Dabwali. Now the last major hurdle was cleared. Tripta and I got married in her hometown, Kathgodam.

When we were a few months in our marriage, Tripta and I compared notes about our first meeting. We shared several comical observations.

First, I was not introduced to any of the sisters in the room. Therefore, I never knew which of the sisters I had come to see for marriage, and there were three of them including Tripta! Also, I was expecting the prospective bride would be wearing a sari and serving tea to me and my entourage the way it is portrayed in Indian movies. But here was a deglamorized girl in a traditional North Indian plain set of clothes - Shalwar Kameez. These old Indian movie notions can be very misleading and deceptive!

The girls were confused too as none of them knew which of the two boys had come to see Tripta; Khrist or me! Wow, what a lack of communication!

In retrospect, marrying Tripta was the right decision. She loves and cares for me despite all my shortcomings – Amen. She is the Kohinoor[*] diamond of my crown and also my backbone. Tripta keeps our home together binding us with love sacrifice and patience in a common thread as a family. She is a staunch believer in her Heavenly Father through Jesus Christ.

My parents and my siblings are all happy with her, though not always my two sons, Fazal and Rahul, since she is the disciplinarian in our home. She loves me dearly and often says, "You are an answer to my prayers," and that by "sending you in my life, God has shown that He loves her." Tripta is a tributary in my life which brought sweet, pure water which overflows throughout our marriage. With that water she washed the dirt which I had accumulated in the dark, deep cold dungeon. When you have a wife like Tripta, a person often changes. Did I?

I believe my parents and Tripta's common God had made His first move by bringing Tripta in my life. Perhaps through her He planned to change me from a passive, nominal Christian to an active practicing Christian. Until now, He had always been protecting me. I never realized that God had made His move. It was not evident to me. But in retrospect, unmistakably, He made His move.

After our marriage in Kathgodam and reception in Hissar, Tripta and I went to Kodaikanal. In Kodaikanal, Tripta started managing the businesses. Soon we were expecting our first child. In India, when a woman expects her first child, traditionally she goes to her mother's house. In our case, Tripta went to our family house in Hissar, because it had better hospitals and better medical facilities. Also, Tripta's mother was now elderly and a widow. Tripta's father had passed away, a few months after our marriage.

Tripta gave birth to a baby boy-our Tiger number one, as I lovingly call him, through a caesarean section after two years of marriage. Our son was in the hospital for about ten days in an intensive care unit just after his birth. He could not pass urine and did not cry loud enough at birth. This was due to fetal heart distress. Tripta's God being gracious, compassionate and loving, did have mercy and Fazal survived the ordeal. And when he came out of the ICU he was a healthy baby. Everybody believed that he had been saved by the grace of Ma's and Tripta's God. Since Fazal was saved by His grace, we named him Fazal. In Urdu/Arabic it means "Grace of God." Fazal brought huge smiles to our faces and our lives.

Despite Tripta's Lord's blessing, I was still under the influence of Satan and not close to God. Though clean from the outside I was not transformed within and remained in the dungeon of worldliness. I refused to attend church and be in the company of believers or give a boost and bring alive the 'Relationship Building Time' as our parents had practiced with us. I stubbornly refused to read the Bible. I would not admit that it was because of God's mercy that Fazal was given a new lease of life. Oh, how our hearts can be hardened towards our loving and faithful heavenly Father!

For me Fazal's survival was a medical wonder. From my perspective, credit went to me and the medical system. How could we possibly attribute the miracle to God? Yes, if credit was to be given, it had to be given to our capacity for decision making, to my family, and my friends, who all worked as a team. For me, it was a case of being at the right place at the right moment and medical intervention. Had we not foreseen such emergency and decided that my wife should go to Hissar for her delivery? Now I wonder how blind a person can be? Yes, I must have prayed and must have promised many things to the supernatural to show His mercies on us.

In a few years, we decided to move to Hissar from Kodaikanal. In me was an insatiable urge to be with my mother. Her hair was getting grey and her body was aging, though she was gaining wisdom. The King of Kings had just played his next move by instilling this urge to be with my mother. He lifted me up from the comfortable squat position in the dark, deep, cold dungeon and walked me to a series of exit gates. Perhaps His plan was to take me out of this darkness? Kodaikanal was the place where I had been most exposed to Satan's world. I could have fallen over the precipice and hit the deep abyss. God knew this, but not me. Therefore, He uprooted us and led our small family to Hissar far away from Satan's influence. Strange are the ways of our God, beyond our comprehension! He has His plans for us. Mortals cannot fathom and comprehend them. Wise King Solomon could not, how could I?

On reaching Hissar, we started a tutorial group in our house. It was meant to help school students who were weak in academics. It was a commercial venture. Tripta and I also started another small venture to make ends meet. We sold some selected products of Oriflame, a cosmetic company.

My mother did not see good future for us in these two ventures. So, she asked my sister, Mamta di, to call us over to Dubai for work if possible. Mamta di was working in Dubai in an international school. She talked to the Principal of the school. I was interviewed on the phone and soon I got an appointment letter from the Principal to come and work there as a Geography teacher. I flew to Dubai in the United Arab Emirates (UAE) to teach in the same school as Mamta di.

The circle was complete. I was back in the field of education. How did it go?

> *Inscribe it in your soul: The Lord our God puts His people around to uplift and protect us.*

CHAPTER SIX:

Rendezvous with Lord's Servants

❦

Blessed are all who fear the LORD, who walk in obedience to him.
PSALM 128:1

L ife is a meaningful journey, and in this worthwhile adventurous exploration we meet galaxies of people and encounter new experiences. For a learner, every experience teaches and opens new possibilities in every area of life, and some people leave a lasting impression. In my journey of life, I met servants of the Lord who brought me to our God as per His plan, purpose and timing. Because of their walk with Jesus Christ they gave me a peek in the spiritual realm which until now I had purposefully neglected and rejected. They formed the tributaries which brought ever flowing cleansing water to my soul.

Moving from India to Dubai in late 1998 meant entering an entirely different culture. In India, I was amid the predominantly the Hindu ways of living and thinking. When the airplane landed at the Dubai airport, I saw a different world. In Dubai and Sharjah, I was now exposed to the Muslim culture dominated by large mosques in the manmade environment.

In the UAE women traditionally wear abaya*, with a hijab*. Some women may add a niqab. Alternatively, some women pull their hijab over their faces so no part of their face is visible. UAE men traditionally wear the dish-dash* also referred as dish-dasha and (keffiyeh)*. Seeing them in their traditional dresses in public I was filled with respect for them. What struck me most about the Arab culture was the regularity at which they prayed. Be it in school during Ramadan or before any function, they boldly profess their faith both in public and private life! Also, the recitation of Quran (Holy Book of Muslims) by mullahs (priests) followed by sermons five times a day, every day, was an eye opener. Their Friday prayers in the mosque reminded me of Christians going to the churches on Sundays. Muslim and Christian believers came in droves during the respective Holy days.

The shopping malls and multi-level buildings displayed their leaps in development, as did the vast number of foreign cars plying the road. I was also astonished by the vision of the great leaders of the UAE and the way they made it successful. They imported soil and planted date palm trees transforming the arid area into almost a living paradise. In this earthly Eden, flowers added color. High humidity, accompanied by scorching temperatures, was a constant reminder of the nearness of a huge water body. The beautiful corniche, embedded and interspersed with date palm trees, made the Aladdin stories that we had read when we were young come alive, though the camels were missing in the city!

Due to Mamta di's effort, the Principal's benevolent nature and the ever-willing hand of the Public Relations Officer of our school, my family (Tripta and Fazal) came to Dubai within one month of my arrival. There was disbelief within the teaching community of our school regarding the rapidity with which this was accomplished, but what Tripta's God unites, nobody can separate.

We were given accommodation in Sharjah. Fortunately, again because of my sisters' efforts, we got a shared accommodation in the same building where she was staying. It was near Sharjah and Dubai borders. Settling in was difficult at first. We – Mamta di, Tripta, Fazal, and I travelled to the same school, the Westminster School, Dubai, in the same school bus. The school buses did not have air conditioning which made the journey very uncomfortable, especially in the summers and in the afternoons. The temperatures would reach about 45^0 Celsius. Overcrowding in the school bus, stifling weather, and the smell of perspiration made the air unbreathable. Consequently, at times some staff or student fainted because of suffocation and dehydration. Traffic jams amidst all this made it worse.

At school, I was appointed Head of the Department of Social Studies and Geography, and later also a House Master. After some years, I was in the discipline committee of the school and I was given the responsibility in school to introduce a new course - Natural Economy, which was later called Environmental Management. The result was that I became the founder staff member of the Westminster Environmental Group. These added responsibilities did not mean additional income. Despite that, I accepted various positions and the challenges. In overcoming these challenges I began to understand more about the dynamics of human conditioning.

Being a private or independent school, the Principal had all power and authority over both teaching and non-teaching staff. There was always the fear of losing the job. As bees know where the flowering plants are, so did many teachers knew the advantages of being ears and eyes of the Principal. This perhaps would explain why teachers were prone to stoop to the level where they had to sneak around and report on others to the Principal regarding trivial matters concerning the running of the departments. They had their reasons; low salaries, perhaps the compulsion of buying a dream house, its mortgage payment, taking care of old parents, marriage of a family member, future education of children, or other factors resulted in feelings of insecurity. Though, conversion rates between Dirham and Indian rupees did help, but only to a point. Man is born free but chooses to remain in bondage everywhere, alas!

Principals thus became man-made gods and due reverence was given to them. In return, blessings in the form of favors were received in terms of increments and a satisfactory annual report. It had its negative aspect too. The principle of diminishing returns came into play. Many good teachers were not motivated in this environment. The teaching effectiveness of some teachers atrophied. Many left.

Realizing their limitations in the school and recognizing there was an opportunity to make money, some teachers took to private tutorials, so did I. Now, instead of making money in business, teaching was reduced to a business, and many teachers focused on this extra income. For me, money now had become the reason to live. God again was not the priority. Money had become God for me. Amusingly, this extra income could not take away the vacuum that had started growing within me it became deeper. As if the one god of money was not enough in my life, soon I succumbed to another man made god: gold.

Dubai is known as the city of gold. People mainly from the eastern hemisphere get caught in the frantic pace of making money and buying gold, little realizing that there is something so precious that money cannot buy that is nearness to the Almighty! In general, people also forget about The New Jerusalem mentioned in Revelation 15, or what Lord Jesus had spoken about:

> *Do not let your hearts be troubled. You believe in God; believe also in me. My Father's house has many rooms; if that were not so, would I have told you that I am going there to prepare a place for you? And if I go and prepare a place for you, I will come back and take you to be with me that you also may be where I am.*
> JOHN 14:1-3

I too was blinded by the glitter of gold and the additional income from tuitions helped to acquire this god.

While I was lost in the attempts to acquire worldly wealth, we had a blessing bestowed on us. We were blessed with another baby boy - our Tiger number two. Rahul came into our lives after six years of marital bliss. Our elder son, Fazal, was very happy when Rahul had arrived in this world. The first day when Fazal saw Rahul he wanted to play with him. He took his hand and tried to drag him out of bed. When Tripta saw this, she screamed fearfully and jumped out of bed, as only a mother could, exclaiming, "Fazal, he is just a small baby; you should not drag him like this!"

With distress in his voice Fazal exclaimed, "But he is my brother, and I want to play with him." Later, she made Fazal understand that he would have to wait for quite some time before that could happen. Poor Fazal!

My whole family, except my father, was present in Sharjah when Rahul was born. Was this planned? No, it wasn't. A childhood friend, Shekhar Rao, and his wife Uma, too were there. Wow! This was exactly the case when Fazal was born—one of our childhood friends was present there.

As our children started taking their responsibilities of life, Tripta started to sing a familiar song in my ears: "James, since the children are growing up you better start going to a church now, and it will be nice to give our children a Christian foundation and fellowship."

The song Tripta was singing appeared illogical as far as I was concerned, and not to my liking. My usual counter was, "One parent is enough; what is the need for the second parent to go to a church?"

Technically speaking, I did go to a church in Sharjah, but would not enter the church until the benediction. Instead of attending the service I would wander away with Mamta di, to tea shops along the roadside just near the church where we would talk endlessly about school politics while enjoying tea. Discussing school politics was hotter than the spices of India and a better option than going to the church to listen to the monotonous sermon of a pastor in shining white crisp gown! Fortunately for Tripta there was no dearth of Christians in Dubai and Sharjah.

In Sharjah and Dubai, the two emirates of the UAE that I know of, the sheikhs have set aside few acres of land in which they have allowed non-Muslims to have buildings for the purpose of worshipping their respective gods. Within these acres there were mainly double storied buildings in which there were many halls. Each hall was booked by different denominations for worship on different days and timing of the week. Thus in one hall there could be multiple meetings of different denominations one after the other, especially on Sundays, and it would appear as if a human factory was continuously churning religious products for many hours in a day.

The only constraint was that the churches were not allowed the use of loudspeakers, unlike the mosques which had loudspeakers pouring out the words of the mullahs at high volume which could be heard at faraway places. Nevertheless, I appreciated the graciousness of the sheikhs in allowing churches in their sheikhdoms, particularly considering that the UAE is a Muslim country. Christian meetings in private homes were discouraged, especially if loud music disturbed the neighbors.

Time went by and later my eldest sister, Madhu di, and Prem joined us in Sharjah. We all lived together in one condominium. Madhu di got a job in a school as an English teacher, while Prem was employed as a civil engineer in a construction company. Once again we lived together as one big family.

Tripta's God again started making a series of moves in our lives. And with each move I would be nearing the exit of the dark tunnel. Tripta's elder sister, Anita Threlfall, who was in Canada started urging Tripta, "Come to Canada for good." Tripta in turn began nudging me and selling me this dream.

This was an idea which I immediately rejected, as I loved – and still love – India. I would not even entertain the thought of immigrating and settling outside India. However, there were two important catalysts that prodded me to reconsider my resolve and to amend my decision about our future as a family.

First, I wanted our children to be in an environment where it was natural to have intermixing of both genders in a school, which was noticeably absent in Dubai schools. In the education sector and in school in particular, co-education was allowed upto grade 4, but it was discontinued after this grade. Though in universities, co-education was an option in the community by and large, there was a thin invisible line segregating the genders.

Second, expatriates could not own property. Later this rule was relaxed, but the new exception applied only to rich people. Paying rent and not owning property seemed unwise. These two catalysts forced me to review our plan regarding our future.

I gave in to the demands of my Eve, Tripta, and started contemplating immigration to Canada. Anita suggested, "James, file your immigration papers yourself. This way you are going to save considerable amount of money which would otherwise be paid to an immigration lawyer or agent."

I asked, "How can this be possible? I have never done anything like that and I do not know where to begin."

"I will help you in completing the papers whenever you have a problem," Anita reassured me. She had filed her and her husband's immigration papers successfully on her own. I relented and chose to trust her judgment and heed her advice. On her direction we started browsing the internet, and over a period of a year we updated records and compiled information. Finally, we completed the application papers and filed them in 2004.

One fine day, Tripta proclaimed to me as if a judge were pronouncing a sentence, "If the immigration authorities ask us any question which might delay the process of immigration, we will take it as a sign from God that He does not want us to be in Canada. But if the process is smooth, then we will take it as a sign from God that He wants us to immigrate."

"Amen," I said. Was she testing God, or was it me testing Him?

An extraordinary event happened a week after filing our papers. I had a strange dream. I saw a unique undulating landscape with crops on it. The clouds were of unusual type. Neither the sky color nor cloud type I had ever witnessed before. Perhaps in youth many of us did not look up towards the sky and that is why I had missed the color and sky type in India and UAE! Or perhaps it signified a distant land where we had not been. When I woke up in the morning, I declared emphatically to my wife, "We will be going to Canada."

How I arrived at this conclusion just by seeing a dream, I do not understand. Yet I knew we would be going to Canada since it was Tripta's God's will and therefore there would be no problems with immigration process. Strange that I saw the dream but not Tripta, after all, she was closer to God.

In the meantime, life as usual was busy in Dubai and brought with it its share of rough patches, which happened by default and not by design. With every rough patch came blessings too. Few of the blessings were meeting servants of the Lord.

Strange and unique are God's ways in which He calls a person to Himself. Yet again, the King of Kings moved. He lifted one of the many exit gates of the long dark tunnel and pushed me towards it. This time, I saw Pastor Mahender on the other side of the opened door. Perhaps what the Lord had preordained in the spiritual world was to happen now in the earthly realm. Tripta handed over the baton to Pastor Mahender and then as time went by he passed it on to two other pastors as if it were a relay race. I think no one was aware of the importance of this moment except the director—God Almighty. Perhaps it was time for my spirit to be transformed. Tripta in partnership with the Lord had already worked wonders with my soul. Pastor Mahender took my hand and walked me toward the exit of the tunnel beyond which was light. This time I did notice the change, though I did not understand the depth of this seemingly innocuous move.

During summer holidays one of our school teachers telephoned me at home and requested, "A pastor has come from India. He needs some help in teaching Hindi to his daughters. He is a Hindu convert. Could you please help them?"

In our family we have been taught to be very respectful and helpful to pastors. Tripta and I agreed to meet him and teach his children. He came with Pastor Iqbal from Pakistan. I had met Pastor Iqbal just once in a church in Sharjah. Pastor Iqbal introduced the gentleman as Pastor Mahender from India. Pastor Mahender was from Bombay (Mumbai). He was a young man of about 35 years, lean, about six feet tall, fair, with a sharp nose. His slightly grey hair was combed back and he had a thin moustache. Since we were meeting for the first time, we started conversing about India, and then went on to the subject of teaching his children. Finally, he inquired, "How much will you charge as tuition fee?"

I replied "No charges."

I said this because we had been taught by our parents not to ask for any fees from a pastor, instead try to help them financially whenever possible.

He smiled at my answer.

I probed, "Why do you smile?"

"God had foretold me that you will not be charging any money," he explained with a smile.

While we were sipping tea and still getting acquainted, my mind was thinking about his reply. It had an unsettling and perplexing influence on me. I thought, 'Oh no! Not one of those who claim things which are not true.' Was he a follower of the occult? Was he a magician? I was in a contemplative mood and such thoughts ran across my mind. I failed to rein them in.

Soon the conversation drew to an end. Time was approaching to say good night. It is a tradition in our parents' home to ask the pastor to pray before he leaves. When it was time for them to leave, Tripta requested him to pray.

Pastor Iqbal, intervened at this point and disclosed, "Pastor Mahender has the gift of prophesy; you can ask him anything you want." I did not comprehend the statement, but out of politeness I requested, "Please pray for us."

Pastor Mahender started praying, and then suddenly stated, "God is showing me a cold country, and you all will be going to that country."

I was baffled and speechless: we had never confided with anyone about filing immigration papers to Canada! How come he knew? While praying Pastor Mahender articulated, "Brother, you cannot lift your right hand above your shoulder because of some injury."

Now this truly startled and scared me. We were meeting Pastor Mahender for the first time, and he was speaking to us about our well-guarded secret of filing immigration papers to Canada and my injury. My wife was bewildered. When the prayer was over she looked at me, and I at her, and with our mouths open, we looked towards Pastor Mahender.

He asked us, "Brother, do you understand the meaning of the vision?"

"Yes,…yes, I…I do," I said stuttering.

But deep inside there was a violent churning of mind and emotions. I was unsure. I faintly remembered a few sentences of the Sunday school teachers. Was he like Baalam mentioned in the book of Numbers (chapter 22-24) in the Bible? Or was he like Simon the sorcerer of the

Book of Acts (chapter 8: 9-24)? Was he a wolf in sheep's clothing? Had he come to pull the wool over our eyes? If yes, what could the reason be? Was he a representative of the prince of air (Satan)? I was genuinely lost in a maze of thoughts. Fear had a gripped my mind and my thinking paralyzed. Pastor Mahender had a crippling effect on my clear thinking. All powers do not necessarily come from God but some do. Did not our pastor warn us about this from pulpit when sharing with the congregation? Some of the miracles done by the magicians of the Pharaoh of Egypt in response to the miracles done by Moses were exactly same? (Exodus 7:8-24;8:1-15) The flood gates of my thinking were now wide open.

My unfocussed thoughts were interrupted by his gentle voice. He was now explaining the vision. What an extraordinary meeting this had turned out to be!

As the seasons changed and we weathered a few sandstorms of the hot desert of Sharjah and Dubai, we came to know Pastor Mahender better. Finally, one day he courteously suggested, "Why do you not attend our church service in Dubai?"

In a gentle voice Tripta responded with caution. "We will give it some thought,"

Later, Tripta and I agreed to go to his church at least once. Since the church was in Dubai, and about 22 kilometres from our home, we requested car pool facility. He graciously agreed to that and organized it. We went to the church to check it out. Curiosity filled our visit. After the service was over we saw people going to him for prayers. Pastor Mahender would pray for them and then interpret the visions he had while praying.

I was rather skeptical about it. I judged that it was no different from consulting a palmist or a numerologist. Yet, I went to the church again and again. It was appealing to my spirit. At times we saw people suddenly falling on the floor. This was explained to us by some church elders, "The Holy Spirit has touched that person."

Whenever we met, I was always on guard like a defensive boxer; both elbows toward my solar plexus and gloves covering my face. 'Fools rush where angels fear to tread', and I felt uncomfortable visualizing myself as unwise. With passage of time we saw Pastor Mahender from close quarters and my perception about him slowly altered. We noted that he would always refer to the Bible for any advice and prayed to His Heavenly Father in the name of Jesus Christ. He would always glorify Christ and never exalted himself.

When we attempted to bless him financially Pastor Mahender would never accept the offering. Once he accepted a small donation from us, he immediately gave it to someone else in our presence. We were shocked and asked him why he did that. Pastor Mahender explained that the person he gave the cash needed it more than him. Because of these attributes I could feel pastor's nearness to God and was convinced to some extent that he was a good man and a servant of God through Jesus Christ.

Slowly, we started spreading the word amongst the teaching staff in our school about Pastor Mahender. They showed a keen interest in meeting him. We started prayer meetings in our home in Sharjah. Thus a Home Group was born. Teachers and a few other friends would come. After sharing the Gospel, Pastor Mahender would pray for everybody and reveal the visions he saw for them. Our guests started believing in what he prophesied when the prophecies came true. However, I did not see them or myself turning to Christ.

I particularly liked his testimonies a lot. Once, during our Home Group meeting, we persuaded him to give his testimony about how he had come to his Lord and Saviour, Jesus Christ. He divulged to us, "I lived in Mumbai, India in our ancestral home. It was a joint family. I was a Hindu fundamentalist and I was such a staunch devotee that I used to drink cow urine…"

Gasping with disbelief one of the teachers asked, "You drank cow urine?"

With patience and understanding in his voice Pastor Mahender replied, "Yes, cow is considered a holy animal by the Hindu community of India and being a staunch Hindu I used to drink that." He continued, "In Bombay, I was a businessman with a sugar coated tongue and great business acumen. Therefore, I had a reasonable amount of cash."

"However, I was possessed by evil spirits which used to torment me at times." Pastor Mahender continued his mesmerizing testament. "The evil spirits, would throw me to the ground and I would start screaming and frothing."

It was scary. Almost inaudible, I could hear gasps among the audience. Then I heard a voice loaded with sympathy. "Was it really bad?"

Pastor Mahender smiled and replied, "It was bad because I had no control over my physical body." He continued his testimony further. "At times my Hindu friends would talk to me about a Christian preacher Mr. Masih[α], because they had learned he drove evil spirits away with the power and authority of Christ. Some of them even suggested bluntly, 'Mahender, why don't you go and meet Pastor Masih? He drives out demonic spirits.'"

His eyes gauged the visible interest amongst his audience and continued with a smile. "In the beginning I was angry and upset with my friends and argued with them fiercely because they had suggested I was possessed by evil spirits, and also because they had the gall of suggesting I should go to a Christian priest!"

"Few months later I decided to go and attend a prayer meeting conducted by Pastor Masih. When the meeting was over, I met him personally. To my surprise while we were talking, instead of saying a prayer of healing or deliverance Pastor Masih prophesized, 'Mahender, you will be preaching the Gospel abroad, start reading the Bible.'"

Pastor Mahender was now speaking in excited tone. "As it is, I was disappointed with him because he had not prayed for my deliverance and moreover I thought that he was fanning the flames of a staunch Hindu devotee by suggesting the unthinkable of me preaching the Gospel! I ridiculed the pastor, by laughing at him and using abusive language."

I noticed, as an individual or collectively, we could not have stopped Pastor Mahender in offering his testimony. He was on fire for his Lord!

Reminiscing, he continued. "Nonetheless, I regularly went to his prayer meetings. On July 12th, 1996, when I was sitting in Pastor Masih's house on the third storey, the evil spirits possessed me and pushed me towards a window to kill me. Though I was inhabited and muted by the evil spirit, my eyes were open, I could think, and tried desperately to resist the evil spirit from pushing me out of the window to the street."

There was silence in the room. I could see that all of us had leaned in our sitting position towards Pastor Mahender. His testimony had captivated our hearts and our ears yearned to hear more. Who could stop him from giving his testimony?

"Seeing this Pastor Masih started praying fervently. Shortly thereafter, a greater force, exerted from the opposite direction threw me back inside the room."

One of the teachers exclaimed, "Thank you, Lord!"

Unperturbed and undeterred, Pastor Mahender continued. "The following day I went to my local Hindu priest and removed the Janeau* or "Janeu" (pronounced "Juh-nay-oo") and threw the Janeu at the feet of the Hindu priest, yelling at him, "Your god is a false god, Jesus Christ is the true God!"

"Later, I studied in a Bible college and started preaching, and just as Pastor Masih had prophesied, I started preaching in India and now in Dubai. Praise be to God through Jesus Christ my Savior for redeeming me and using me to glorify Him," said Pastor Mahender.

We were electrified by this testimony. I could sense the change in the atmosphere in our house. Consequently, with the passage of time our friends wanted to hear more prophetic messages and Biblical teachings from Pastor Mahender. Seeing their hunger and keenness, we unwittingly opened our house for more meetings because we saw the happiness it brought to our friends. Strangely, I was a facilitator without believing in the package.

As the number of people coming to the Home Group increased Pastor Mahender cautioned us of the unwritten government policy of not encouraging people to meet in houses to praise, worship, or share the Scriptures. So we decided to play it safe and requested people not to arrive in groups but preferably in ones and twos. Tripta would close the windows and draw the curtains during the time of praise and worship. We sang in low volumes and when the meeting was over we suggested people disperse in small groups.

The parched souls and spirits could not be satisfied by intermittent showers. Our friends wanted to be drenched with the perennial flow of the Word and the testimonies of the servants of Tripta's God. Sensing this, we decided to invite other servants of God to our Home Group. Perhaps in my life, the Lord's time had come for another door in the tunnel to be lifted and exchange the baton with another servant of His choosing. The King of Kings had now made a small hole in the dark tunnel and I could see an awakening of desire in me to know more about Him.

While we were impressed by Pastor Mahender's prophesies and sharing of the Word, I wanted to meet Pastor Masih. There were two reasons for that: first, to check the veracity of Pastor Mahender's testimony, and second, to hear his own testimony. I asked Pastor Mahender. "Could you please give me Pastor Masih's address?" I enquired.

He casually replied, "He is presently in India; but soon he will be coming to Dubai."

Not long after that, Pastor Masih arrived in Dubai. Pastor Mahender remembered my request and gave me his address. I made time to search and locate his house. With trepidation I rang the doorbell. The door opened, and out stepped a short man. He was stout and had dark complexion, black hair and equally black pupils. He was probably in his fifties. I introduced myself and requested, "Could you please come to my house and hold a prayer meeting?"

Pastor Masih peered right into my eyes, and with gusto replied, "Surely; but only if somebody can take me and bring me back."

I understood the problem. He did not have a driving license. Without blinking an eye, I uttered, "I will do that; you please come."

We agreed on a day and time and I left. When my feet hit the loose desert soil outside the multi-storeyed building, I raised both my arms towards the sky, and my hands formed a fist, and I let out a victory cry that would even put Tarzan's victory cry to shame!

On the appointed day, I went to Pastor Masih's condominium to bring him to our Home Group. He gave a wonderful testimonial. "I used to collect 'Protection Money'[*] from people in one locality in Bombay for a certain criminal gang. After Christ called me, I decided to give up my wrongful actions. Now, gangs do not believe in letting their members just go. Usually, deserters are killed, as the gangs believe the deserters will disclose to the police the modus operandi of the gang which could put the lives of the other members at risk. Consequently, I was taken hostage by my own gang, and taken to the boss who inquired, 'Why do you want to quit?' I declared boldly, 'Because Christ has found me. My old self has died, and now I am a new man.' Hearing this, the boss was angry and he ordered his men to bind me and keep me locked in a room. The name of Christ was like plague to the boss."

"The following day the boss called me and divulged, 'I wanted to kill you because of your decision. However, the whole night I was not able to sleep. A voice inside me forbids me to do so, and now listening to the voice I am letting you go.' The boss then threatened me, 'If you ever blabber to the police you will be dead.'"

Taking a deep breath, Pastor Masih continued. "After I left the gang, people in general came to know about it. Now I had to face another set of problems. Since I no longer had the gang's protection, even peace loving people started harassing me. The wheel had turned a full circle. However, the Lord protected me. The very fact that I am with you all today validates what I have just said."

Oh, what a testimonial it was! Just goes to prove that stories regarding gangs are a hit amongst the believers too! Pastor Masih's God be praised!

Taking a sip of water from the glass Pastor Masih continued. "I had to find a job now. Who would give me a job and why should they? My bad reputation preceded me and people still doubted my transformation and feared me let alone giving me a job. Nobody was even willing to refer me. Nonetheless, the Lord opened a door and I joined the work force. However, I stayed in the huge house which I had rented earlier when I was a gangster."

"After my disassociation with the gang, the flow of cash had trickled down and since my job was not a high paying one, I did not have enough income to pay the rent. One day when I was coming back home after my work the landlord sauntered towards me and demanded the rent money. Since I was not in a position to pay the money, I requested some extra time. The landlord warned me, 'If you do not pay me by tomorrow, you will have to vacate the house.' How drastically life changed because of following the Lord's calling! People who had been afraid of me had started threatening me!"

"The next day I was not able to pay the money, hence I had to vacate the house. I, along with my wife and our young son, huddled under an umbrella on the roadside in the monsoon rain with our belongings. With resentment in his voice my small boy then challenged, 'Father, you said Jesus will look after us, then why are we standing here on the pavement? Why is He not helping us?"

I replied very prayerfully and in faith. "Jesus will definitely help us, son."

"A few hours later, the landlord came out for some reason. He saw me and my family standing in the rain. His heart melted. He took pity on us and approached me urging, 'Today you go and stay in the house, but tomorrow you should leave, as I want to sell the house and a buyer is coming to see.' I praised the Lord with muted voice and agreed."

"The following day, before the arrival of the buyer, we left the house. Some hours passed and we were still out on the pavement with our belongings. I still did not know where to go and did not have any plan. Then I saw a servant of the landlord coming hurriedly towards us with an expression which betrayed inner turmoil and fear. When the servant reached us he literally begged us in a trembling voice, 'Please, sir, please, come back. My master wants you back in the house as a tenant.'

"This surprised us greatly. Was a quirk of fate at play? We went back to the house with our belongings. I then meekly asked the owner, 'Why have you changed your decision and called me back?'

"With fear in his voice the owner replied, 'The prospective buyer came to the house and liked the house. He also agreed on the price, but before signing the sale deed the buyer wanted to consult his Hindu family priest. The Hindu priest performed Pooja.* After it was over, the priest's face was ash colored and he told the buyer in a fearful voice, 'Do not buy this house.' Why?' asked the surprised buyer, with a confused expression.'

'With a perplexed reaction, the Hindu priest explained. 'While praying I saw a vision that outside the main door was an angel standing with his sword, ready to behead anybody with intentions of buying the house.' The priest then embarrassingly added, 'Their God is mightier than our god. So, let us go from here and no matter what, do not buy the house.' The prospective buyer and the priest then left hurriedly on trembling legs with pale faces.'

Pastor Masih continued with his testimony. "Several years passed and the owner failed miserably in his attempts to sell the house to anybody because the story of the priest's vision and recommendations had spread like fire. Eventually, the owner realized he would not be able to sell it to anyone. Therefore, he offered the property to me at much lower rate. By now, I had learnt the lessons of life well and had saved some money from the job I was doing. We made a down payment from our savings account, and in some years I paid the amount in full. Our compassionate God made it possible to buy the house and now we are the owners of the prime property!" All of us in the Home Group, were bewildered at the work of Pastor Masih's Lord.

Out of curiosity, I asked Pastor Masih about the veracity of the testimony of Pastor Mahender coming to the Lord. Pastor Masih validated his testimony.

Tripta's God then made His next move. He lifted yet one more gate from the dark tunnel and again pushed me further towards the exit. I could see reflected light. On the other side of the gate was yet another of His servants, as if two were not enough! Perhaps a skeptical person like me with a science background needed more proof of His existence, His being alive and working. The baton was then exchanged between the two servants of God.

Once we had gone to a prayer meeting in our friend Mr. Ronald Parker's house in Dubai. There we met a God fearing pastor from Pakistan, Pastor John[α]. He was probably in his fifties, five feet five inches, with a wheatish complexion, lean with thin hair combed backwards. He shared the Word of his Lord and gave many testimonials. I liked his testimonials so I called him to our Home Group. He agreed graciously.

Pastor John arrived at our house at the appointed time. Our friends were awaiting his arrival with bated breath to listen to his testimonies and message. Imagine teachers who discipline students were now behaving like good students themselves as if the head teacher was on the round! The prayer session started, followed by some of his testimonials:

"I was from the family of mullahs or Muslim priests in Pakistan. My family had been mullahs for generations. I had persecuted Christians in Pakistan, and I also burnt the Bibles. One day when I was working in my office, I saw a very bright light in my room. Startled, I asked with alacrity, "Who,…who… are you?"

"'Your guess?' the bright Light whispered.

"With delight in my voice I responded, 'Allah'. I took the name Allah because I believed that if God had to come and meet me then it had to be Allah," Pastor John explained. Gently the Light responded, 'No.'

"This started a series of questions and answers back and forth, and each answer was refuted by the light. Exasperated I gave up and said, "You, you… now tell me, who,…who you are?

"The light then revealed, 'I am Christ.' Immediately I fell to the ground and repented," Pastor John commented. There was stunned silence amongst the listeners. We all were looking at each other's faces with our necks preening over each other's shoulders and heads.

Unfazed Pastor John continued. "I renounced my Muslim faith and because of this my wife divorced me and took our little son with her. I started reading the Bible and undeterred by circumstances preached the Gospel of the Cross. Embarrassed by this turn of events, the Pakistan government started persecuting me.

"I was arrested and put in prison. I was hung from a ceiling fan with my hair tied to the fan. The fan regulator was then turned to 'ON' mode. The fan started revolving. I swung in the room. I was shrieking loud but none came to my rescue. My hair was pulled by the forces in play. After sometime I fell down with a big thud, bleeding, in pain with almost no hair on my head. Despite this torture, I did not renounce Christ."

Many of us gasped audibly. One of us commented, "They cannot do this."

"They did that to me, sister," Pastor John said with a smiling face.

He continued. "A few days later, my ex-wife visited me in the prison and gave me some food to eat. I ate the home-cooked food to my heart's delight and content and wondered why she had come to visit me. When I finished eating, my ex-wife started laughing derisively and loudly proclaimed; 'Now you are going to die, because the food has been poisoned with the venom of Cobra.' I survived the poisoning, because my loving Shepherd had another plan for me."

There was disbelief amongst many. How could an ex-wife do that to her ex-husband?

There were many more testimonials which he shared with us yet we were hungry for more and more.

Of the many testimonials Pastor John gave that day, I liked the following one the most as it was about Pastor John's God's faithfulness on full display.

"One day," said Pastor John, "I was walking through the city with my long uncombed hair, dirty ragged clothes, torn slippers and a foul smelling body. I had not had a bath for many days as I was homeless and penny less since I accepted Christ. Some people thought I was a madman so they threw stones at me!"

One of the teachers in the Home Group interjected, "Yes, I have seen that in our country too, I mean throwing stones at a mad person because they believe evil spirits reside in them and…"

Pastor John interrupted, "Undeterred I kept walking in the city looking for a restaurant. I was desperate for food since I had not eaten for many days. I was famished, my intestine and stomach were making rumbling sounds. As I walked, I saw a restaurant on the side of a road. I decided to go and eat in that restaurant. With no money in my pocket, I entered the restaurant to have a lavish meal. Seeing me some people left, as it was a high-priced restaurant and nobody wanted to sit next to a beggar, especially a beggar who was stinking and looked like a madman!

"Surprisingly, I was not thrown out of the restaurant despite my shoddy appearance. I took a seat and drank water. The waiter brought me the menu. I decided to have the best expensive food because I believed, my Heavenly Father, the King would make provision for the payment of the bill. And because, the Heavenly Father was the King, I should eat the best food since by heritage I was a prince. I ordered good non-vegetarian food. With arched eyebrows and side glance the waiter scrutinized me while taking the order since he knew the bill would be very high, and perhaps thought, how could a beggar possibly pay the bill?

"Nevertheless, the food was served, and I ate to my heart's content. Thereafter, I washed my hands, went to the payment counter, and obdurately declared, 'I cannot pay the bill!' Audacity of a mad beggar! When I finished speaking to the cashier, the cashier responded with a smile on his face. "You do not have to pay. The bill has already been paid by your friend while you were eating.'"

Unaware of any friend, Pastor John was amazed, and asked the cashier, "Who was he?"

The cashier was taken aback because he had assumed Pastor John knew who had paid his food bill. Pointing at the exit door the cashier then confided, 'Your friend just left.'" Pastor John concluded. "I ran outside the swinging exit door and looked on both the sides of the road in search of my friend. I could not find anyone on the empty road. Then I understood who my friend was. I came back in the restaurant and looked at the bill, and to my amazement noted the amount tendered was exactly the cost of the food served plus a tip for the waiter"! Wasn't Pastor John's God a loving God, a Provider-Jehovah Jireh?

At tea time, after the meeting was over, people would socialize. Pastor John showed us a picture of his young son. Pointing to it and with a sense of a father's pride and longing, he emotionally shared with us, "I will be meeting my son after a long time. My son expressed his desire to his mother to meet me. I have not met him since he was a baby. My wife had taken him away when I had surrendered to the will of God and had started preaching the Bible. My son is coming to meet me in Dubai. I made my position clear to him that he can come and stay with me, but there would be no compromise in my faith in Christ. I would continue to do the work my Lord had ascribed to me and if that was OK by him, he would be welcome!"

These testimonials shook us from our deep reverie. I forgot the sermon. Rattled by Pastor John's testimony, I felt that some invisible force was leading me towards a spiritual journey I had never chosen to embark upon and had shunned by choice. I now stood at the end of the tunnel with no gates and was blinking. After all, I had spent almost my entire youth in the spiritual dungeon which was dark, deep and cold. Standing outside at the end of the tunnel, I saw the world from a different perspective. After a long time my spiritual journey would perhaps start with my willing participation. Perhaps a few more baby steps and the Lord's vision for me would then be clearer to me. Perhaps I would be a part of the heritage which was preordained for me. These servants of God were the God directed tributaries which brought sweet, fresh, life giving water in abundance to my soul. I started to view religion through a different prism. How could I possibly deny these testimonies? I could not forget them for a very long time. Perhaps the time had come to stop looking at other people's beautiful perennial gardens, streams, and fountains. I could no longer assume that my own soul and spirit were in full blossom. I had to look at my own garden which had nothing in it and make it pleasing to God.

Stirred by all these testimonies, I decided to give Tripta's God a try, as in my opinion, I did not stand to lose anything. I began to attend church regularly with a different frame of mind. I even remained for the entire service! God bless all the servants of our God. They all are doing tremendous work of the Lord. May Lord use them more and more.

One day in our house, Pastor Mahender prophesied, "Brother, you better start reading the Bible; God is going to use you."

I had a hearty laugh and retorted, "This is not possible."

But he did not change the prophecy and stood on it like Rock of Gibraltar. After this episode of prophesy regarding God using me for His work, Pastor Mahender would remind me continuously at regular intervals, "Brother, read the Bible, God is going to use you for His work."

Neither of us would change our stands, and a few seasons passed. However, Pastor Mahender was so confident of the prophecy that he enrolled me in a seminar which was about Gospel knowledge, teaching and preaching. The teacher of the seminar was Pastor Joel, from India. He was not very tall, about 35 years of age, with black short hair, and wore glasses. Pastor Mahender informed us that Pastor Joel had an awesome testimony, he was well-educated, a fiery speaker, and very strong in the Word. It was said that people walking at his side could sense the presence of the Holy Spirit in him.

The seminar was held in Dubai, and I did attend, though half-heartedly. Pastor Mahender also gave me a particular responsibility in his church. The congregation was told that prayer requests could be given to me.

While all these transformations were taking shape within me, one of the many prophecies of Pastor Mahender regarding us came to be true. We got our Permanent Residentee Visas for Canada in 2006. How true were Mahender's words about our immigrating to a cold country: Canada! We had been selected without a hitch; our interview was waived – a clear indication that Tripta's God wanted us to be in Canada, the sign which we had thought would come from Tripta's God if He wanted us to immigrate to Canada.

Pastor Mahender's delight knew no bounds when we shared this news with him. He cautioned us: "Now do not change your mind about going to Canada, because God wants you to go. He is going to bless you, and because of you many people will come to Canada and many people will be blessed." How many did we bless? Did we?

> *Inscribe it is your soul: Plans of the Lord never fail.*

CHAPTER SEVEN:
A Glimpse in the Spiritual Realm

⚜

Let the one who is wise heed these things and ponder the loving deeds of the LORD
PSALM 107:43

Bidding farewell is never easy. On one hand it opens a new world of joy and hope, on the other hand there linger pangs of separation from dear friends and colleagues. We were no exception. After bidding farewell to our friends and colleagues in Dubai in 2006, we went to India to spend some time with family and friends before finally bidding them adieu.

We flew from Delhi to Taipei, Taiwan, and then to Vancouver, Canada. The flight was of about 26 hours of back breaking journey crossing many time zones. By the time the flight landed in Vancouver, I understood the feelings of a caged animal. But once our feet touched terra firma we were relieved of that feeling and enjoyed inhaling the fresh air.

We travelled in the Pacific Coach Lines bus from Vancouver airport to downtown Victoria. In between there was a BC ferry ride from Vancouver Tsawwassen Ferry terminal to Swartz Bay Ferry terminal in Victoria. This was our first ferry ride and we enjoyed it to the hilt. The ferry was massive, about 160 long, with passenger and crew capacity of approximately 2000, and vehicle capacity of about 450. It was painted white and on it was written in blue 'BC Ferries'. It had several decks. The small islands in the Pacific Ocean, fresh cool air, liberty to walk on the sunny deck, unbridled view of open sky with clouds floating, birds flying, and a great expectation of seeing a big whale made the ride unimaginably refreshing and enjoyable.

After a ferry ride of 90 minutes we were in Schwartz Bay, Victoria. We boarded the Pacific Coach Lines bus again to continue with our journey to downtown Victoria. The first thought which struck me as I looked at the landscape near Michell's farm on Island View Road, Saanichton, was, 'This is the place I saw in my dream in Sharjah in 2004!' The distinctive appearance of the sky was similar and was still etched fresh in my memory. The topography and landscape were also similar.

Usually I have selective amnesia, but in this case I remembered every scene even after two years! A week after we had filed our immigration papers in 2004, I dreamt of a place I had never walked in, and the color of sky, I had never seen or witnessed. The following morning I had declared to my wife, Tripta, "We will be going to Canada." Was some supernatural cosmic power at work?

The drive to downtown Victoria was of around 55 minutes on Highway 17 and was an uninspiring one. I felt this was not a place I would like to stay for long. It was very quiet, a laidback kind of rural life. The reason for such an impression was because we were coming from India, a nation of more than a billion people. Back in old cities of India we had rickshaws, bullock carts, cows, buffaloes, cats, dogs, monkeys, horses, donkeys, and depending upon the province, camels, and elephants crossing the bustling roads amongst the ocean of moving people and vehicles. In Dubai and Sharjah there were multi-storied buildings and traffic jams. What do I see on Patricia Bay Highway, extensive farmlands. There was light traffic on the roads, and few buildings. As the bus rolled into the city the view improved a little, though not enough to lift my sagging spirits. Seeing multi-level buildings of downtown Victoria my faltering spirit soared like an eagle but soon landed on the ground with a thud. Why? Even before I could speak, the bus had arrived at the downtown bus stand.

Anita was waiting for us at the bus stand and was genuinely happy to see us all. A few years older than Tripta and competing with her in height, she is fair with a round face, glasses, and short black hair. She took us to her house in Langford, Victoria. At their residence we met her husband Gerry. He was around 45 years of age and was 5' 6" with short black hair that was greying, well-trimmed moustache and glasses. He was well dressed too. God bless both Gerry and Anita for opening their home to us. It was all God's plan. The next morning we went downtown to register with the Victoria Immigrant and Refugee Centre Society (VIRCS), a non-profit organization which helps new immigrants settle in Victoria. My heart was troubled with what I saw in certain small pockets of downtown Victoria.

In India, we had seen people living in poverty and begging on the streets. In Victoria we saw similar sights in some places. It was difficult for me to accept this scenario in a first world country. In addition, in downtown Victoria there were drug addicts and marginalized people on the streets in broad daylight. Surely this was not the place we wanted our two young sons to be? Fazal was ten years of age and Rahul was just six. When we learned that there were government sponsored drug sites where people could inject themselves. We were taken aback. Why was the city encouraging this kind of lifestyle by providing free needles? This was beyond our comprehension. From our perspective, it was a convoluted solution. Surely there must be a reason behind it, which we failed to understand. Our minds flashed back to India and Dubai where we had not seen this kind of government sponsored drug injection sites. All the stories of Canada that we had treasured had lost their luster and left us unsettled for a moment. Did we come to Canada to expose our children to such sites?

Then, we heard that parents were not to leave children below 12 years alone at home. They had to be accompanied by a person 15 years or older. Again, from our perspective it was a challenge, as our boys were under 12. The question looming large was, if one of us has to stay home with children after their school, how would we provide food for our table? How would the bills be paid? The thought of state intervention in family life did not impress us. We had to find a way of meeting this requirement. After all, we had immigrated to Canada for our children to have better prospects and quality of life.

To us the law seemed lax for burglars. We were given to understand that if a burglar entered our house and got injured on our property, he could sue us in court.

Divorce rate and number of single parents was high. All these loose ends within the social fabric disheartened us and our social antennae went up alarmingly. Our picture of a glamorous Canada as the epitome of an exemplary society was broken.

In general, Indians believe personal interest should be sacrificed or kept at bay for the sake of the family. The social adjustments evident in Victoria are alien to Indian society. Here the society catered mostly to the concept of an individual: I, me, and myself. We had heard about its prevalence in the west, nevertheless the reality hit us hard. I wondered if I wanted to stay in Canada!

Perhaps I was opinionated and judgmental. But these harsh realities touched my raw nerves. Did I live a cocooned life in India all these years? Probably - yes. The litmus test was yet to be observed – the life of Christians in Canada.

I wanted to see for myself the Christian way of life amongst the believers in Canada. We had heard remarkable stories about it. I thought it would be at its pinnacle in the West. With this frame of mindset, we went with Anita and Gerry to the Jubilee Christian Church Community (JCCC) in Langford on the first Sunday of our arrival.

I was uncomfortable in the church. There were some inmates who had come from William Head Prison to attend service. This petrified and perturbed me. There were some from marginalized section of society too. I was again gripped by paternal protectiveness over our sons. I was convinced that it was the wrong church to attend, therefore, the wrong country to live in. Was I being paranoid about it? Did I want to leave? Yes! I wanted to run out of the church and Canada!

After coming back from church, I phoned my friend, Mr. Raj Chaturvedi, who was residing in Dubai. Both of us went to the same church in Dubai. I sought his advice about the prevalent social conditions. He was a believer with wisdom beyond his years. He counseled, "James, think about it in a cool manner, and take your problem to the Lord in prayer." It was a sagacious insight: I should not trust my instincts and colored vision but to take it to the Lord. God bless him for the sound advice. I did exactly what he had asked me to do, but I did not get an answer. How could I possibly get one, when God and I were not on the same frequency?

The following Sunday our family again went to the JCCC. Our fears were not allayed. While our views did not change, we did not mind giving it another try. I promised myself that at the first sign of anything wrong I would quit coming to the JCCC. As of today, I am still waiting for the first sign!

Gradually we became comfortable with the congregation and our sons made friends with other children. Being a small community church, everybody knew everyone else. Soon we recognized that we were embraced by them, and the congregation had accepted us. We imagined that it dawned on them that our family was going to stay and eventually become members of the church, and probably not run away to another church!

Pastor Bob Greene was very welcoming. He was 5'8", fair, had short white hair, and blue eyes that were always beaming. He made us feel wanted, and we felt he was a genuine servant of God. God bless him and his family for his faithfulness to our Lord. After the church service, he would often ask me one question: "How are you doing?"

My reply invariably was the same: "God is looking after us, and He will continue to look after us." Since when did I invoke *God's name in my life?* I did not notice when it had started, but it happened. Did I have faith in the statement? No.

Then why was I repeating the same every Sunday? I cannot explain. Probably I was now hoping that there was somebody who would look after our family in this land to which we had come by choice. Probably someone who was: omnipotent, omnipresent, omniscient, invincible, righteous, slow to anger, forgiving, compassionate, a provider, a healer, and one who could give us peace. Who could that be? I probably was able to identify what I was searching for but could not give it a name. Probably this was a case of unconscious mind overruling conscious mind. This perhaps explained my responses to Bob's question.

Somewhere around this time, probably in the month of October 2006 there was a posting for positions as Correctional Officers. I did not know what it meant. All I knew was the good salary that was offered. After inquiring, I came to know the nature of the job. However, it was not a deterrent to me, at the end of the day it was all about earning for my family. I felt responsible for the decision to come to Canada, and as a man considered it my duty to provide for my family. I did not want to be just a biological father to my sons and a ceremonial husband to my wife. I even planned how to invest the income. I had started counting the chickens even before they were hatched! I confided in my wife, "Tripta, with the money coming in, you could go for further studies and then you could have a career." Wow! I was indeed a man of foresight!

A day before the physical test, my friend Rhodes[α] came by to show me where the test would be held. I had befriended Rhodes in Victoria. He was a wise and humorous middle aged man, about 5'8", and had a moustache. He was an Anglo-Indian, and was working in the BC transit as a bus driver. I met him while commuting on the bus. He not only befriended me, but guided me as well.

We drove in Rhodes's car that evening to the test site. Once Rhodes had shown me the test site, he brought me back to our place. When the day came to an end, I went to sleep with no anticipation of what would happen next.

In the middle of the night I woke up startled hearing a voice whispering and stating as if it was a decree: "This job is not for you, James."

I did not know who spoke, nor recognized the voice. Thinking it was a dream, I tried to go back to sleep and succeeded after a few restless moments. The next morning when I woke up, I remembered the message delivered to me by a soft voice. Nonetheless, I went to take the test half-heartedly, and did not succeed. I was not upset about not making it; but was lost in deep thoughts about the voice I had heard the previous night. Later I came to the conclusion that perhaps God had spoken to me just as he had called Prophet Samuel when He was a child (1 Samuel 3). This story of Samuel had left an indelible impression on me when our Sunday school teacher had taught us. Now 45 years later the story re-played in my mind.

One night, in early December 2006, I was woken up from my sleep by some supernatural cosmic power. While still in bed, the power took both my arms and spread them out across the bed. A few seconds later, my right foot was placed on my left foot. Next, the intriguing movement that was flowing through my right hand was led by the cosmic power to my left rib cage just below the diaphragm, and I felt my right hand jabbing me in the rib cage area with a help of some imaginary sharp tool. Immediately after my right hand formed a cup in which the imaginary liquid oozing from the imaginary wound was collected. The imaginary liquid was then applied all over my body by my right hand. I presumed that the imaginary liquid was blood. All these were involuntary movements. How could I sleep after that?

Everything that was enacted on me in bed clearly depicted Crucifixion of Christ! I was not scared of this experience, but mystified. I neither lost a wink of sleep over it nor my tranquility. However, thereafter I started reflecting. I suspected that the supernatural cosmic force that was in contact with me was somehow related to Christ. Was it The Holy Spirit? Still, being a man of reason and caution, I waited for a few more concrete proofs.

Did they materialize?

> *Inscribe it in your soul: Let not the mind rule over matters of faith.*

CHAPTER EIGHT:
Jehovah Elohay –
The Lord my God

"Forget the former things; do not dwell on the past. See, I am doing a new thing! Now it springs up; do you not perceive it? I am making...."
ISAIAH 43:18-19

After the reenactment of the Crucifixion of Christ episode in my life, a series of intriguing and inexplicable incidents occurred as if some sort of alignment was planned. On the canvass of my life there appeared to be many dots. The questions were: Who had put those dots? What did the dots represent? How many dots were they? Where in the canvass were they? The most important was: who had the marker? These questions were careening in my mind and I felt like a nucleus around which the electrons were rotating in a fixed orbit. In my case, the questions were my electrons. I was expecting these dots to connect and a picture to emerge. And when the expected happened I surrendered unconditionally, accepted it, welcomed it, and embraced it with open arms. What did the image look like?

After landing in Canada in September of 2006, possessing a car became imperative, primarily because we had to drop off and pick up our children from their school, Tripta had to take the public transit to work at 5.20 a.m. and I had to reach my work place. On Sundays we had go to church and Tripta also had to do the weekly purchase of groceries. These travels became cumbersome between September through March when it rains and sometimes it snows. Summer, early fall and late spring were easier.

Tripta and I had brought our international drivers licenses with us from Dubai, presuming that we would be allowed to drive a vehicle with it until we got our Canadian driving license. Time had now come to make use of it. Keeping this in mind, I took the knowledge test in October 2006 and cleared it. Since I had the international driving license, the graduated road test was not required. However I had to take the road test. If I cleared it, I would be given class 5 passenger vehicle license. I needed a vehicle to practice for the road test.

We started looking for pre-owned cars. We went to car dealers and started reading 'Buy and Sell' column of various newspapers with the intention of buying a car. As the date for the road test drew near, we were getting desperate. We mentioned this to Nola when we visited her home. She suggested, "I am selling one of my cars. If you are willing to buy it I will lower the price since we all are from the same church."

We were naturally thrilled. The offer had come to us at the right moment. And she was willing to give it to us at a discounted price!

"First we'll give the car a test drive for a few days, and only then we will confirm," Tripta gently responded. Nola agreed and gave her car to us.

I started practicing. About a week before the test date, our neighbor, Kim Munro, knocked at the door of Anita and Gerry's residence where we were staying. My wife invited her in and they started conversing. Just before leaving, Kim inquired, "Somebody wants to give away their car as an unconditional gift, and as you do not have a car, I thought of you all . . . would you accept it?"

Tripta was speechless. Once she recovered her demeanor she happily chimed, "We will be delighted to accept this generous offer".

"When can we possess and become the proud owners of the car?" Tripta enquired excitedly.

Kim replied, "The donors would give you the car within a few weeks, and it would be shipped from Vancouver."

Victoria is an island, and Vancouver is on the mainland, so Tripta thought perhaps we would have to pay the shipping charges (which we assumed might be substantial). As if reading her mind Kim added, "Even the shipping charges will be borne by them!"

Befuddled, Tripta inquired, "Why do they want to give it away as a gift?"

Kim gently and reassuringly answered, "The donor is a pastor, and he got the car as a gift. Now they wanted to give it as a gift and a blessing as they are buying another car." Had not our parents taught this to us during our daily devotion time! Remember? Freely, freely you received, freely, freely you give. Perhaps my mother was reflecting from Matthew 10:8 and extending it so that we recall this lesson from our childhood.

Within few days we got a Chrysler 99 automatic model- FREE and delivered to our home! And yes, they also gave us two extra pairs of new tires along with the winter tires which the car had at that time. Incidentally, that year it snowed a lot in Victoria, and I was new to driving in snowy conditions!

Later, we came to know the pastor was the father of: Kim!

Tripta's God did take care of her and our needs – He gave us a FREE car before I got my class 5 driving license of Canada. Isn't He the best provider? *Think, James, think!*

The dilemma which we faced now was how to back out of the agreement with Nola. We found ourselves in an awkward position of having to say that we could not buy her car. After all, we had committed to buying if the test drive proved satisfactory. We tried to think of various excuses for not purchasing the car. Ultimately, we concluded we should tell her the truth. We did. She accepted the truth and was delighted that we had got a car as an unconditional free gift. Since I had practiced driving in her car, she was gracious in allowing me to use her car for the road test. I took the road test in her car and cleared in my first attempt. Praise be to Tripta's God.

Now we had to have a plan for work. We realized that our skills, experience, and training would not get us teaching jobs in Canada. It did not matter that we had degrees, teaching licenses and more than a decade of experience as teachers in India and in an international school in Dubai.

The plan that we formulated together as a husband and wife team was to keep our personal ambitions in check. We did not have much money; consequently both of us could not attend school simultaneously. Faced with this reality, Tripta offered to work in a hotel as a breakfast server. She sacrificed her career of teaching for some time and successfully coaxed me to pursue a higher degree.

We thought having a Master's degree would help me get a good job outside Canada, just in case we decided to leave Canada for good. And if we succeeded in planting our feet firmly in the Canadian soil, some teaching assignments possibly would come our way in Victoria. We also mutually agreed that after I complete my education and get a job, Tripta would start her career in education by getting a certificate or degree if possible.

I went to the University of Victoria (UVic) between October and December 2006, to seek admission into Master of Educational Psychology and Leadership Program. Since it was mid-term, I had a slim chance of being admitted. I requested that the secretary of the Student Academic Advisor "Please accept my application, and forward it to the committee. I shall get admission in the program, because *my God* wants me to be enrolled in it."

I must have spoken with such conviction that she presented my case before the committee. A few days later the office informed me that I had been granted admission in the Master's Program. But there was a condition: transcripts of my degrees from India were to be submitted by a certain date. The e-mail also suggested clearing an English language exam, either the TOEFL or IELTS! The battle was now half won. All Praise to Tripta's God!

We were not satisfied with a partial victory. We sensed victory and now we aimed to complete the campaign.

JEHOVAH ELOHAY – THE LORD MY GOD

I went to the University again. This time I sought an appointment with the Student Academic Advisor- Dr. Rachel[α]. During the meeting with her I pleaded, "Please waive the English Proficiency Test for me, because I had studied in an English-medium school, and in the University the medium of instruction was English. Moreover, I had taught in English-medium schools in India including an international school in Dubai, which was affiliated to the IGCSE system in UK. And before coming to Canada I had taken the IELTS examination and cleared it."

She responded generously, "James, IELTS score is relevant only for two years, and in your case it is way past two years." However, she gave me her word that she would discuss with the Dean, as she knew that students in India studied English, and in my case she could see that I did not need to take the Exam. Hurriedly, before she could change her mind I blurted out, "Please forward my case to the Dean, I am sure the exam requirement will be waived and I shall be admitted, because *my God* wants me to get admission." Audacity at its pinnacle!

Now twice in a row I had involuntarily articulated words which I did not usually associate with- *"My God."* My self-confidence gave me rich dividends and my words proved to be prophetic. I soon received an e-mail from the Dean stating my TOEFL exam had been waived. With this the half victory changed into a complete victory saga.

God be praised!

Ponder, James, ponder on His resources!

Now the other hurdle was getting transcripts. Getting transcripts is a difficult process in India, but by now I had observed where there is Tripta's God's hand, rough obstructed passages change into smooth unobstructed passages. I received my transcripts within a very short time as my friend, Dr. Rakesh Seth, went personally to Kurukshetra University to pursue the matter. Rakesh initiated it and Tripta's God took over and completed the work in a record time. Hallelujah!

Did the matter end with that? No, I still had other obstacles on my pathway to attain a degree. I could not fathom and understand them, but Tripta's God did.

After gaining admission we realized financing my education would be a problem. The department secretary suggested the option of applying for student loan and also recounted some successful stories of students getting it. Some friends recommended I strategize a game plan required to secure the loan. They advised, "James, just fill in the application form, and when you come to the question which asks whether you have any money in the bank or not, just respond negatively." I was uncomfortable with that.

We had some money in the bank which we had brought from India, so I could not truthfully claim I did not have money as asked on the loan application form. For me it was not right and I could not omit this information. This was not the way our parents had brought us up. I filled in the application form with all the correct information, including the financial statement, and predictably, the loan was refused.

The government and the education loan policy is right. However, because of my honesty, I did not get the loan. Consequently, the problem of financing my studies stood staring at me. Probably finding Aladdin's treasure was easier to find than money for my studies. However, Tripta faithfully kept on praying to her Lord. Tripta's Lord used Anita for playing the role of a benefactor. She played a masterstroke with an elegance of a genius and recommended, "James, why don't you go to the VIRCS and ask them if they have any government scheme to help recent immigrants to settle in the job market?"

I went and met my case manager in the VIRCS who'd been assigned to me when we first came to the centre. He gave me a patient hearing and then declared, "James, you are a lucky man. The federal government has just launched a scheme for recent immigrants to help them tune their qualifications to facilitate in settling. We shall apply and see how it works for you." Both of us worked on the application and submitted it.

Several days slipped away and I did not hear from him. I was apprehensive. After a week or two had gone by, he phoned me and excitedly shouted at the top of his voice, "James, congratulations! Your application has been approved. This scheme is much better than the standard student loan, which has to be repaid with interest. Under this scheme you have to pay about 33 % of the fees. The rest would be paid by the government." After holding his breath for some time he delivered the punch line: "and you do not have to pay it back!"

Man cannot understand the ways of God. The same is also written in the Bible,

"For my thoughts are not your thoughts, neither are your ways my ways," declares the LORD. (Isaiah 55: 8)

God is the Provider. He is a compassionate God. By now I had started thinking about God more and more, and started inching towards Him. Slowly, I realized the lens through which I used to view God was changing and mercifully I was not holding that lens! *Reflect, James, reflect!*

I finished my Master's degree in about a year and a half. It was nothing short of miracle. We had just come to Canada in September 2006. I was working on weekends and holidays, getting tuned to the social fabric, climate and so many other factors which only an immigrant can understand. I completed the Master's Program in a year and half or so! *Contemplate, James, contemplate!*

As if these blessings were not enough, Tripta's God kept on nudging my soul.

One Sunday in early December 2006 in the Jubilee Church I saw a man named Victor Hollefreund, fondly called Vic, comes in front of the congregation during the 'Prayer Request and Testimony Time'. He was short; his hair was grey, wore spectacles and was probably in his early sixties. While speaking Vic was literally in tears. "I am going to die as my Prostate Specific Antigen count is increasing and my doctors are not very hopeful." The dire judgment was announced by the doctors. He requested prayers for healing which were offered immediately. Later, I came to know that Vic had been a pastor in Canadian Armed Forces before taking voluntary retirement. Later he joined the Monk office, Victoria and is currently leading a retired life.

The following Sunday, Vic came forward during the testimony time and facing the congregation he reiterated his earlier account and added that his PSA count had increased even further. He was heartbroken. Believers were shaken. Prayers for healing were offered. I was stirred by Vic's passionate plea, but I did not pray. I concluded, if the doctors have already diagnosed, what can prayers do? To me, the doctors were omniscient and specialists.

After coming back from the church service, as usual we had a nice family time. We gobbled the famous Indian Chicken curry for lunch and saw a Hindi movie on TV. Tripta read the Bible to our children and prayed with them. When night silently crept in and the moon was high in the firmament, we retired to the unconscious world.

Time had now come for the creator to make me realize His Sovereignty which, up to this point, I had denied. The King of Kings made one of His many lightning moves.

I had a dream. I saw a doctor stepping in the operation theatre. He was wearing white overalls and a stethoscope was hanging around his neck. He examined the patient who was lying on the operation table. After examining the patient he took a pink piece of paper. After scribbling a note, he handed me the note with his diagnosis and declared to me, "Vic is now OK." Then a voice commanded me, "Pray for Vic right now and coming Sunday you should go and pray for Vic in the church with him."

Startled, I woke up and looked at the watch. The time was 2:02 a.m.

I tried to analyze my dream for some time and after failing in the attempt, I went back to sleep without praying. I did not understand to whom I should pray and why I was chosen. To me, Vic was merely an acquaintance and therefore there was no empathy. Heart like a stone?

When I woke up in the morning, once again I tried to decipher the dream and yet one more time I did not succeed. I shared the dream regarding Vic with my wife and confidante. She too could not decode it. We never spoke to anyone about this, since we did not understand the significance and the magnitude of it and thought it as just another dream. Much later I understood the importance of the pink slip.

The Sunday after I had the dream, I saw Vic in the church, but didn't have the courage to approach him to take his permission to intercede on his behalf and pray. I still had my doubts about effectiveness of prayers and intercessions. Once the church service was over, we drove home, but I felt miserable about not praying for Vic.

Following Sunday, before the church service began, with all the courage that I could muster I approached Vic, and meekly implored, "If you do not mind, can I pray for you?"

He agreed. Midway while praying and mumbling, I blurted, "Our... uhm ... God has healed you."

These words just rolled off my tongue. I felt I was powerless to stop them. In fact, I had no clue that these words would be vocalized. I had never intended murmuring them, yet I had stuttered in a meek audible voice. It appears spiritual truth found words. Did Vic believe in those words? Only he can comment. Did I believe in those rumbling inexplicable words? No. We hugged each other, and tears flowed down my eyes.

After my almost incoherent and unintelligible soliciting to the cosmic power, I went to a corner of the main hall in the church and cried and sobbed to my heart's content and slumped on the floor. While sitting on the floor I prayed. The more I moaned and groaned, greater was the urge to pray. I petitioned my request to God, "I,...I (sob), have misused your name (sob), I have given a false,...false hope to Vi, Vi, Vi, Vic,...Vic (sob). Not for my,...my,.. name (sob, sob), but for your name *God*, and for your glory, please,...please, heal him. I will never,... never,... repeat this mistake, but please,...please,... please,(sob) heal Vic (sob, sob)."

I felt miserable, bad and moved into the 'Red Zone'. I started procrastinating, but kept on pleading. Once the service was over, the matter was forgotten!

Did you notice, subconsciously I used the word *"God"* as if coming from the core of my heart and mind? Was this a mistake?

Be calm, James, be calm!

A few weeks passed. One Sunday, Vic came in front of the congregation during 'Prayer Request and Thanksgiving Time'. He proclaimed, "I went to see the doctor. He instructed me to undergo some more tests. I underwent those tests and the doctors are baffled that the PSA count has moved southward. They cannot explain it, but they are happy for me and I, too, am ecstatic. Thanks to the prayers of James, who had revealed to me, 'Our God has healed you.' Now I have to get some more tests done after a few weeks, and then they will update me as to where the case is heading to."

Even more than Vic, I was relieved and thanked the cosmic power! Strange as it may sound, but it was true. Vic was thanking his God through Jesus Christ and I was thanking the supernatural cosmic power for the same incident!

Some weeks passed by Vic once again came to the pulpit in the church and gave his testimony. "The doctors have now declared that I do not have prostate cancer, as the PSA count has gone down drastically and now they will review my case after 6 months!" Hallelujah! Do you remember the pink slip mentioned earlier?

Celebrate, James, celebrate!

After Vic's incident my cognitive faculties started considering what had happened. My confidante and I would discuss this quite often.

Cancer struck Vic again two times between 2007 and 2012, and Vic did undergo some treatment, but by God's grace, he is as fit as a fiddle. It appears that Vic has some fondness for the hospital and goes there at regular basis! *Accept, James, accept! Throw away the caution and take the leap of faith!*

Sometime later (2013) the doctors found polyps in his bladder. The doctors investigated the polyps that grew and after biopsy found that everything is fine. Most of the time our Heavenly Father had foretold Vic's health would be just fine: polyps or no polyps.

These series of extraordinary cloudbursts of events changed my perception about God, and brought me closer to the Almighty. These events were so life changing that my views changed completely about God. All the rays of these incidents were falling at the focal point: God. The picture formed was bright, sharp, and magnified. It became my 'Red Sea Crossing'.

These incidents opened my mind. I was now viewing the world through a different prism. I had rationalized that I did not have the skills to heal or prophesy, yet they were happening. I reviewed some of the critical incidents up to this point which happened in my life. My scientific background could not explain any.

What my mind definitely accepted was this: Tripta's Lord was using me as a vessel to deliver His plan. I also realized that my mind was not supporting me in arriving at any logical conclusions; therefore, it would be better to go ahead with my heart. With this understanding there was a distinct, radical paradigm shift. Now the picture that emerged was that God takes care of the needs of His people; He loves them unconditionally and provides for them, heals them and protects them. These were just a few of the many facets that I came to know, understand, and witnessed in the lives of people around me and in my own life.

With this light hovering over me no longer was the God of Israel just the God of my great grandfather, grandfather, father, mother, sisters, brother, Tripta and my two sons Fazal and Rahul – He became My God too. In early 2007, I put a 'No Trespass' sign for Satan in my soul and spirit! The grip of Satan was broken and he was decimated and he gave a concession speech in his kingdom. I was no more a puppet in his hand. Consequently, the predator and prey relationship ended. The weathervane of my soul pointed towards Christ. I repented and submitted to Jesus Christ unconditionally and unreservedly and without fear of the unknown. I accepted Christ as my personal Savior, my anchor, and my rock.

His righteousness was on me, I was justified and my Salvation was done and became a sealed deal. He became my shield and reward (Genesis 15:1). The bird had come to its nest to roost. The dichotomy in my thoughts and action were gone. Peace which I, a desperado, escapist and fugitive, could not find amongst more than the billion population of India, in the Himalayan Mountains, desert of Dubai and Sharjah, forests, lakes, or golf courses of Victoria, suddenly dawned on me. Peace which comes only from Him. Peace which cannot be given, stolen, bought or sold. He indeed was Jehovah-Shalom. It was checkmate. I lost, yet I won. I was redeemed, stood justified, was saved, was born again and given eternal life. I was no more "An Almost Atheist" but a follower and a believer in Christ. God-phobia (fear) changed into God-philia: love for God. The foundation laid by my parents became suddenly active.

With this happening my river had the greatest tributary in the form of the deposition of the Holy Spirit. The Spirit of the Sovereign Lord, brought warm living water in me which thawed the frozen port of my attitude, and believers were now welcome. The warm water also cleansed the polluted shores of my heart that had reigned up to this point of my life. At last I was transformed! How do I know? Simple. Over years the desires of the sinful nature have abated and fruit of The Holy Spirit, as recorded in Galatians 5, have flourished. Some of the Gifts of the Holy Spirit as inscribed in 1 Corinthians 12 have blossomed.

What did I do for it? I just accepted Jesus Christ as my Savior.

After I had run the bend of the u-turn there was a great hunger to read the Scripture, to know more about the Lord. I wanted to become sound in doctrine and move closer to Him so that He is more in me. My insatiable thirst was quenched by reading about 7-10 chapters per day. For me this was a mammoth reading. I would just read them and not meditate. I would pray and He would speak to me.

What did He confide in me? Did He?

> *Inscribe it in your soul: Peace and internal life comes only from God through Jesus Christ.*

CHAPTER NINE:
Doubts, Directions and Some Clarity

*Show me your ways, LORD, teach me your paths.
Guide me in your truth and teach me, for you are God
my Savior, and my hope is in you all day long.*
PSALM 25:4-5

Although I had accepted Jesus Christ of Nazareth as my Savior, I was still in my shell because I was not strong in the Word and therefore lacked confidence. Knowing my Achilles heel, Satan gleefully galvanized to action. He was relentless to pursue me and drag me back either in his kingdom or at least in the neutral territory. After all, he had to salvage his image, reputation, and kingdom.

Since early 2007, the Lord used me to bring healing to the sick and prophesy as if it was His divine plan. I would often wonder: What was happening? Why me? Consequently, I was scared at times because I thought what if the work was being done by the evil one? Very seldom, these negative thoughts visited my subconscious mind and frightened me. I had to tread slowly and wisely.

The best and time-tested ploy used by Satan was to sow seeds of doubts in my fertile mind. It was not just one seed, but rather a minefield of them. And the sowing did not stop in the first few months of accepting Christ as my Saviour; he tempts me even today, though the frequency is tapering off. Thomas, a disciple of Christ did not believe Christ risen from the dead and he went to the extent of saying:

> *So the other disciples told him, "We have seen the LORD!" But he said to them, "Unless I see the nail marks in his hands and put my finger where the nails were, and put my hand into his side, I will not believe."*
> JOHN 20:25

In my case, some believers helped me, guided me and boosted my confidence. And the Lord was there too!

Facing this dilemma of doubts, I would often phone Pastor Mahender and ask him many questions. Pastor Mahender was very patient with me. He always suggested, "Read the Bible, meditate on the Word, and keep on praying." At this stage of 'Transformation' in my life, I could trust him and Pastor Bob.

Pastor Bob helped me a lot in this personal Spiritual journey. Whenever I requested him to help me remove my challenges and doubts, he would take time out from his busy schedule just to meet me. He encouraged me a lot by answering questions which were beyond my ability to comprehend at this stage of unbelief, doubts and lack of Biblical knowledge-which was incidentally zero. He too encouraged me to read the Bible. Bob would often suggest:

> *As for you, the anointing you received from him remains in you, and you do not need anyone to teach you. But as his anointing teaches you about all things and as that anointing is real, not counterfeit--just as it has taught you, remain in him.*
> 1 JOHN 2: 27

As far as I was concerned, until January 2007, the Bible was a fictional book which had all the ingredients of a Hollywood movie! The very book which I never wanted to read, was being recommended and foisted on me. I had to read it and find the truth on my own and try to understand the inexplicable. I did a sudden Volte-face! It was incredible to imagine that I would be reading the Bible! Anyway, at their behest, I started reading the Bible. And to my surprise, I developed an unquenchable thirst for the divine word. The thirst was deep and my mind a sponge. I just wanted to know my Lord and also to have a relationship with Him. I started asking questions, and both the pastors were there to help me. Even though at times I questioned the authenticity of what I read, the desire to keep reading was ever increasing!

My scientific background would not let me accept the supernatural things. Even today there have been times when my scientific background makes a comeback. The Holy Spirit was however working within me. I, "An Almost Atheist", did not know the difference between Gospels and other books, Old and New Testaments but the eternal Spirit would lead me. In the beginning it was simply amazing. The Spirit would impress on me to open a certain book in the Bible, a certain chapter, and a certain verse. I just did not know where in the Bible the book was! I had to open the list of contents and from there to take the clue.

Once the Spirit said, "Open and read Isaiah 6:6-9". It is written:

Then one of the seraphim flew to me with a live coal in his hand, which he had taken with tongs from the altar. With it he touched my mouth and said, "See, this has touched your lips; your guilt is taken away and your sin atoned for." Then I heard the voice of the Lord saying, "Whom shall I send? And who will go for us?" And I said, "Here am I. Send me!" He said, "Go and tell this to people...."

"These verses are for you, James." The Spirit of wisdom and of understanding disclosed to me. In my human wisdom, I interpreted this as the Holy Spirit confiding in me that there was a plan for me and my sins had been forgiven.

Reading the same in the Bible is different, but when the Lord suggests reading: it is exhilarating. On 25th April, 2009, the Spirit of the knowledge recommended me to read Jeremiah 10:10, where it is written.

But the LORD is the true God; he is the living God, the eternal King.... The Holy Spirit was disclosing that He indeed is the true Spirit. He was revealing Himself to me!

On 29th April 2009, while I was reading the book of Zechariah 14:21, where it is written, *Every pot in Jerusalem and Judah will be holy to the LORD Almighty, ...* The Spirit of Christ indicted me. "James, you too were unclean and common, till I chose you to spread my Gospel. Now you are clean and useful. I am going to use you to spread my work through healing and prophecy." On 19th June, 2009, again the Lord led me to read the above book, the same chapter and verse. Again, in unambiguous tone the voice stressed, "These verses are for you, James." Messages like these started flowing to me, guiding me to open the Bible and read a certain Book, chapter and verses. For any wise man, this would be ample proof that indeed the Advocate was persuading me to believe that He was surely delivering me a message from our Heavenly Father.

In mid-2011 I was going through a rough patch as my scientific bent of mind and the inherent doubts associated with it took control of me. Woe to my Science degree! However the Lord reinforced His presence in my life.

On 24th July, 2011, when I was in the Jubilee Church standing about one foot away from the back wall of the church while the service was taking place, a very great force pushed me to the wall. In panic I said, "Imagine, as if I am placing Holy Books of all religions right in front of me. After doing that, I am going to call out the names of the Holy Books of all the religions one by one. When I do this, I want you to take my right hand and put it on the Holy Book which you represent, and I will know who you are."

I kept both my hands on my side touching my thighs and I called out "The Bible."

The Holy Spirit lifted my right hand and placed it on the imaginary Bible which was in front of me. Then my right hand came back involuntarily to my side touching my right thigh.

Then I took the names of few other Holy Books of different religions, but my hand did not move at all. I tested the spirit as suggested:

DOUBTS, DIRECTIONS AND SOME CLARITY

> *"Dear friends, do not believe every spirit, but test the spirits to see whether they are from God,...This is how you can recognize the Spirit of God: Every spirit that acknowledges that Jesus Christ has come in the flesh is from God,...."*
> 1 JOHN 4:1-2

I chose a slight variation this time from the above experiment. I inter-mixed the names of the Holy Books of different religions but nothing happened. Then I spoke: "The Bible." My right hand again lifted and placed on the imaginary Bible which was right in front of me, and then it came back to my side touching my right thigh. With such conclusive evidence, I realized the Spirit which had been talking to me over a period of time was the Holy Spirit.

John 14: 16-17 says, *"And I will ask the Father, and he will give you another advocate to help you and be with you forever- the Spirit of truth...."* As these verses have been spoken by Jesus, it signified to me that there has to be Jesus Christ. Since "The Spirit of truth" will be given by the Father, it clearly signified existence of - Father.

With this I also understood two very important concepts. The concept of 'Trinity': Heavenly Father, Son (Jesus Christ) and the Holy Spirit. I also understood the Unknown Spirit had to be, 'He.' and not 'She.' as in the above verse and many other places it is inscribed in the Bible: 'Father' and 'He' and never 'Mother' or 'She'.

Praise be to God for removing all the doubts from my mind, for Him being who He is:

A patient God!

Where would we be if the Lord was not a patient God?

> *Inscribe it in your soul: It is wise to follow the cue from the Holy Spirit and seek the Spirit of discernment from the Lord.*

CHAPTER TEN:
Jehovah Jireh – The Provider

Can a mother forget the baby at her breast and have no compassion on the child she has borne? Though she may forget, I will not forget you!
ISAIAH 49: 15

To have a roof over one's head is considered to be topmost priority amongst the people of the Indian sub-continent. It was also our priority. When we were in India and were about to come to Canada, Tripta asked me, "When will we have a house in Canada?"

"You do not have to worry, we will have a house within a year or two," I answered, tongue in cheek.

Within a few months of inhabiting Canada, I realized the dream which I had sold to Tripta was not going to happen within the time span I had given to her. It could not happen because of several reasons. This is a common immigrant story in Canada, no matter what the qualification or experience of a person was. Our academic degrees were not accepted by the Ministry of Education, British Columbia. Therefore, just like any other immigrant both of us started work at entry level jobs. Consequently, I did not see a promising career in the near future and with meager wages purchasing a house was a mirage in a hot desert. Besides, we had not come to Canada with substantial money. From the perspective of Indian sub-continent, age was also not on our side. I was already 44 years of age, and Tripta was 39. The average longevity amongst Indians is about 69 years. This took the wind out of our sails in the pursuit of our dreams to purchase a house within a year or two.

When we had arrived in Canada we were sharing accommodation with Anita and Gerry in Langford, Victoria. Within two spring seasons, our two sons had reached pre-adolescent stage. I thought of moving in a rental house and living independently as a nuclear family unit. However, this was a bone of contention between Tripta and me. Tripta was convinced we would not be able to get a place to rent within the small budget we managed. Her stand was to stay with Anita till we had a better bank balance in the savings account. I on the other hand, was obdurate in my approach and thought we would be able to get an affordable place to live, and the earlier we moved the better. I advised Tripta, "It would be tough in the beginning, but later it would work out." I firmly believe when the mountain is too steep and tough to climb, mountaineering skills are exhibited best- a case of survival of the fittest. As usual, my wife's wise counsel prevailed and we remained in her sister's house.

On December 11th, 2006 when fast asleep at night I was spiritually transported into space. I still remember it vividly – Oh! How could I ever forget? It could be equated with what the Prophet Ezekiel experienced:

> *He stretched out what looked like a hand and took me by the hair of my head. The Spirit lifted me up between earth and heaven and in visions of God he took me to Jerusalem,...*
> EZEKIEL 8:3

I could possibly be wrong to compare it to Ezekiel's vision, though I must say my experience cannot be counted as a dream. It was the first and the only time that I experienced spiritual transportation.

In the spiritual state, I was taken to a place which appeared to me as a subdivision of newly built houses. My spirit then stood in front of a house and I saw its facade. To my spirit apparently it was a small house. Alarmed, I exclaimed, "This is too small a house to live in!"

Then, the Spirit of the Sovereign Lord took me around the house to see the side view. Seeing the profile, I felt it would be spacious for four of us to dwell in. Even today, I remember the noise which I heard when transported around the house from the front elevation of the house to the side elevation. It was like a door pivoting on its squeaking hinges. The house that I saw had a 4-digit number, and the numbers were 3 – 2.

My spirit then started its journey from this subdivision to our shared accommodation. It stopped right above my sleeping physical body, as if it were identifying my physical self. It looked at my physical body and then dove straight into my body. I woke up with a start and saw the time at my watch – it was 2:40 a.m.

Clarity, James, clarity!

The next morning, I told the incident to Tripta. This started several futile, disappointing and demoralizing days of trying to seek by human endeavor a house that was seen by me in my spiritual form. We would often go and look for houses numbered 3 – 2 in the vicinity of our neighborhood and if we found one, I would then compare the shape and size of it. We assumed and hoped that I would be able to connect the two worlds. At times we also came across houses with the same number. However, since the front and side elevation of the house which I had seen in my spiritual state were different from the one we actually were looking at, I would rule it out. For our endeavor to be successful, God had to give us clearer indications, and they were not forthcoming. Soon we realized that there would be many houses with these numbers, size and similar shape. When this dawned on us we gave up the search and left it to the Lord and put our faith on Him to let it materialize in His good time.

In January 2008, one of our friends, Giles, was reading a local newspaper at his house. His wandering eyes arrested a public notice published by the Langford Municipality. The notice was for the public to apply for a house under an 'Affordable Housing Program'.[*] He brought the newspaper clipping and came to Anita and Gerry's house.

Over a cup of tea, Giles gave the public notice clipping to Tripta and advised, "Tripta, apply for a house under this scheme." Tripta replied with gratitude. "I will give this to James and ask to him to apply."

True to her words Tripta gave the notice to me just before going to sleep at night, and requested, "James, Giles gave this to me today. Please read it and apply."

I read and laughed sarcastically when I realized what she was asking me to do. I chortled because the reason she used to give me for not moving out to a rented house, townhouse or condominium was "We will not be able to afford it…" and now she wanted to own a house! That was unbelievable. How could she be so fickle minded and have the gall to ask me to apply? Nevertheless, her decision was final and I did not have the right to appeal. The following day, I got the application form, but did not apply.

The earth rotated for about two or three more times. Then a day before the last date for submission of form, Tripta inquired in a concerned voice, "Did you apply or not?" I thought I had muffled her unbridled dreams and desires! But I was wrong.

"We cannot afford to rent a house and now you are insisting to apply for a house under a program, where we would have to buy it, if we qualify?" I replied curtly.

Unfazed by my lack of manners she insisted I apply by the next day. To be rid of the persistent idea and frothy optimistic enthusiasm, I submitted to her suggestion. "I will apply tomorrow." Declaring that, I walked out of the room and house in annoyance. I came back when the volcano of my volatile anger had erupted in the darkness of the cold and numb night and good sense prevailed.

In order to apply the very next day, we had to read the application form right away. We took the application from our bedside cabinet and read it. It was a very simple application.

The following day, even though I had not intended to, I submitted the application. In the beginning of the month of February, 2008, the Spirit of truth impressed upon me and spoke to me: "I will give you a house under the Affordable Housing Program." I did not take it seriously. I laughed aloud saying, "God, this must be the joke of the century. I cannot afford a rented house and you are speaking of owning a house!" I rested my case with that.

On February 4th, 2008, the Lord guided me to read from the Bible. He commanded me to open and read from the book of Genesis 13:17-18, where it is written, *"Go, walk through the length and breadth of the land, for I am giving it to you." So Abram went to live....*

I realized The Spirit of the knowledge was indeed speaking specifically to me and with specific intent. I then interpreted (in my own human wisdom) the above quoted scripture as: The Lord is commanding us to go from Threlfall's residence because He was giving us a place to live. Even then I was not sure!

After about three weeks or so, I received a phone call from the municipality informing me, "You have a slight chance of getting a house and you might qualify."

This electrified us, and we went into a high energy orbit. I went on my knees to God and beseeched, "Lord, I had never dreamt of owning a house in Canada with this meager income and savings, but now since we might qualify for it, please... have mercy and give us a house."

Around 21st February, 2008 we received a letter from the municipality notifying us that we had qualified, but were third on the waiting list!

Our prayers now became more frequent, earnest and emphatic. We desperately wanted this to happen as it would truly be a faith bolstering and confidence building step for us. After a few breath taking days had passed the municipality verbally apprized us, "There might be a remote chance that persons ahead of you in the waiting list may not want the house, and if and when they confirm, the municipality would contact you."

The pitch and volume of our SOS's to God reached their crescendo. We were now just waiting for things to happen. One day, The Spirit of wisdom and of understanding gave me a verse*:*

> *So that your faith might not rest on human wisdom, but on God's power.*
> 1 CORINTHIANS 2:5

This is what we were waiting for, and we clung to the verse and started claiming it for ourselves. Our days and nights were filled with anxiety, but we tried to trust in the Lord. Remember it is written:

Immediately the boy's father exclaimed, "I do believe; help me overcome my unbelief!"
MARK 9: 24

One night as I was going to my bed to sleep, The Spirit of grace softly and tenderly called me, "Tomorrow you will get a phone call from the municipality about possession of the house." Naturally, I was elated and felt like shouting 'Hooray!'

The following morning, when I was getting out of bed, in my ears I heard the sweetest music of my life. It was very pleasing and soothing. I wanted to hear more and was drawn to it. But it stopped after a few seconds. I believe it was not from the fallen world. In retrospect, I think the music was heavenly music, and the angels praise the Lord with that kind of music. This is my belief – not that I have been to heaven!

In anticipation, my feet grew springs, and I spent much of the day lost in thought. I was shaken up from my dreams while working in aisle 4 of my workplace, Fairway Market in Langford. At 09:30 a.m. my cell phone buzzed. I answered the call in great anticipation and expectation. A shrill and highly ecstatic voice imploded my ear drums and left them scarred, "Congratulations, you are the proud owners of a house!" the municipality secretary informed me. I was given a word that we would get the house in the month of April 2008, as currently it was under construction. Was not that enough to make me dance on the floor with wild abandon?

How could I praise our majestic God? I did not even have words. But my heart sang praises of Him. We had forgotten all about the spiritual transportation incident of December 11th, 2006, but our God had not. The house number that we dwell is 3372. It is indeed a house given to us by our Lord.

Our God did not stop blessing us. Having a house led to other important matters. Since we had been residing with the Threlfalls, we had been using their kitchen appliances. Now we had to have appliances of our own. We started looking for them and concluded they would cost us a fortune if we went for brand new ones. Subsequently, we started looking for used appliances. Deep inside I was not comfortable with the idea of settling into a house provided by **my** Lord with second-hand appliances. Did you notice the use of the word **"my"** in the preceding sentence?

As usual, we took our dilemma to our God and supplicated for the brand new kitchen appliances. Few days after our prayer, and while working in aisle 4 of Fairway Market I got a phone call from the municipality. The secretary quizzed me, "Do you possess a driving license?"

"Yeeeeees." I was not sure where the conversation was heading.

She then questioned, "Does your wife possess a car?"

"Uh...Yes." By now I was puzzled.

The secretary then inquired, "How many cars do you have?"

"Ma'am, we have one car only." I was lost by her inquisitive and invasive queries.

Sensing eagerness in her voice, I asked, "Why are you asking me such questions?"

Unable to contain her excitement any longer the secretary announced in a high pitch and at the speed of almost 10 words per second. "The Mayor wants to celebrate the selling of 30th house under the 'Affordable Housing Program'. Since you are the proud owner of the 30th house, he wants to give you a gift- a car!"

I was overjoyed and without thinking blurted out, "Is it possible to have some other thing other than a car?"

The spokeswoman encouraged me to ask. I uttered hurriedly, "I... would be happy to have chicken,...sorry, kitchen appliances."

I then proceeded and gave her a list of kitchen appliances which she noted, but as a wise woman, refrained from promising me anything.

After a week or so and what appeared to me as an eternity, I received a call from the municipality requesting us to come to the municipality hall for the celebration of the 30th house sold under the 'Affordable Housing Program.' I had not disclosed to my wife anything about my conversation with the secretary. The reason was very simple: Who would ever ask for new kitchen appliances instead of a new car? In retrospect, I was feeling foolish about the entire episode.

Tripta, our two sons and I arrived well on time in the municipality hall. When the festivity started, the Mayor took the mike and spoke in general. Then with theatrical dramatics which only a politician can bring, disclosed his revelation. "A company is pleased to inform they would be giving the Roy's five new kitchen appliance FREE!" Yahooo! We got a fridge, a dishwasher, a cooking range, washer and a dryer. There was unbelief in the audience and pin drop silence. It was broken by deafening applause. While the audience was applauding for the municipality and the donor company, I eulogized our Heavenly Father, municipality and the donor. When invited to say a word, my emotions were unleashed and my voice betrayed me. I choked. I tried and failed to give comprehensive words to my turbulent emotional thoughts. Further magnanimity was offered when Tripta's aunt, Mrs. Laj MacArthur, gifted us money to buy a new microwave oven.

Later, I asked God what should be the name our house? He whispered "Bethel." To understand why He wanted us to name the house 'Bethel', He commanded to read the following passage:

> *Jacob left Beersheba and set out for Harran. When he reached a certain place, he stopped for the night because the sun had set. Taking one of the stones there, he put it under his head and lay down to sleep. He had a dream in which he saw a stairway resting on the earth, with its top reaching to heaven, and the angels of God were ascending and descending on it. There above it stood the LORD, and he said: "I am the LORD, the God of your father Abraham and the God of Isaac. I will give you and your descendants the land on which you are lying... When Jacob awoke from his sleep, he thought, "Surely the LORD is in this place, and I was not aware of it." He was afraid and said, "How awesome is this place! This is none other than the house of God; this is the gate of heaven." Early the next morning Jacob took the stone he had placed under his head and set it*

up as a pillar and poured oil on top of it. He called that place Bethel, though the city used to be called Luz.
GENESIS 28: 10-19

We took the possession of the house in the month of April, 2008. I requested one of our church members, Nick[α], to make me a wooden name plate with 'Bethel' inscribed on it. He graciously complied. It still hangs in front of our house. He also helped us a lot with settling in. Similarly, Roger Corbett, from our church helped in assembling our garden shed and cementing the front portion of our house. There were others, too. God bless all who came to help us! May we help those in need.

The Lord then started engaging me as a conduit for His purposes.

Perhaps now our Lord was on overdrive. The following incident was one of the many incidents in the series of revelations which took place in early 2007.

To discuss my employment and my student loan, I was in VIRCS to talk to my case manager. While waiting to meet him, I met a Chinese girl who had recently emigrated from China. We were exchanging notes regarding problems faced by immigrants. While I was talking to her about her job opportunities, I inquired, "When do you have an interview for the next job?" She replied, "I am going to give two interviews in the next two weeks or so."

While we were still exchanging notes with each other, I felt the Spirit of wisdom and of understanding settling over me and urging me to say a prayer for her right then and there. I entreated her, "Could I pray for you?" In a quiet, gentle and graceful voice she replied, "Despite the fact I am a Buddhist, I am willing." I said a prayer for her and passed our Lord's message to her. "Our Living God is foretelling me, you are going to get a job within the next two weeks." I also suggested to her, "Once you get the job you must come to our church to exalt the name of our Loving God."

She agreed. I then gave her my cell phone number. She got the job within two weeks and phoned me to share the exciting news, "James, I have got the job!" With happiness in my voice I reminded her of her promise: "Now you have to come to our church and give a testimony."

She refreshingly acknowledged and declared, "I will surely come." She came to the Jubilee Church to testify to that! God be praised for upholding my faith, for showing this girl who He is and making her a witness of His glory.

The following incident happened in our house in 2008. My wife needed a little guidance in a certain computer program which was giving a slight problem. We sought help from our friend, Melinda. She came with her husband Vic to our home to help Tripta. We had a nice time laughing and discussing many things over a cup of tea. During tea time, Melinda and Tripta left Vic and me in the guest room downstairs, and went upstairs in the study room where the computer was. After the problem was solved they came down and we sat down on the sofas of our sitting room. Just before their departure we prayed. During prayer the Holy Spirit revealed "Melinda would be getting a job within 20 days." Around ten days earlier, and prior to this revelation at our home, the Lord had spoken to me in the church when Melinda had come and asked me to pray regarding her job. The Lord then too had disclosed that "She will get a job in 30 days."

I gave them the message which the Lord had given to me. Melinda, wise lady that she is, heard the message with a smile but did not comment. We continued talking about various things, uplifting each other by sharing our joys and sorrows as Christians are supposed to do. After sometime they left.

One week had passed since the revelation and nothing had happened. After about two weeks, in total, when we had just entered the church and prior to the service, Vic came running to me, and in an excited tone inquired, "Do you remember when we came to your house the last time?" "I do not remember," I said, after pondering momentarily. In an excited voice, Vic added, "There is a testimony to be given by my wife Melinda."

By then, I had guessed what the testimony could possibly be. I thanked God for keeping His promise. When it was time to give testimony, Melinda got up and revealed that she had got a job out of the blue in the government sector, and what James had prophesied had come true! Melinda had actually got a phone call for an interview from a job placement organization informing her that there was a job posting and an interview the very next day. Melinda then navigated to say her Lord's story…the job she got was tailor made for her!

God's interest in us did not stop. His blessings just rolled on and on like a snow ball.

In January 2011, Tripta suggested, "James, we should buy another pre-owned car."

Tripta was talking sense because the rainy season in Victoria starts anytime after September and continues till late March. Light to moderate snowfall occurs once in 3-4 years and that too only for a few days, compared to the heavy snowfall in North and East Canada. On her way to the medical office where Tripta worked she had to change three different buses in the morning and then three buses again from her office to reach our house in the evening. About half an hour was wasted waiting in a bus shelter to change buses on her way back in the evening. The bus shelter had only a roof but no side walls. The wait was worst in late fall and winter season when the rain was heavy and the wind howled. Snowy conditions did not help; neither did short days.

While Tripta worked in the medical office, I worked in Thrifty Foods in Colwood. At times, during our coffee break, I used to go out and have coffee with my friend, Sofie Hagens at the nearby Tim Hortons. Once when we were going to have coffee in our break, I saw a red sports car on display outside a pre-owned car dealer's office. The moment I saw it, I fell for it. I shared my interest with Sofie to buy it and later also with Tripta. I even suggested to Tripta, "We should buy this car and we could even paint the whole town red while driving in it!"

However, since it was expensive for our budget, we dropped the idea. Instead I went to differrent pre-owned dealers to look for a cheap pre-owned car. In the meantime during the 'Prayer Request and Thanksgiving Time' in the church, I requested, "We are looking for a pre-owned car for Tripta; please let us know if somebody is selling a good, reliable and cheap car." After waiting for a week or two I became desperate and in frustation started going to new car showrooms. I once even placed a deposit on a new Hyundai car. My friend Ashu[a] dissuaded me from buying a new car, citing the financial constraint about buying a new car. He bluntly put it: "James, you cannot afford it." Ouch! it did hurt. Who advised 'Friends should do plain and simple talk?' It hurts! On serious note, it is always nice to have honest friends who give sound advice.

Realising he was speaking the truth, I took the deposit back. Fashion changed with the seasons but there was no sign of a car for us. With that we put the dream of buying a new car at hold.

It was now time for our Heavenly Father to work on our dream. He intervened and we were blessed for the umpteenth time. Simple, is it not?

Becky[a] from 'Always Towing', and also a member of our church started raising funds for 'Cops for Cancer'. This she was doing in different places in Victoria. To raise funds, she was shaving her head and selling tickets for CAD $ 5.00 each. The winning prize was a 1990 Chevorelet Cavalier. For fund raising in our church, she arranged a BBQ, but we did not buy any tickets.

One day, in the month of November, 2011, just before we were about to start our Home Group at 7:00 p.m., our phone rang. I picked up the phone and recognised Becky's voice.

Full of excitement and out of breath, she blurted, "Guess what?"

"Sorry, no clue," I replied. With intensity and bubbling excitment in her voice, Becky replied, "Tripta has won a pre-owned car!" I was too astonished and stunned to comprehend the news. I asked her twice. "Is it true? Is it true?" She confirmed both times and had a hearty laugh at my expense because of my disbelief. After a few hours, Becky came to our house with a bouquet of flowers, a card, and a photograph of the car. Exhilarated Tripta asked her, "How did this happen?"

Becky then explained the whole story to us. Recounting the details she disclosed, "I was raising funds in the downtown area by selling hot dogs. A gentleman walked up to me and gave me a CAD $ 5.00 bill and requested, 'This is the cost of the ticket, put the name of a person who you think needs a car most and put it in the draw.' In return I gave him a hot dog. Before putting the name on the ticket, I thought about a person who needs the car most. I then remembered that Tripta needed a car. Unhesistatingly, I put her name on the ticket. The rest was unbelievable yet true!"

Oh yes! The car that Tripta won was red in colour and an entry level sports car with a sunroof! We might forget or forgo our dreams and desires but our Lord redeems them and gifts us if they are within His will.

Where would we be if He was not the Jehovah Jireh?

> *Inscribe it in your soul: Our Lord is interested in all aspects of our lives and not just spiritual. He is our provider.*

CHAPTER ELEVEN:
Jehovah Rapha – The Healer

Heal me, LORD, and I will be healed; save me and I will be saved, for you are the one I praise.
JEREMIAH 17:14

While God revealed His plans for me, He also refined me. He led me like a father leads his child when he is learning to walk. While travelling in this spiritual journey I thought the Lord was now leading me to take water baptism. As per my logic it appeared to be the next important step.

In 2007, while doing Master's Program from UVic, our family attended the family camp organized by our church at the Cowichan River Bible Camp held at in Duncan. Duncan is in north of Victoria and is about 51 kilometres from our house. The camp has about 80 acres of land. It boasts a large field, has around 10 family cabins and is an ideal choice for family outings. It also has luxurious trees, play grounds, huge dining area, a chapel and the Cowichan River divides the property.

I decided to take water baptism (baptism by immersion) in the family camp. In Dubai, when Pastor Mahender had mentioned to me about taking baptism, I would not show any interest and fend him off saying, "I was baptised as a child, and I do not believe in God."

However, with events unfolding the way they were, and I accepting Christ as my Savior and Lord of my life, I decided to be baptized. To me, what it meant to be a follower of Christ was not crystal clear. While I was in the doldrums I was sure the mist would dispel, and the picture would be clear. Yet I knew God was using me for His glory

I strongly believed that on December 11th, 2006, the Lord had baptized me with the Holy Spirit and I should not backslide. The following verse echoed in my mind:

> *Surely no one can stand in the way of their being baptized with water. They have received the Holy Spirit just as we have.*
> ACTS 10:47

When the big day arrived, I became very sick. I was shivering with a high fever and was tempted to cancel the baptism. Fear of getting cramps in the cold waters of Cowichan river also played its part in this decision. However, better sense prevailed, and I received water baptism.

Even today, I can remember the moments very clearly as if they had been etched on a rock. My flesh was numb, but not my mind. During baptism pastor Bob and three others immersed me in the freezing water in a horizontal position with face towards the sky and then pulled me out. As I came out, I was gasping for oxygen, and my head jerked upwards towards the sky. I believe that my head was pulled by the Spirit of Christ. The Holy Spirit then took my right hand towards my forehead and then moved downwards towards my waist. Once it reached there my right hand then moved to my left shoulder and across to the right shoulder. This movement of my hand signified a Cross. I believe that with this symbolism my role in this world was made amply clear to me. These unique moments were captured by the camera. Melinda also noticed and spoke to Tripta and me about it.

While my child-like walk in the Lord progressed, Satan became restless. I started falling sick quite often after my baptism. Perhaps in this way Satan wanted to break me and tell me, "See for yourself the God who calls Himself Jehovah Rapha, is not so." He clearly hoped he would bring me back into his fold of darkness and deceit. But God is indeed Jehovah Rapha. When faced with health issues related to non-communicable diseases, I went to Him just like the persistent widow who went to the judge again and again till the judge was worn out and settled the case in her favor (Luke 18:1-8).

My first exposure to health issues started with a toothache. I went to see a dentist. After examining my teeth he recommended, "James, three of your teeth need root canal treatment and four need normal fillings. Thus seven of your teeth need immediate attention, but before I start working on your teeth, I would like you to go and have an appointment with a gum specialist as you need treatment for the gums first."

On the recommendation of the dentist, I took an appointment with a periodontist and went to meet him in the clinic on the date and time given to me. After he had examined my gums he declared, "Your gums are receding."

The periodontist presented me two options: "First, would be scaling. It could help your gums to come back to their original position. And if this is not successful then there would be the second option-a surgical procedure." He proceeded to tell me, "There was an 80% chance that you would need a surgical procedure. Unfortunately, you are in the category of those people who would have to undergo surgical procedure."

I went for a second opinion to another periodontist, who confirmed the earlier diagnosis and treatment.

Just as a tiger is driven out from his hiding in a jungle by beating of drums and yelling of people, the fear of a surgical procedure drove me to our living God, and I prayed and prayed for healing.

A date was fixed for me to go to the periodontist. The expected day arrived. I prayed and went to meet him. As I sat waiting for my turn in his clinic I underwent an anxiety attack. I prayed, and my anxiety abated. In few minutes the periodontist came. I requested, "Please do scaling only." After scaling was done he told me, "Come and see me after four months so that I could analyze the result."

For the next few months I prayed and pleaded my case with the Lord, trying to convince Him. "I do not want to undergo surgical procedure, so please let scaling be sufficed by your grace!"

After the end of four months, I went to the periodontist again. He examined my teeth and with awe and amazement in his voice declared, "You do not need any surgical procedure. Your gums are much better than before. If people start getting their gums in place just by scaling, how will I feed my family?"

God heeded my prayers, and I gave my testimony in the JCCC about our Jehovah Rapha.

Once the issue of gums was settled successfully, I went to the dentist for three root canal treatment and four normal fillings which were required. The estimated total cost came to about $4,000.00, a bill I couldn't repay easily, so I went back to my Lord imploring my case yet one more time.

After soliciting my case to the Lord, I went to the dentist on the appointed day and time and requested, "Please do not do root canal treatment in any of my teeth instead do normal fillings on all my seven teeth." My wife was working part time, and I was studying and working part time. We had our regular bills to pay, so the decision not to have the root canal treatment was solely based on prayers and monetary considerations.

He tried his level best to convince me of the futility of my decision, but I stood firm and did not relent. He did normal fillings in all my seven teeth as I had desired. Of the three teeth which had been deemed to require the root canal treatment, two are still there and one was extracted after a few years.

Since I was covered under a medical plan for normal fillings and extractions I had to pay only a nominal amount. Praise be to God. He not only saved my teeth, but also our expenses!

Jehovah Rapha's healing touch and grace in my life continued. Earlier, I had talked about getting high fever frequently during the River Bottom Family Camp in 2007. High fevers continued for about three weeks. At persistent directions and advice of my wife, I went to see our family doctor. He suggested, "Let's do a blood test." About a week after blood test was done, I received a phone call from our doctor's office advising me, "Could you please come and meet the doctor? It is not urgent." An appointment was arranged.

When the day came I casually walked to meet the doctor. He looked at my test results and pronounced his diagnosis. "You had been ill because of a viral infection. The viral infection had run its course and would ebb soon, as would the fever. However, I stumbled upon another factor of concern in the test result, which is why I have called you." Looking at the test result he pointed out, "Your sugar level is high, James."

I was aware that my physical activity level was almost zero, I had a pot belly, was middle aged, overweight, ate a lot of food with carbohydrates, and had a family history of diabetes from my father's side. Therefore, I was a textbook case. I also understood, it might not be true because I had cut down on sugar consumption long ago. Consequently, I challenged the clinical result which indicated high sugar level in my blood. I told him gently and politely, "This is not my test result." Have you ever tried saying that to a doctor?

"What do you want, James?" My startled doctor asked me.

"A second blood test for sugar- please, because I know my God is going to heal me if this is my actual test result."

My family doctor ordered a second blood test. I went back to my ever reliable support system- our living God. A day or two after I went for the second blood test. About a week later, I received a call again from the doctor's office. The Medical Office Assistant requested me, "James, can you please come and see the doctor, it is not urgent."

I took an appointment and went to meet the doctor at the given time. He shared the latest blood test report with me and to his surprise (not mine) the sugar level had dropped. Hallelujah! Just by a prayer, without a change of diet or increase in physical activity or intake of any medicine in few days the sugar level dropped! Since then my sugar level keeps on fluctuating with volatile readings of my waistline and fluctuating weight. But whenever it happens, I turn to our Heavenly

Father who then takes over my sugar level issue in His own safe hands and brings me in the green zone of health.

God did not withhold His healing touch in my life, it just continued...

Around 2008-09, I injured myself in the stomach area at my work place while lifting heavy boxes containing groceries. I reported the matter to the manager and he asked me to go home, take rest for few hours and also to meet a doctor. After taking some rest at home, I went to see our family doctor the same day. Unfortunately, he was out of Victoria and was on vacation. The receptionist advised, "Mr. Roy, would you like to meet the other doctor -Dr. Longfellow[α]?"

"Yes, please."

I was ushered to the medical examination room. After my physical examination, Doctor Longfellow declared, "You have a hernia. Next week your family doctor is returning, so it will be good to have second opinion." Begrudgingly, I agreed.

Our family Doctor examined me a week later and declared, "You don't have a hernia; but to be on the safer side you should see a physiotherapist." Then he booked an appointment with a physiotherapist and also with a specialist.

I agreed, hesitatingly. Why did I hesitate? Simple. I was relying on my God to heal me and the doctor's suggestion was in contradiction to my attempt to put my belief and trust in God.

On the appointed day and time, I went to meet the physiotherapist. She examined and diagnosed, "Your muscles are taut, and the chances of a hernia are 50-50."

Wow! Three different opinions from three different medical professionals for the same medical problem! The physiotherapist sent this report to my family doctor and at the same time she started physiotherapy sessions. She worked on the taut muscles of my shoulder and back.

During all this time, I had been going to the Lord in prayer and confiding in Him. He responded in a hushed voice, "You do have a problem but it will be healed by my grace."

Knowing the plan of the Lord, my faith soared so high that during the 'Prayer Requests and Testimony Time' in JCCC, I declared with confidence personified, "Dr. Longfellow's diagnosis is: 'I have a hernia,', my family doctor is saying, 'I don't have a hernia,' the physiotherapist's diagnosis is – 'my chances of having a hernia are 50-50,' but my living God is foretelling you do have a problem but it will be healed by my grace and the specialist will declare you do not have a hernia."

In the meantime, after about 40 days, I went for my appointment with the specialist. After examining me the specialist declared, "You don't have a hernia."

Without a second thought, I responded, "I am not surprised by your diagnosis because, our Heavenly Father, my ABBA, had already disclosed to me that I will be healed." He smiled at me and then we bade goodbye to each other. It was time to give testimony in the church and I did that.

In God's eyes, there are no diseases which cannot be healed by his Mercy. Be it terminal, chronic or non-chronic. Such classifications have been made by man not God. One such disease is Cancer. Other than Vic's Prostate Cancer, there were a few more incidents of the dreaded disease, where the Lord showed what He ordains none can change. A case that comes to my mind was about a school boy named Ralph[α]. Around 2007 Anita and Gerry invited Pastor Dan Mclean and his wife Pastor Susan Mclean, of the Victoria Miracle Centre in Victoria, for dinner. The Victoria Miracle Centre began in 2001 after some healing meetings in Nanaimo and Victoria. Susan loves her God, is passionate about the Word and prayer. Dan is a prophet and evangelist. God bless both of them for the work they have been doing for the Lord. As per our custom of praying just before guests leave, we all agreed to pray. Before the prayers started my son Fazal, who was in Division 6 requested, "Could we pray for my classmate Ralph, who has been diagnosed with Skin Cancer?" We all agreed in unison and prayed. Once the prayers were over, the guests went home and we went to sleep.

That night when I was praying, God revealed to me that Fazal's friend did not have Skin Cancer. The next morning, I mentioned to Fazal, who was only 11 years of age, "Let your friend know he does not have Skin Cancer." Fazal did not do so, since it was contrary to doctor's diagnosis, and perhaps he did not have the courage to say to his friend or did not believe it or did not want to give his friend a false hope on the basis of a prayer and no sound medical investigation and diagnosis.

The following day, I requested of Tripta, "Please tell Ralph's mother about what God has foretold regarding her son's diagnosis." I presumed it would be easier for Tripta to talk to her since she met Ralph's mother at the school. Tripta did not convey the message. I was a little upset with her. That night I showed my annoyance to Tripta, and urged her to tell God's plan to Ralph's mother the next day.

The following day, Tripta mustered courage to reveal to Ralph's mother about God's assurance. I am sure, out of politeness Ralph's mother must have given an ear to what Tripta had to say. Perhaps she must have been skeptical too about the message. After all, she barely knew the bearer of the message.

About three months later the boy was taken to the hospital to start the radiation process. As a precautionary measure the doctors consulted with each other for the last time and ordered another test, which showed Ralph did not have Skin Cancer! *Rejoice, James, rejoice and praise God!*

Later, Ralph's parents came to the Jubilee Church. His father, a pastor, gave testimony regarding the miracle, "The Lord be praised for the miraculous healing, which made it clear to me that our God is an awesome and wonderful God and indeed the Jehovah Rapha."

Yet one more beautiful testimony about the Healer. In the month of April,'08, we moved into our new house and we invited the church family to our open house. Prior to the 'Open House' there was the usual Sunday church service. During the 'Prayer Request and Testimony Time', Barb Corbett came forward and stood near the pulpit. She requested for prayers for her son, Charles. He must have been about 4-5 years old. Tears rolled down her eyes and cheeks as she spoke about her son. In a broken voice she revealed her innermost fears about Charles' medical condition, "I ...please ....please (sob) need prayers for Charles (sob) because he cannot hear (sob).... so his cognitive skills...(sob) are not to the normal level for his age. In previous consultations the doctor has divulged to me…(sob) that there is a remote chance Charles might have to undergo surgery."

Looking at her disheveled hair and hearing her sobbing, I was reminded of:

> *My sacrifices, O God, is a broken spirit; a broken and contrite heart you, God, will not despise.*
> PSALM 51:17

As she was unfolding her prayer request, The Spirit of the knowledge settled on me and advised me to let her know: "Charles will be healed by God's grace."

After requesting prayers for healing, she returned to her seat. I went to Barb and politely and gently unraveled to her God's promise of healing her son. I said, "Barb, our Lord wants His name to be exalted. When the doctors declare that Charles has been healed, your family should testify, glorify and magnify our Lord." After that I invited her family to our 'Open House'. Encouraging her I said, "I shall pray diligently to the Lord again and reconfirm about God's plan for healing Charles."

When the church service was over some members of the church came to our house. Barb came with her family. Once the 'Open House' was over, I shared with everybody about God's will in Charles life and asked them to join in prayer. While I was praying I felt some invisible thing which was entrapped in Charles ear lunged out in the palm of my right hand which was near his ear. It was eerie. It was so powerful and forceful that I had to shake my hand a couple of times in downward motion. It then jumped from my palm to the floor and out it went the main door. After the prayers, I reminded Barb, "Our living Lord has healed Charles by His grace."

Two weeks passed by. Barb and family came to the church and gave her testimony. "We had gone to a doctor, who declared that Charles could hear partially. His case has now been referred to a specialist." After her testimony, I went to her and boldly assured, "Our

God does not leave His work half done. Charles would be healed completely by God's grace."

Two weeks passed by and I was becoming impatient. In my daily prayer time at home, I would periodically go to God for reassurance about Charles and inquire, "You will heal him, won't you?"

"I have already healed him completely." The Spirit of truth would repeat it. He never chided me for asking the same question again and again. Then I marveled at our God's patience. We tend to "Sssssssshhhh!" our children for asking the same question again. Oh! What a stark contrast!

At last, the Sunday following the meeting with the specialist came. We reached the Jubilee Church on time. The church service also started on time, but Barb's family was not there. I was waiting impatiently for them to come to the church even if they were late and give their testimony exalting our Lord. Whenever the church door opened, I turned around towards the main door hoping they would step in only to be disappointed. I started praying to God reverently to remove all obstacles which might be in their way to the Church.

Finally, they came and I took a deep sigh of relief. The Church elder announced, "Now is the 'Prayer Request and Testimony Time,' please let us know what God did for you this week." I was exceedingly happy for now it was the time to exalt our Lord and hear a great testimony. But no, they did not get up to praise the Lord!

I was disheartened and now full of doubts. Had I correctly heard the whisper of our Lord? Was Charles really healed? I was deflated. Despite my doubts, I wanted to run to them, shake them, shout at them and say, "Come on, give the testimony." The negative thoughts which were roaring inside my mind weighed more heavily, and I stayed stuck to my chair. At last, they got up. I was elated, for I knew what they were going to share. And they said it! Halleluiah, praise be to the Jehovah Rapha. The specialist had declared Charles was completely healed!

Our God will never fail those who seek refuge in Him and trust Him if it is in His plan. The Corbett family had sought refuge in our Lord, and our Lord healed Charles by His grace. The specialist dismissed his case. Praise be to our God!

Did God stop His healing touch now? No. Sometimes my mind wonders, would it not be better if I do not fall sick at all rather than falling sick and then being healed? After all, when one is sick there is an insurmountable amount of stress at play. But then it appears that there had to be a reason for falling sick which I as a human being was not able to comprehend. Was the Lord drawing my attention towards something? Yes, there was a reason.

In 2008, I was diagnosed with hyperthyroidism (overactive thyroid). I used to get physically exhausted while working in Fairway Market. At night, I would just hit the bed and fall into deep slumber. While sleeping, I would get temperature, which resulted in sweating and shivering. I could not have a continuous sound sleep, was breathless, with a high pulse rate, and developed an aversion to the smell of food. I was frustrated at the helplessness of not being able to do anything to stop it. The weighing scale reading shifted to the left by about ten kilograms in about two months without any exercise, change in diet or any other life style changes. After few weeks, on Tripta's persistence, I went to the family doctor's office just to find our family doctor was out of Victoria again!

The locum doctor ordered a blood test for me. When my blood test results reached the doctor's office, his secretary asked me to come and meet him. I was at his office at the appointed time and date. The secretary ushered me to the examination room. Soon the doctor came in. He peered at the report and read it to me. Somehow, Murphy's Law played its role: the doctor read all the results; except for the results related to my thyroid and I was declared fit!

A few weeks after the doctor's diagnosis while sitting in the church and listening to the sermon of our pastor, my heart palpitation increased. I rose up from my chair, walked outside the church, and squatted on the ground under the awning of the door. It was raining gently and the world at that moment appeared to be very beautiful and peaceful. I was in love with the world, the beautiful work of our Creator. The pitter-patter of the raindrops, the sound of the tires when vehicles drove through the rain on the road, the smell of the flora and soil in the air, the mist curling up and down in the lower layers of troposphere and the gentle breeze gave me a fresh realization that I was alive to appreciate creation. Suddenly, life appeared to be more precious. My palpitation increased further and so did my breathing. I knew it could not be heart attack as I was neither sweating nor had pain.

After the service ended, I went inside and spoke to Tripta, "I am not feeling well, let's go home." Perhaps my slow speech and pale face said it all.

"What happened?" Tripta asked with all seriousness in her voice.

Panting and puffing, I replied slowly, "My... heart palpitation... is... increasing."

Tripta immediately dropped cleaning the dishes that she was doing and we drove home.

Later in the night around 8 p.m., my heart palpitations increased again. Tripta telephoned Khrist, who is a consultant in Cooperative for Assistance and Relief Everywhere (CARE)* in Atlanta in the United States. He is a year younger to me, is reasonably fair, supports short hair, has a round face and reasonably big eyes with black pupil and is the wisest of all the siblings. Because of his tender heart and philosophical understanding of life my father often called him a sage. In a worried tone she said, "Khrist, this is the second time in about 8 hours James' heart palpitation has increased."

Jesting he inquired, "Did he see any beautiful girl?"

With displeasure in her voice and with impatience Tripta retorted, "No...no, he was in the church when this happened around 11:45 a.m."

"Take James to the emergency immediately," Khrist responded with urgency in his voice.

Initially I resisted this suggestion. Tripta however overruled all my arguments and drove me to the Victoria General Hospital (VGH). When we reported to emergency department the Medical Office Assistant (MOA) welcomed me with sweet smile and a barrage of questions, "Sir, how are you feeling today?"

"I have heart palpitations and that is why I am here in the emergency ward."

"Did you drive by yourself?"

"No, I drove him," Tripta intervened.

"Were you sweating, Mr. Roy?"

"No."

"Did you feel any pain?"

"No." I replied, perplexed.

"Were you breathing heavily?"

By now I was annoyed. With irritation in my voice replied, "Yes ma'am, and I was panting and puffing."

"Ok, it seems you are in for a heart attack. Your lips are pale too. Please sit down."

Ironically, despite the initial unofficial diagnosis by the MOA, I was not rushed to the emergency ward and had to wait. Symptoms of heart attack were apparently not sufficient criteria for getting emergency treatment!

After a delay of about half an hour we were taken in a room in the main hospital. Once we reached the room the nurse told me gently and politely, "Mr. Roy, we will be taking your blood sample for test and will do an ECG. Could you please put this hospital gown now?"

"Thanks," I replied and took the gown.

After the blood sample was taken, I changed into the crisp clean gown given to me and lay on the bed waiting for the nurse to come. When she came back, she stuck some weird wires of different colours on my chest, toes and fingers. That was enough to give me a heart attack! It was late night and I wanted to sleep but could not due to anxiety. This stress caused the ECG warning alarm to go, summoning a hurried and worried nurse. Seeing nothing out of the ordinary she would heave a sigh of relief but soon got annoyed as the warning bell went on frequently. Once she even advised, "You are under stress, try to think of something else and not concentrate on your medical condition."

Usually we always keep a Bible in our car, but somehow on this particular day the Bible was not there. Since we did not have the Bible with us, my wife could not read verses from it to seek solace for me and her. Instead she started singing hymns at low volume in the room. It reminded me of the scripture of praising the Lord in all circumstances. Kudos to her for following the Word. Praising God at this time of distress and anxiety helped us a lot. God took away a lot of our anxiety. I also realized and understood the importance of knowing some Bible verses by heart and resolved that henceforth I should make a concerted effort to do so. I ruminated it would be a nice idea for such times in the future and if led by the Holy Spirit, they could be quoted to strangers too if and when they seek prayers or Biblical advices.

Fortunately, when leaving our home to go to VGH we had not left in haste. I had taken with me a copy of all my medical reports which my family doctor had ordered over a period of time. It was here in emergency ward while going through my personal medical records the doctor diagnosed I had hyperthyroidism. This was corroborated with the blood test results taken at VGH .The blood test results were later posted in the e-health system. He gave me Metoprolol, a medicine to slow my heart palpitation and advised me, "Meet your family doctor tomorrow."

"Will do, doctor."

We left the hospital and were at our home around 2:30 a.m.

After booking an appointment with my family doctor, I went to meet him the next day. He asked me some questions, and later saw the latest blood test report which came electronically from VGH. Having read the entire report, he confirmed, "James, you have hyperthyroidism."

He told me to continue with Metoprolol and also gave me some other medicine to control my anxiety. The doctor also booked an appointment with a specialist, which was one and a half months later.

However, I did not start with the anxiety control medicine because I said to myself, "I would go to the Lord for this purpose."

When the health scare of hyperthyroidism started there was no fear of dying, but thoughts of imminent death were planted by Satan and I succumbed to them, even though it is well known that no one dies of hyperthyroidism if they receive early treatment. I became very irritable and my family was tormented because of it. Nonetheless, I sincerely believed that my Healer, my Loving God, was neither irritated by me nor would He turn His back on me.

Daytime was usually good because of my busy work and the symptoms either did not occur or went unnoticed. But in the quietness of the night the symptoms were all too evident. With the frequency of the heart palpitations and breathlessness increasing, my anxiety also increased. There were times when the spirit in my heart would move as if it wanted to come out of my body. I was unable to have a sound sleep. Gradually, I started fearing nights. Sometimes I would weep bitterly, crying to the Almighty Father to take hyperthyroidism away from me. He would always speak to me through the scriptures, and I would cling to His Word desperately like a survivor clinging to a straw in the ocean.

One fine day I suggested to Tripta, "Dear, I would like to sleep downstairs as we do not have a washroom upstairs, and I have to empty my bladder couple of times during the night. Also, I do not want to disturb you by tossing and turning in bed while trying to sleep." She did not respond positively, but I persisted and they say persistence pays. Well, it did. I moved downstairs with my bedding in our sitting room.

Again I took my case of hyperthyroidism to my Lord in prayer and He promised, "I am going to heal you without a medicine going in your body for its treatment." I was glad at His promise.

The following Sunday, I gave this testimony in the church: "My loving Heavenly Father is going to heal me of hyperthyroidism, and this will happen before I meet the specialist. My Heavenly Father has also promised me that He would heal me because of His grace and without any medicine for the treatment of hyperthyroidism." After giving my testimony I came back from the pulpit and sat on my chair in the church when again there were heart palpitations! I was bewildered by this because I thought God had healed me.

Later when the church service was over, I met Shiver[α], a servant of Christ, in our Church, and asked her about reoccurrence of heart palpitation. She suggested, "Healing is different from restoration, and you should start praying for restoration also." I just hoped she knew what she was saying! God bless her for the insight.

On September 9th, 2008, while reading my Bible in my 'Relationship Building Time' at home The Spirit of the knowledge gave me three readings: 14th, 15th chapters from the Gospel of John and from the Gospel of Mark, 16:18 "...*they will place their hands on sick people, and they will get well.*" On September 10th, The Spirit of Jesus guided me to open and study the book of Acts, chapters 3 and 4. In the book of Acts, chapter 3, Peter healed a crippled beggar. This was a clear indication to me that God was going to heal me. On September 11th, the Holy Spirit directed me to read the Gospel of Matthew, chapter 9:1-9 and chapter 10. When I read chapter 9, I came to know that Jesus healed a paralytic man. I took this as a reconfirmation from God that He was going to heal me of hyperthyroidism.

What hit me hard was:

"Follow me,".... (Matthew 9:9)

Was the Lord hinting something to me?

On September 12th, The Spirit of his Son directed me to read whole of Psalm 23, and also Psalm 91:3-16. Some important verses which caught my attention were from Psalm 91:

- *Surely he will save you from the fowler's snare and from the deadly pestilence.(v.3)*
- *For he will command his angels concerning you to guard you in all your ways;(v.11)*
- *"Because he loves me," says the LORD, 'I will rescue him; I will protect him, for he acknowledges my name."(v.14)*

Ah ha! There it was!

I was very elated to read these reassurances and reinforcements God gave me, particularly because they were from the Bible.

One day I received a phone call from our family doctor. "James, the specialist wanted a few tests to be done. These tests are related to nuclear medicine. Can you go and get the tests done?"

I picked the necessary papers from his office and went to the Royal Jubilee Hospital on the given date and time.

In the nuclear medicine unit I met a young technician who was wearing a Cross on her necklace. She must have been in her mid-twenties. Being inquisitive by nature I asked her, "Are you wearing the Cross as a fashion statement, or is it because you are a believer?"

She replied, "I am a believer."

This was good tidings to me as we could speak unhesitatingly. We started exchanging testimonies. I recounted to her many testimonies where God had used me to heal people and to prophesy. I also disclosed to her my God was going to heal me before the appointment with the specialist, but He wanted me to go through all these processes for a definite reason which could not be fathomed then. Before starting the scanning for MRI, my suggestion to her was, "Since you have instructed me not to talk and lie motionless, could you please share your testimony while the machine is scanning?"

I still remember how excited she was. Her hands were flying all over and she was smiling excitedly while sharing her testimony. After every two or three sentences she would say, "I can't believe this, I can't believe this." And by "this" she meant giving her testimony to a stranger, a patient undergoing MRI test. Once the tests were finished, we bade goodbye.

On November 6th, The Spirit of holiness spoke to me through the Word yet one more time. He directed me to read Psalm 121. My mother always read this Psalm whenever any one of us would leave our hometown. I liked verse 7 in particular: *The LORD will keep you from all harm- he will watch over your life;* .On 4th December, The Spirit of Christ gave me another passage from the Bible:

Cast all your anxiety on him because he cares for you. (1Peter 5: 7)

I would get all these assurances from our Almighty God time and again. I was just being led by the Holy Spirit to read these passages. All these passages were related to protection or care, or both, and following God.

Despite all these assurances, reinforcement from the Bible, and my own resolutions, Satan would come with his nefarious strategies. Just as a virus attacks a computer and destroys all data, Satan attacked me again and again and tried to uproot me from God's kingdom and my faith. Because of this destroying resemblance between the two, I call Satan a 'Virus." Once this virus even said, "When Christ could not save himself from death on the Cross, how can he save you?" Was this not the line of thought of some teachers of law and elders when they mocked Jesus during Crucifixion? Satan pushed me into negative thinking, day in and day out. He was always attacking and playing with my mind. It became his battlefield. His strategy was to divert me, to change my outlook towards God. It acted as centrifugal force[*] and tried to pull me away from our Loving God. However, our living God never let Satan take the anchor away. He acted as a centripetal force* and lifted me back from the negative zone and moved me into His positive territory by giving me Scripture references to read. Between the two, my mind would meander like a river shifting between God's and Satan territories within a very short span of time.

One Wednesday morning around 10 a.m., when I was off work and sitting in the couch of our sitting room and reading my Bible, I felt an urge to pray. I kneeled on the floor and prayed. All of a sudden I broke down and started crying bitterly and loudly to God, "God," I sobbed, "I do not want hyperthyroidism. Take it away from me; Christ said, ask anything in my name in faith and you will be given, so I beseech you my Heavenly Father, in the name of your son Jesus Christ with all the power and authority, He gave to us, heal me completely."

While I was praying on my knees, The Advocate spoke yet one more time assuring me that He was going to heal me because of His grace. The Spirit of his Son then directed my hand towards my neck, where the thyroid is located, and then moved my hand down towards my urinary passage and then towards the floor. In my human wisdom, it meant that God would heal me this way. Any medical logic to that?

I then submitted my request to the Lord in prayer: "If this is what it means, then, Lord, let me urinate now. I will take it as a sign of confirmation of your healing." As soon as I had said this there was an urge to urinate. Satan now stepped in and whispered, "This is just a coincidence; demand another sign." Gullible as I was but in earnest I immediately petitioned: "Oh Lord, if I urinate now let it be done with pressure." As soon as I said that, there was a deep satisfaction within me which meant I would urinate with pressure. "This is just a fluke, ask for more signs," the deceiver, whispered. I appealed for the third time, "Oh God, if you want me to be healed by your grace, when I urinate, let me urinate for a longer time than normal."

This time, the accuser, Satan, did not further implant anything in my mind. Was it a mere coincidence that Christ was tempted three times after baptism by Satan and I too who was redeemed by the precious blood of the Lamb, Jesus Christ was tempted three times? (Matthew 4:1-11).

As soon as I had put my third condition, the Spirit of counsel and of might pulled me up from the floor and pushed me towards the washroom which was two to five steps away. I went in the washroom. All three conditions which I had put before our Healer were met. Surprisingly, when I had started praying my bladder was not full to its capacity!

In this entire episode, what I was unable to understand was how Satan could play with my mind while I was seeking and praying to the Lord? Then I recalled that Satan had come in the presence of the Lord with other angels as per the book of Job. In fact, the Lord had talked with Satan (Job 1:6-12). I also recalled that though Adam and Eve walked in close proximity with the Lord in the Garden of Eden, yet Satan came in the same garden and the first sin was committed.

Time passed by and the date to meet the specialist arrived. He read all my reports and also did some tests, quizzed me, and then pronounced his diagnosis: "You are now OK." My wife, who had accompanied me, was naturally elated as were my two sons. Of course, I was too!

Praise be to God for keeping His promise! I was healed without taking a medicine for treating hyperthyroidism! The only medicine that I had been taking was Metoprolol to slow down my heart palpitation. The specialist also stated, "You should stop taking Metoprolol."

After returning home, Tripta phoned Khrist and shared the good news and then asked, "Should James continue taking Metoprolol?"

He suggested, "Continue with it for some time but he should wean off from it."

The following day I went to meet my family doctor and shared the wonderful news with him. Then we discussed regarding stopping the intake of Metoprolol and mutually agreed that I should be tapering on Metoprolol.

On his recommendation I reduced from two doses per day, to one dose per day and then finally stopped the single dose after 15 days."

Getting rid of the Metoprolol was not easy, especially the second dose, as by now I was psychologically dependent on it. This reliance on medicine was one more aspect which I hated, as I wanted to count on God and make Him my security blanket. This dependency on medicine added stress which affected my health a lot. I would imagine things which were not happening, and would feel I was under some sort of attack from within my body.

When the anxiety would reach its peak, I would ask my wife to read some passages from the Bible for me. She quite often would read from the book of Psalms. While reading she would personalize the verse by inserting my name. Rather than "your" or "I," Tripta would insert "James." For example, she would read Psalm 23, as: "The Lord is your (James') Shepherd, I (James) shall not want..." In this way she was able to personalize the Biblical passages, and after some time I would feel better.

At times, I would phone Shiver and her husband Danny[α], who prayed for me. It took around 7-8 days to finally put a stop to the intake of Metoprolol, but because of the grace of my Lord I was able to get rid of it, and I became dependent on God, rather than on medicine. Hallelujah!

In this journey with the hyperthyroidism I came to realize the name of Christ is all-powerful and my faith in Christ increased even more. During nights when I was woken up by the pounding of my heart against my chest, I would start praying to our Heavenly Father, and as soon I would say, "In the name of Christ, palpitation become normal." The palpitations would start ebbing from the crest they had reached! Why wouldn't my faith soar high like a glider?

Yet one more positive outcome of the hyperthyroidism was fall in my blood sugar level. When it had all started, in one of my blood test reports my sugar level was high. When I shared my concern with doctor regarding high sugar level, he said, "I am more concerned about hyperthyroidism and would deal with sugar level issues later."

Whenever I prayed for the healing of my hyperthyroidism, I would also pray about sugar level. God, as usual, came to my rescue. The sugar level dropped from about 7.6 mml/L to about 5.9 mml/L in a period of three to six months without any change of diet or exercise or medication!

Once again, with a smile on my face and a thankful heart, I went in front of the congregation one Sunday morning and confidently and gleefully reminded them of my testimony which I had given to them few Sundays ago regarding the promise of our Lord healing me. This time, I declared to them all, "My Heavenly Father has kept His promise, and

JEHOVAH RAPHA – THE HEALER

has healed me and His promise of healing me without medicine has been fulfilled." Praise be to Jehovah Rapha!

Is He not our Jehovah Rapha?

> *Inscribe it in your soul: Our Lord was Jehovah Rapha in the Old Testament, in the New Testament and will remain so till the end of the world.*

CHAPTER TWELVE:
Our Lord is Omnipresent

―――✦―――

For he spoke, and it came to be; he commanded, and it stood firm.
　　　　　　PSALM 33:9

Our Heavenly Father created the world and human beings. We delineated and demarcated the world into countries. We recognize the man-made political boundaries, and the need of having documents to cross these boundaries. But our Heavenly Father never recognizes any of these boundaries nor does He need any paper work to cross the border! Geographical limits can be insurmountable to us but it does not interest our Lord and they cannot limit Him or His works. He transcends all political and geographical boundaries.

His omnipresent attribute has helped me a lot, when I was in doubt or when my stubborn reasoning or my scientific way of thinking came in my way. Also at times there were doubts or unbelief and I did not trust God's plan which He revealed to me just because they were overwhelming. During such times, I would telephone Pastor Mahender for confirmation. Our Lord would divulge the same plan to him as well! Surprised! Isn't that great? This is especially shocking given that Pastor Mahender was unfamiliar with the players involved, nor the background of the problem. I would always get buoyed by this reinforcement and my faith would skyrocket. And this happened when I was in Victoria, Canada and he in India or Dubai.

Once I got an e-mail from Melinda requesting a special prayer. This must have been in 2007. She got the prayer request through a prayer chain. A lady was denied permission to cross the border in a foreign land where she had gone for some work. I was informed that the lady's visa had apparently expired. When I prayed, the Spirit of the knowledge revealed, "Within a few days the lady's visa problem would be over, and she would be allowed to return home." Prior to sending the Lord's revelation to Melinda, I asked Pastor Mahender to pray about it. Our Lord gave him the same answer that He gave me. I disclosed the Lord's plan via e-mail to Melinda who had requested me to pray. After a few weeks I received an e-mail back from Melinda, informing me that the lady who had not been allowed to cross the border was allowed to and she had reached her own country. Praise be to God!

I was lucky that the Lord had revealed the plan to me when I was praying to Him. This however does not mean that He knocks at the door of our heart and mind only when we pray. Umpteen times He has woken me up from deep sleep just to give me a message. Under such circumstances I always wondered, 'Lord, why not give the message to me when I am praying or wide awake?' But the beauty of it is that despite waking me up from deep slumber in the midst of dark night, I was never tired or short of sleep the next morning. He took care of that too.

One day in May 2007 while I was sleeping at home in Victoria, I was woken up by the Holy Spirit. The Spirit revealed, "Your sister Mamta, who is in Dubai would be flying to India shortly and after that she would be going to the United States."

The following day, when I remembered the message of the Spirit of glory, I telephoned Mamta di who was working as a teacher in a school in Dubai. It was night time in Dubai and she was fast asleep. Nonetheless, she woke up and I spoke to her and delivered the Lord's message little caring that she was almost half asleep. After about 12 hours, she telephoned me back and in a surprised tone said, "How did you come to know about it?"

"The eternal Spirit revealed it to me," I disclosed. Then my sister took me into confidence and in a hushed tone divulged, "I had indeed applied to do Master's program from the Cleveland University, Ohio, in English and was waiting for admission to..." I broke the conversation in the middle and confessed to her, "Do not worry, you surely would be given admission to the University, because the Holy Spirit has revealed it to me." We both were happy and before she put the phone down she reminded me, "Do not tell anybody about it."

Later, when she was granted admission, she disclosed to Ma. Ma was overjoyed.

A few days later while talking to Ma on the phone, Ma confessed her stress over the monetary concerns. Then and there I submitted my prayer request to the Lord about the strain that my mother was feeling regarding Mamta di's financial status and its implication. The Spirit of the Lord revealed, "Mamta would not only be paying her tuition fee from her previous savings but she would also get an assistant's job in the field of education, and because of her work in the United States she would be able to meet her financial obligations of boarding, lodging and transportation." I disclosed this to Ma, and upon hearing this, her tension ebbed.

Mamta di left Dubai in late June 2007 and reached India. Later she arrived in America in August 2007. When my sister reached America, everything happened as God had spoken. Praise be to our Provider!

Yet another example of God not being confined or controlled by man created geographical boundaries concerned Prem. Madhu di and Prem were no longer working in their parent's schools in India but were in Dubai since 2004. Madhu di was working as a teacher and Prem was working as a civil engineer in a private company. Once in 2008 summer holidays, when Madhu di was in India, and I was speaking to her on the phone from Victoria, she confessed, "I am concerned about Prem's job." She further elaborated. "In Dubai, because of the recession, large numbers of people were being laid off, and Prem's company might lay him off too. Please pray for him."

I prayed to God about it. The Spirit of the knowledge revealed "Prem's job is safe, and he will not be asked to leave immediately but he should change his job in about a year and half time." I gave her the Lord's message.

On 15th May, 2009 I received an e-mail from Madhu di informing us that "Prem has received an appreciation letter from his company and also a cash award. The company declared, 'His services would be required by them until January, 2010.'"

Did our Lord not say that?

In our Lord's time, Prem did change his job and went to another company in Dubai within a year. In April 2011, Prem left Dubai to help his parents run their family business in South India.

God is not only omnipresent but is also omniscient.

Pastor Dan and Susan invited us to their house towards the end of December 2010. After a delicious dinner we had a prayer session. While I was praying the Holy Spirit settled over me and declared, "Somebody close to you is flying…." Pastor Susan immediately cut in and asked her daughter, "Where is Russel^a right now?" Her daughter replied, "Russel is flying…."

The episode was gratifying for me as there was immediate confirmation. God knew Russel was in the plane and probably He was sitting next to him!

Is not our God just everywhere?

> *Inscribe it in your soul: The Lord ensures when He speaks to a person, the message is delivered to the right person at the right time and not redirected, delayed, or delivered to a wrong person. Often, we might add color to the message and make a mess of the message because of our human wisdom or emotions.*

CHAPTER THIRTEEN:
He Loves, He Cares

⁌⁋

The LORD is my light and salvation-whom shall I fear? The LORD is the stronghold of my life – of whom shall I be afraid?
PSALM 27:1

In Psalm 145:13, it is written, "*...The LORD is trustworthy in all he promises and faithful in all he does.*" How these words have proven to be true in our lives!

One of the many promises that God has given to me is "I will look after your family's needs." He provided for many of our needs like housing, cars, and finances for my studies and my wife's studies, and many more in India, Dubai, and in Canada. There are uncountable instances of His mercies and grace which we clearly see in our lives. Whenever I am in doubt, I always meditate and look at the rear-view mirror of my life and it reflects the immense wonderful works that He has done which we could never have achieved in our strength and wisdom. My faith in Him then increases and I walk towards His open welcoming arms with all doubts dissipated.

One such example involves our car, a 2003 Oldsmobile Alero, which we purchased from a pre-owned car dealer. As it was a pre-owned vehicle it did not come with a warranty and we did not opt to buy any warranty. Within half a span of a fly's life, car brakes started grinding and squeaking. I went to the dealer who had sold us the car and drew his attention towards the screeching brakes. Casually he suggested, "Go to our repair workshop and get them checked there."

Fearing a substantial bill, I asked, "What would they charge me for it?"

"Not for checking. But definitely for material and labor costs," he retorted.

With a heavy heart I went to the work shop and got a rough estimate. It included replacement of rotors, brake pads, brake drums and calipers for both front and rear tires. I came back to the salesperson with the estimate and after consultation with him booked an appointment for the repair work.

On the appointed date, I went and gave my car for repairs. The manager asked me to return after a few hours. When I returned the beaming car mechanic said, "Repair work is done, we dealt only with the front wheels' brake issues, and have replaced what was essential."

"What about the rear wheel?"

The manager interrupted our conversation and answered, "We thought the rear wheel brake problem does not require immediate attention, hence we have not fixed it."

Full of anxiety in my voice I inquired, "Can you please give me the bill?"

Guess what?

The bill they gave me was zero dollars! ABBA, our Heavenly Father, be praised for the zero dollar!

God's promise was not limited only to our needs but also extended beyond them. God never promised there would not be any tough times, but He did promise during the tough times He would lead us out.

The righteous person may have many troubles, but the LORD delivers him from them all; (Psalm 34:19)

There were times when Yahweh warned me of a particular danger. One such incident is related to ingestion of food. Our parents had taught us to pray before every meal and this had become a ritual for me. However, this ritual gained significance and acquired new meaning when God opened my eyes and stepped in. I was so cocooned in God's love and in His assurances that I never thought food could present any threat to us and if it did, our Lord would warn me. As few seasons went by, I started believing that God would never say, "Don't eat this food because it is going to harm you", until the day it happened.

During my lunch break in Fairway Market, I prayed to God to bless the apple that I was about to eat, when the Spirit of his Son warned me: "Do not eat the apple." I was startled and surprised because that was the first time the Lord had warned me not to eat. I complied. Because of human curiosity, I picked up the apple to have a closer look. To my surprise, I found the apple had a reasonable thick coating of wax!

The second time when the Lord warned me, I had not even prayed! Tripta and I had gone to visit our friends at their house. At the time of departure, they gave us a box of delicious Indian sweets. On the way back as I was driving, Tripta gave me a piece of sweet to taste. As soon as the sweet touched my taste buds I felt a bout of dizziness.

I muttered feebly under my breath, "God, why is my head acting funny?"

"Sweets are not good for your health."

"Why?"

"They are rich in sugar," He stated.

I did ruminate about His explanation and was despondent of being deprived of the tasty, mouthwatering Indian sweets in Canada. I knew very well that He would not reconsider changing the answer but gave me an option to believe or not to believe or even after believing to do or not to do. I chose to be obedient.

Hesitatingly I asked, "Is it OK if Tripta eats them?"

He replied in the negative.

"Can my sons Fazal and Rahul have them?" I asked guardedly.

"Yes, they can."

Such is the protective care our God lovingly extends towards us.

The beautiful part is: His love is for everyone, not just for few chosen ones. And His love endures forever. The most delightful part being He wants to be intimate with us and that is why He knows us by our names, the same way as He knew Saul and Ananias (Acts 9), Peter (Acts 10). Imagine, right from the day He created Adam and Eve and as of today He knows all of us by our names! And that will make how many of us? Uncountable stars! Not only does He know us by our name but also where we live as He knew where Peter was living and directed Cornelius to send men to bring Peter to his house (Acts 10: 5-6). Do you think He knows our lineage too?

If He did not love us why would He send His only son in flesh and give us another chance?

> *Inscribe it in your soul: The Lord loves us and knows us by our name, where we live and is interested in are daily affairs no matter how trivial they are.*

CHAPTER FOURTEEN:
Jehovah Shammah – The Lord is Present

❧

> *Suddenly the fingers of a human hand appeared and wrote on the plaster of the wall, near the lampstand in the royal palace....*
> DANIEL 5:5

In the Old Testament, God spoke directly to His people. Later He used prophets to speak to them. Then there was a time of silence followed by coming of the only begotten Son of God, Jesus Christ into this world in flesh. After Christ was crucified and rose from the dead, the Holy Spirit –the Advocate was given to us.

> *Suddenly a sound like the blowing of a violent wind came from heaven and filled the whole house where they were sitting.... All of them were filled with the Holy Spirit....*
> ACTS 2:2-4

I strongly believe even today the Holy Spirit is active.

The Lord started revealing His plan to me in the year 2007. Once while at home I was praying to our God in my 'Relationship Building Time', despite the force of gravity, my hands were involuntarily lifted, and my fingers started writing something in thin air. The fingers formed words and the words formed sentences and the sentences declared our Lord's Sovereignty. I was startled and intrigued when it happened for the first time. Needless to say it was the work of the Holy Spirit.

After a few months, I sought a meeting with our pastor and Vic, an elder of the Jubilee Church and showed them what was happening. Vic recalled that in the Bible, in the book of Daniel, the fingers wrote on the wall when King Belshazzar was having a party in his royal palace (Daniel 5). In my case I was writing on a thin wall of air! Vic's Biblical knowledge proved to be comforting to me. Had he not cited this example, I would have been scared, doubtful and ignorant. This was one of the many ways of communication God used to deliver His messages and does it even today.

Then God led me to another way of communication, but the common factor remained the same: it was through the Holy Spirit. In March of 2009, during my lunch break, I was eating lunch in my car. After finishing my lunch, I opened my Bible and started reading. Then I observed an astonishing work of the Lord which left my mouth agape. The Spirit of the Sovereign LORD wanted to give me a message and to receive it the Spirit of Jesus impressed upon me to take a sheet of paper and a pen. I usually have both in my car therefore with ease I picked them up; then the Spirit of truth started writing on a sheet of paper! My hand was being used by The Spirit of the LORD to inscribe! The message from the Spirit of the knowledge was about what I had to share during our Home Group meeting on that Friday. The Spirit of glory wrote down the name of the book, chapter and verses from the Bible. Later, The Spirit of the living God went on to write the entire explanation. He drew references from different books in the Bible. From then onwards, this method of communication has continued.

The Lord then chaperoned me into yet another way of expression. He sure knows ways to surprise me!

In the month of April 2009, God sprang one such surprise on me. Instead of giving me a message in advance for sharing the Scripture in our Home Group, He proclaimed, "Today I will be with you in the Home Group, and I will then lead you in sharing the Word with others." That would be extempore! For a person who had just started sharing God's Word this was unfair! It was difficult to follow the command of the Lord but since I had no choice in this matter, I accepted it. Since then I understood the veracity of the statement, "The one God chooses, He uses."

Our Home Group meeting started. After 'Praise and Worship' it was time to share God's Word. All eyes were on me. My heart was racing like a Ferrari at high speed. Then the Lord empowered me with the Spirit. The Spirit of the living God spoke and shared the entire message. It was the most authoritative message I had ever shared. The Holy Spirit was quoting from the Bible, from a number of different books, giving examples from all over the Bible, and there was a perfect flow of the message. When it ended I could not believe it since I never knew the topic I would be speaking on until the message started flowing out of my mouth. It ended after about 45 minutes!

Yet another way in which God has guided me is through the Scriptures. He guides me to open a certain book in the Bible and then goads me to read some verses from a chapter. I remembered, when I was young, I would laugh to myself when pastors claimed "God speaks through the Word." I was never able to comprehend how the Bible spoke. Today the shoe is on the other foot; now I proclaim that God does speak through the verses in the Bible. On 29th April 2009, when I was reading the book of Zechariah 14:21, where it is written *"Every pot in Jerusalem and Judah will be holy to the LORD Almighty, and all who come to sacrifice will take some of the pots and cook in them...."* The Spirit of the Sovereign LORD commanded me to pick up a pen and inscribe in my Bible 'You too were unclean and common, until I chose you to spread my Gospel. Now you are clean and useful. I am using you to spread my Word through healing and prophecy ministries.'

May the Lord Almighty lead me to where He desires, and use me as He wants. May the Lord mold me in such a way that I may always remain at the center of His will. Amen.

Should we not desire God to be the potter of our lives?

> *Inscribe it in your soul: Be sound in the Word, for the Lord our God might use anyone of us to give sound Biblical advice to our family, friends, believers, and non-believers.*

CHAPTER FIFTEEN:
My Lord, My Guide

Bless those who persecute you; bless and do not curse.
ROMANS 12:14

While reading the Bible and listening to sermons, I learned that the apostles, disciples, preachers, evangelists and many others over the course of history of our planet were persecuted. At times, believers have animated discussions regarding news emanating from different parts of the world where Christians are persecuted, even today.

How then could I be left out even though it was a very low level of condemnation? How I wish I had a choice in this matter! But then condemnation draws an individual to a closer relationship with the Lord. Only during the time of condemnation a person understands to a very small extent what Christ must have undergone. After condemnation the true light of humility, patience, understanding, and humanity sparkle.

Once, while asleep the Spirit of the LORD gave me a message which I was instructed to give to Donald[a]. The message was, "James, will be severely criticized and your work is to defend him." When I woke up, I wondered about the message. On Sunday, I conveyed the message to him. After contemplating in my human wisdom, I came to the conclusion that nothing would happen to me since the Lord is with me.

But I was wrong! I learnt when the precipice of doubt comes people can sway the emotions and reasoning of others.

In 2008 I was openly criticized for the first time in a Home Group. At least this was the first time I came to know of it. The aim of the Home Group was to share the Word, sing hymns in praise of God, pray, and uplift each other. However, in this particular meeting of the Home Group the Lord's name was neither uplifted nor exalted.

When the meeting started one of the Home Group members stated, "James is a man of God. God's revelations through him have come to pass." As soon as this thought was shared, a believer, who does not believe in present-day prophecies, opened verse after verse from different books of the Bible to prove all prophecies have already been fulfilled in the Bible. Was it just a difference of opinion? Whatever the reason, the end result of the relentless tirade was that the meeting was adjourned as nobody was willing to listen to anybody. The purpose for which such meetings are held was thus hijacked and sabotaged. Distaste, acrimony, infighting, and factionalism reached its peak. It became chaotic. The difference of opinion brought about segregation in the Home Group.

I came to know about this disturbing event the following day. But I was not able to gauge the undercurrent, its effect, and the spillover it would have in our church. I was happy, sad, and hurt regarding the incident. Happy, because I, it had come out in the open, believers in the church would now talk freely about it and the matter would be settled once and for all. I was saddened and hurt because to a certain extent, I took this attack personally.

By Sunday, within two days of this incident, many members in the church came to know about it. After giving testimonies for about three and half years almost every Sunday of God's blessings in our family, some people being healed in the name of Christ, with many prophecies coming true, and with glory being given to God, I thought people would be able to see clearly and understand objectively that God was working in my life. And it was not me who claimed anything in the Home Group.

People were divided in their opinion. I got looks of disbelief from some, and a few ignored me. Others were not bothered at all because they believed Christ was working through me. Was I imagining? Fortunately, there were no barbed comments directed at me. The Pastor and at least one elder believed in me.

Strangely, nobody asked me directly for my perspective. It was only after about three or four months that one gentleman from the church came to me and asked my opinion about the outburst in the Home Group. I expressed to him, "I see myself as a servant of God."

The experience of alienation, disdain and arched eye brows, led to a low phase in my Christian life. I was in a dark abyss of despair. I was hurting inside as I was just a beginner in my faith in God. With this experience I could relate to the persecution of apostles in the book of Acts though the intensity and magnitude of hostility towards me was almost negligible. During this time, the Lord spoke to me and questioned, "What are you doing to show people of different churches of Victoria that I am the same God of the Old Testament as I am today?"

I was dumbfounded – here I was, hurting, in my shell and sad. And there the Lord was giving me an assignment! Did God want me to be the small glow worm to spread the message of His grace and mercy? Little do we understand the ways our Lord works? Unconsciously, I did want to wriggle out of our Lord's proposal but because of my experience in walking with our Lord, I knew that to heed, have faith, and remain obedient would be a better option.

In confidence, I shared my thoughts with Pastor Bob, "The Spirit of the LORD is surging within me to spread His name in the churches of Victoria, and because of this, I would not be coming to the church for few months." He was very supportive. He blessed me by praying for me, and encouraged me to go ahead.

I was still not strong in the Word. I believed the Lord was perhaps swelling within me an urge to share testimonies of His work in my life. With the upwelling of the water from the ocean depths nutrients are churned and brought on the surface of the ocean on which the fish feed. Is that why He wanted me to give testimonies so that people feed on it and have no doubt that our Lord is the same as ever? At this point I did not have an answer to the 'Why' of the Lord's directive.

Several questions troubled me. To which churches should I go? Would pastors of various churches allow an unknown person without any references to give testimony in their churches? However, I also knew if it was indeed the outpouring of the Spirit of the Sovereign LORD on me to spread His Word, then the Lord Himself would find a way for me to proceed.

I decided to visit the Chapel at William Head Prison in Victoria. The Chaplain used to attend the Jubilee Church with some inmates. I approached him in the church and asked him in a friendly tone, "Could I come to your chapel in the prison to testify regarding the Lord's work in my life?"

He agreed.

The Lord's hand saw that approval by the prison authorities was given. Once He confirmed, I confided in him about my predicament of not knowing the Lord's Word as well as he did. Would he allow me to give testimonies to the inmates? He did not have a problem with that. How could he when the Lord did not have a problem? God used the Chaplain to bring me out of the state of stupor I found myself in after the knockout at the Home Group. God bless him and his family.

The inmates of the prison embraced me with open hearts. When the time came for me to speak, I gave many testimonies of the goodness of our Lord. How well he had directed my footsteps and my life in the path He wanted me to jive. He took my hand and led me through my 'Red Sea' moments, and transformed me from a person who had labeled himself "An Almost Atheist" into a completely new person. Besides, I was still His work in progress. Moreover, I shared with them the testimony about how our Lord extended Ma's life in this world, for which all my siblings were grateful to our God. Elaborating on it I recounted to them how one day in 2008 the Spirit of his Son brought to my light, "Your mother would soon be resting in peace." Pastor Mahender, who was in India, and another African pastor who had never met Ma was visiting Victoria prophesied the 'home coming' regarding my mother. I shared this sad news with my brother and sisters. We prayed earnestly to our Heavenly Father to grant her few more years.

One day while travelling in the city bus, the Spirit of the Sovereign LORD settled upon me and revealed to me two important things: first, the Lord had answered our prayers and our Ma would live longer. The Lord gave these verses of confirmation:

> *In those days Hezekiah became ill and was at the point of death. The prophet Isaiah son of Amoz went to him and said, "This is what the LORD says: Put your house in order, because you are going to die; you will not recover." Hezekiah turned his face to the wall and prayed to the LORD, "Remember, LORD, how I have walked before you faithfully and with wholehearted devotion and have done what is good in your eyes." And Hezekiah wept bitterly. Then the word of the LORD came to Isaiah: "Go and tell Hezekiah, 'This is what the LORD, the God of your father David, says: I have heard your prayer and seen your tears; I will add fifteen years to your life. And I will deliver you and this city from the hand of the king of Assyria. I will defend this city.'"This is the LORD's sign to you that the LORD will do what he has promised: I will make the shadow cast by the sun go back the ten steps it has gone down on the stairway of Ahaz.'" So the sunlight went back the ten steps it had gone down.*
> ISAIAH 38:1-8

When I read the passage, I took this as a promise from our Lord that our mother would live because our Heavenly Father, our ABBA, had heeded our prayers.

Second, the Spirit of the Sovereign LORD revealed manifestation of His plan for my mother: not only would she live long, but also that she would come to Canada to visit us. We had been praying for both, and the Lord answered both. I then revealed to the inmates that my mother came to visit us in Canada in 2009. Praise be to our Heavenly Father through His son Jesus Christ!

I continued and stated that while my mother was staying with us in 2009, she confided in Tripta, "Few months prior to coming to Canada, I had been on my deathbed, and I could sense death approaching, I prayed to God if my time has come please see that one of my children is with me." Could there be any better confirmation?

When I finished sharing my testimonies in the prison chapel, I prayed with them. When the service was over I went back to our house to share my experiences of the prison ministry with my family. My happiness knew no bounds because I was doing what the Lord was leading me to do.

After some days I heard some extremely inflammatory rumors. The heresy was again started against me by the believer who had ruthlessly ambushed me earlier in the Home Group. This time, though, there was a new vein of attack. The rumor was that 'James calls the Evil Spirits.' The insinuation was that James was a follower of Satan. In my opinion the basis of the gossip was because I sat on the flight of steps leading to the altar and prayed for the congregation in the William Head Prison!

These two assaults from the believer within a span of few months sent me reeling. I was blind-sided, brutally mauled, ferociously torn apart by those comments and did not know how to respond to soften their impact. I realized I was not impenetrable and was also too fragile to weather frequent insinuations. The excruciating pain resulted in an emotional turmoil which was magnified in the loneliness of the nights. The shadows were getting longer and darker but I believed the sun would, rise the darkness would disappear, and there would be no shadows.

After some time, I started making a case to counteract and defend myself against the two allegations. I sought references from the Bible and was totally engrossed in preparing my rebuttal when the Spirit of grace reminded me, "James, you can't handle this situation, but I will handle it for you. Furthermore, the Home Group will close after some time."

The Spirit then directed me to open the Bible and read from the Gospel of Matthew 10. I started reading the chapter, and was relieved when my finger pointed to the following verse:

It is enough for students.... If the head of the house [Jesus] has been called Beelzebub, [demon] how much more the member of his household! (v. 25)

The Chapter given to me by the Spirit of truth acted like balm on my wounds. Recovery was slow from the intentional blows. Even though the Lord had spoken, I was still in pain because it was playing in my mind constantly. The worst were the nights when I would wake up from my sleep and cry until sleep overtook me. This awakening in the nights and crying continued. The days were also harsh. The backlash of these escalated personal attacks was serious. Self-doubt was one of them. I started regressing and my mind became a fertile place for Satan to sow seeds of doubts. One such seed was of racial discrimination.

In this state of mind, I could not trust anybody within the church and found myself withdrawing from many. I fortified my psychological, mental and emotional walls so nobody could reach me easily. My soul was now desperately seeking somebody who I could trust in Victoria. Also, I was searching for a person who had the gift of discernment between evil and Holy Spirit and the gift of driving out evil spirits. Shadows of doubt that had crept in, had to be driven out.

The following Sunday when we reached the Church, one of the elders was standing outside the main door of the building. Seeing him in this unusual place, my sixth sense told me something was wrong. When I was about to greet him, he said, "James, can we speak?"

'Oh,' I thought, 'here we go again' We went away from the crowd and then he asked me, "What happened in the William Head Prison Chapel?"

With a quizzical look I responded, "What happened?"

"There is a rumour that you called the evil spirit while praying with the inmates." The elder slowly and cautiously opened the topic.

I was speechless, and could not believe his words and tears started rolling down my eyes. The elder reassured me, "Do not worry, I believe in you."

I did not want to step into the Church with the elder, but we did. On entering the church, I faced questioning looks of the believer as if asking loud and clear, "Why are you here? This place belongs to the followers of Christ and our Heavenly Father only."

Since we were early, I took few more steps inside and saw reaction of few others. They maintained their distance. Though it was not being verbalized but their body language betrayed them. I was being treated like a 'Harijan*- the Untouchables' of India. The dagger was being thrust deep inside my soul and was being twisted. It pained. I winced. My eyes upwelled again with tears yet I continued moving. Was I imagining again? Time perhaps took a long break.

Within few minutes our Lord's hand showed again. He restored my honor which was snatched away while doing the Lord's directive.

Vic came to me and said, "Today is the Holy Communion, I want you and Tripta to come at that time and help us...."

Tears started flowing down my eyes, "Are you sure? With all this?"

"I am positive," Vic declared boldly.

My sagging self-confidence got a boost. At least somebody still trusted me and was willing to call us to help with the Holy Communion service which is taken in loving memory of Jesus Christ who died on the Cross for sinners.

The simple but bold act of Vic said a lot. Possibly the Lord was working through him. Obedience to the Lord is always the greatest offering. Plausibly, had not Vic been obedient to the Lord's whisper, I would have been a lost sheep. The gesture meant the Lord, Vic and some others, believed in me and that was why they decided to call me to help with the Holy Communion service. Remember the role of Barnabas in bringing Paul and the disciples together after Paul's transformation? Had not Barnabas acted as a bridge between the fearful disciples and Paul, probably things would have been different (Acts 9).

The undisguised hatred of the believer in the church did not deter me a bit. By now the Lord had made it very clear that He was still my Shepherd and He held me close to His bosom. He made me stand in the eye of the cyclone which is always calm. I now understood, no matter how much the wind may roar or shriek, my Lord will keep me in the eye of the cyclone under His protective wings.

In another Home Group, the believer had tried to deflect the meetings umpteen times. The person had tried to be the center of most of the meetings and picked an argument with another Christian. In a belligerent manner on two different occasions the believer shouted at me. Once I was threatened, "You will have to go back to India; this kind of wrong... does not happen in Canada." Ironically, when my college friends were harassing me in the hostel in Hissar, they had told me to go to a Christian country as India is a Hindu country. At that moment I felt that I was stateless; I belonged neither to India nor Canada. The former, my motherland, and the latter my land of immigration.

Ironically, Donald, who was told to protect me by the Lord, never protected me. At least it was not visible to me. It appeared acquaintance with the believer was more important than being a friend of God. That is why it is important we choose friends carefully. I also wonder when people comment, "Only if I knew the will of the God, I would do it." In this case Donald very well knew our Lord's will since he was told about it yet he chose to ignore it. No regrets; he too has a right to think.

The Home Group where it all started wounded up. Was this the way the Lord wanted it to end? Remember what the Lord revealed to me earlier, "James, you can't handle this situation, but I will handle it for you. Furthermore, the Home Group will be closed after sometime." As for me, I am still in the church but the Lord has revealed to me that I will be leaving the Jubilee church to exalt Him. When and where, I do not have any clue. I wanted to disembark the boat of JCCC many times but did not, because the Lord's beacon is not yet flashing green. Disobedience to the Lord is not an option for me.

Despite these incidents, and a broken but rejuvenating spirit, I continued my journey of visiting churches of Victoria. As I continued these journeys, I could clearly see hand of the Lord leading the way. The following incidents happened between August and November of 2009.

Once, Gerry and I visited Central Baptist Church located in Downtown Victoria. I was in awe by the number of people (approximately 300- 400) in the church and the paraphernalia. I prayed to the Lord, "I don't know how you do it, but God, you have to see that I get an opportunity to share my testimony in this church." After all, there was a shoal of fish right there before me.

The church service started, and when we were about 15 to 20 minutes into service, the pastor announced, "This is not something we do regularly, but today, being a 'Thanksgiving Sunday', we would like to invite people to share their testimonies, thanking the Lord for the wonderful work He has done in their lives. Whoever wants to share can come up front and give thanks."

As soon as he said this, I knew it was our Lord's doing. I hesitatingly rose from my seat and looked at the pastor. Our eyes met, he nodded, and there I was, unabashedly in front of the large congregation, giving thanks to the Lord for keeping His promise of healing me from hyperthyroidism without any medication! Praise be to Him! Once the service was over we returned home.

Another incident occurred when I went to United Gordon Church (UGC) at Langford. UGC allows testimonies on only one Sunday each month, and I happened to be there on that particular Sunday! Not only this, they allowed me, a visitor to share my testimony, just like Central Baptist Church!

Yet another door opened when Gerry and I went to Victoria Miracle Centre. We were 10 to 15 minutes into the church service when Pastor Susan announced, "It is time for giving testimonies and I request only those who had gone to a conference come forward and give testimonies."

Since no one came forward to share their testimony, I asked aloud, "Could I share my testimonies?"

Pastor Susan hesitated slightly and then said, "Sure you can." Remember, usually a visitor is not allowed a testimony in most of the churches!

While I was giving my testimonies, I saw a gentleman Bob Newstead getting up from his seat and giving a small piece of paper to Pastor Susan. She read it and then interrupted me, "We have a word for you. A gentleman, who has the gift of prophecy, has prophesied about you. He has written on this piece of paper, which is now in my hand, that you will be doing the work of the Lord."

"While the gentleman is referring to the future, I am doing the same in the present," I replied with a knowing smile. With this reassurance I could now gallop and not canter in my walk with Christ.

Later when the altar call was given, I was called to the front by Pastor Dan and Pastor Susan to pray for those who wanted to be prayed for. We had a good praying session. Many people came forward and we prayed for them.

The pastors are doing a wonderful ministry of the Lord and the church is led by the Holy Spirit. Both are marvelous shepherds and have brought many to Jesus. I have been to one of their street ministry meetings in Victoria. I was amazed to see the youngsters of their church doing this ministry and being led by Christ to do so. God bless them for blessing so many.

In retrospect, I am grateful to those who openly spoke against me. Blessings on them. This is because with each derision, whether it was due to lack of not knowing the Word properly, or my accent, or my English, or overconfidence, or some other reason, I came closer to the Lord. He took my battle, and He fought it. Not only He fought, He won. Praise be to him. Blessed be His name!

After visiting about 12 or 13 churches in Victoria, I returned to JCCC, a happy and contended man. I do not know how many people's faith was strengthened or how many gave themselves again to the Lord because of my testimonies but what I know was this: my own faith was strengthened and that I was obedient to what He said.

Should we not be glow worms of our Lord in our workplace, outside our workplace, at home, in all seasons and in all circumstances?

> *Inscribe it in your soul: In our times of gigantic despair, horrendous trials, turbulent dark times and deepest trenches the Lord never forgets or forsakes us. Rather He gives inner strength to endure it, fights our battles and sails the boat through cascades and high waterfalls to the port He has pre destined.*

CHAPTER SIXTEEN:
The Lord My Protector

But you will not leave in haste or go in flight; for the LORD will go before you, the God of Israel will be your rear guard.

ISAIAH 52:12

It is prudent to seek refuge in God and take protection under his wings. This way we are guided, strengthened, uplifted and the impossible becomes possible. When He is the Commander –in –Chief, the war is His. He not only protects us, but leads us and we humans just have to wait, watch, and be ready to unfurl the victory flag. I have been a witness to this truth not once but many times, not only in my life, but also in the lives of many believers.

A part of the Lord's plan for my life was to do some evangelical work in India. Without the armour of God, that would not have been possible. Without His strength, I could not have been able to cover extensive geographical distances on buses and trains which I did in 2009.

In 2007, the Spirit of the Sovereign LORD settled upon me and disclosed, "You would be travelling by air," Then added, "James, you are going to do my work in a place far away from Victoria. The place is in the eastern hemisphere, and your flight will be crossing enormous water bodies." However, when and where was not disclosed.

In November 2009, when I boarded an airplane to fly to India, I had a vague idea that perhaps besides doing my personal work, the Lord might use me for His work. The questions were: when and where in India will the Lord initiate it? Or will it be some other country?

The idea of going to India delighted me. It set my spirit ascending like a soaring eagle. The thoughts of the airplane landing in the country where I was born, spent my childhood, youth, and early adulthood filled me with joy. I anticipated being with parents and friends, inhaling the air of my motherland and the fragrance of the soil. The anticipation of it gave my life a new dimension.

While these thoughts were exhilarating, I was also keen to meet some pastors who were doing our Lord's work, had Spiritual Gifts from the Lord and who were using these gifts to glorify Him. Did I know any of them? No, but Gerry and Anita knew and they were kind to give their names and whereabouts. I decided to meet these pastors to see how the Lord was using them, to discuss any doubts I had in my mind regarding my walk with Christ, and to know more about the Word of God. The places that I went to were in different neighbouring provinces in North India.

Dehradun, in Uttarakhand: After the airplane had taxied and halted in Indira Gandhi International Airport New Delhi, I went to Sarai Rohilla Railway Station in Delhi and then took the Mussoorie Express train to Dehradun city. It is the capital of Uttarakhand and is situated 248 kilometres from Delhi in the Doon valley of the Shivalik mountain ranges of the lower Himalayas and is northwest of Delhi. Dehradun is the gateway to Garwhal region. The train started in the evening around 7 p.m. and the journey was 12 hours long.

I stayed at my maternal aunt, Mrs. Kishori Greenwold's house. At 65 with salt and pepper hair she welcomed me with a warm hug and smile. Madhu di also came to Dehradun from Sattal. Our plan was to meet my niece, Arpita, my sister's daughter who was studying in Luther W. New, Jr. Theological College in a small town near Dehradun called

'Kulhan.' It is about 11 Kms northeast of Dehradun. The college is nestled in the valley of the foothills of Himalaya Mountains.

After having an early dinner, I went to sleep and slept like a log since I was jetlagged. In the middle of the night, I was woken up by the Holy Spirit and was advised to sit on the bed. I complied and started praying. Several detailed, mind-blowing, spiritual revelations followed all led by our Lord.

The eternal Spirit revealed, "James, you would be giving testimonies in the Theological College tomorrow," and "In India you will need my armour."

The Spirit of counsel and of might then proceeded to clothe me with the full armour of God. The Holy Spirit lifted both my hands and gave me the helmet of salvation. The Advocate gave me the sword of the Spirit in my right hand and swung it in thin air. The Spirit of Jesus then put the shield of faith in my left hand, the breastplate of righteousness on my chest, girdled the belt of truth around my waist, fitted my feet with the gospel of peace. As soon as I was clothed with the armour, I was pushed down forcefully on my bed from an external invisible force and I fell into deep slumber.

When I woke up in the morning I recollected the wonderful experience, I had had with the Holy Spirit the night before. The Spirit of the knowledge then advised me, "Open your Bible, read from the book of Ephesians Chapter 6:10 - 18." I opened the Bible as commanded and started reading:

Finally, be strong in the Lord and in his mighty power. Put on the full armor of God, so that you can take your stand against the devil's schemes. For our struggle is not against flesh and blood, but against the rulers, against the authorities, against the powers of this dark world and against the spiritual forces of evil in the heavenly realms. Therefore put on the full armor of God, so that when the day of evil comes, you may be able to stand your ground, and after you have done everything, to stand. Stand firm then, with the belt of truth buckled around your waist, with the breastplate of righteousness in place, and with your feet fitted with the readiness that comes from the gospel of peace. In addition to all this, take up the shield of faith, with which you can extinguish all the flaming arrows of the evil one. Take the helmet of salvation and the sword of the Spirit, which is the word of God. And pray in the Spirit on all occasions with all kinds of prayers and requests....

The imagery represented weapons of a Roman soldier. The weapons are both for attack and defense. Equally important was that the Lord was telling me to stand firm, be ready, be prepared, and be alert as in India the battle would be against the spiritual world on a greater scale. I was happy because I inferred that the Spirit of holiness made me aware of this and had symbolized this by suiting up the armour Himself. The boon was that the armour of God makes a person victorious and invulnerable. Therefore, I would not be harmed in this evangelical journey. It also meant that the Lord's work for which He had brought me will definitely be in India. I rested in comfort knowing that the Lord will be my protector in this entire undertaking. Did the confidence stay with me?

The following day Madhu di and I went to the Theological College to meet Arpita. After alighting from the city bus at Kulhan, we walked into the campus which was just on the other side of the road. We went to Madhu di's friends who were the staff in the college and stayed in the staff quarters in the college campus. There we had a wonderful time sharing our testimonies about God's goodness, mercy, grace, and also had prayer sessions in their homes.

While we were having these sessions, Arpita came excitedly giggling and smiling, she victoriously declared, "Uncle, you have been permitted by the college authorities to share testimonies with students in the main hall of the college."

What transpired without my knowledge was that the previous night, Madhu di had asked Arpita to inquire from her Principal about the possibility of my sharing testimonies to the students of the college. The Principal gave her consent! God be praised for keeping His promise. Even in my dreams I had never imagined to give testimonies of the greatness of our Lord in a Theological college. Interestingly enough, though I can communicate fluently in hindi, I was asked to speak in English, and was given an interpreter for conveying my message in hindi as the audience was multi-lingual.

THE LORD MY PROTECTOR

An interesting incident took place while we were there which showed Lord's favour yet one more time. The last bus from Kulhan to Dehradun city was at seven in the evening. Knowing this, I told the person in-charge (PIC) of the meeting, "Please see that the meeting is over by 6:45 p.m. as the last bus leaves at 7:00 p.m." The speaker nodded his head in agreement, and I was a relieved man.

Though the PIC had agreed, it appeared in his zeal he totally forgot of our understanding. Like a true Indian, he spoke, and he spoke, and he continued. I started panicking. With each passing second I was sweating and frowning more and more. I started praying to the Lord, "Lord, give the speaker wisdom to understand our plight, to stop speaking, and give me a chance to exalt and glorify you. After all, I was the guest speaker!"

My prayers were not answered. He spoke, and he continued. I was dreading having a very short time to speak and the increasing possibility of missing the bus. It was at this time the Lord opened my eyes, and that changed my prayer request.

Instead of asking the Lord to give wisdom to the speaker to cut his speech short, my prayer to the Lord was, "Heavenly Father, let the speaker speak as much as he wants, but you my Lord <u>have</u> to arrange a vehicle for our return." I dared to use the word "have" in the above prayer because of my intimate relationship with Him, as between a son and his father and not because God has to do what we humans want or demand.

When I finally got my turn to share my testimonies, I took my time because I realized we would definitely miss the last bus. At the same time, my faith was on our Lord for providing some means of transport so that we would reach our aunt's house before the bats would take to the sky.

When my testimonies were over, way past the time of the last bus to Dehradun city, we left hurriedly. We reached the bus stop, and we inquired of the people, "Has the last bus to Dehradun left?"

They confirmed it by nodding their head sideways instead of up and down, rolling their eyes towards the sky and saying, "It just left and it was overcrowded."

We desperately started waving our hands at passing vehicles in an attempt to draw attention of the commuters in their private vehicle to stop and give us a ride. But none stopped. It was now getting close to sunset and we were getting worried. We started praying, and sure enough, our prayers were answered.

The Lord sent a college staff in their car with whom we had earlier shared our testimonies in their house. When they saw us standing on the main road, they stopped and were gracious to give us a ride. While on the way they confessed, "We usually do not go to the city this day of the week, but today we are going for an important work which we could not delay any further."

They stopped the car about 100 m from our aunt's house. We then bade farewell to each other. Did we not pray to the Lord for arranging some mode of transportation for us? God be praised for being faithful! After a few days, I went to meet other pastors in a different province.

In Himachal Pradesh: After I left Dehradun I visited Kasauli and met Pastor Ashok Massey of Kasauli Baptist Church. Kasauli is in the province of Himachal Pradesh in Solan district, about 26 kilometres southwest from Solan. It is a gaze-arresting hill station and has some old buildings from the British era. The beautiful snow clad Himalayan Mountains in the distance, the old tall evergreen Cedar and Pine trees, the chirping of the birds, the wind blowing, the promising dawn, the settling dusk, and the view of the town at night made me desire more and more of the natural beauty of Kasauli.

I met Pastor Ashok Massey in his work place – a public sector bank, State Bank of India. I introduced myself as brother–in-law of Anita and Gerry Threlfall. He was thrilled to meet me and wanted to know about their welfare in Canada. I shared with him about their career and Christian walk of life and later asked him to share about his walk with Christ. His face lit up and in excited tones the pastor gave me plenty of testimonies about how the Lord was using him for His glory. "The Lord was using me to drive demons out, heal people…" While listening to Pastor Ashok Massey, I recollected the following verses written earlier:

> *My message and my preaching were not with wise and persuasive words, but with a demonstration of the Spirit's*

> *power, so that your faith might not rest on human wisdom, but on God's power.*
> 1 CORINTHIANS 2:4-5

Pastor Massey concluded, "…God was doing miracles amongst the locals and visitors from other geographical regions both national and international. Such miracles were being done irrespective of region, language, caste, colour, creed, socio-economic status, religion and nationality. You know James, God does not show favoritism."

Hearing his testimonies, I was impressed to see our Lord working there.

One testimony which the pastor shared with me is worth mentioning. With a big smile on his face he said, "Kasauli Baptist Church had been partially burnt by Hindu fundamentalists on 11-11-2008. Later the Hindus themselves came to rebuild the church. They paid money for construction material, and for labor. After the renovation was completed, the Hindus commented, 'The church looks better than what it was before!' Even communal riots were not able to divide what the Lord did not want divided; rather people came together all the more!"

When he concluded his testimonies, I rationalized and came to the conclusion that he could discern and also drive out the evil spirit. I became bold. Cautiously and with great hesitation I asked Pastor Massey, "Do you think I have an evil spirit residing in me?"

Shocked by my statement Pastor Massey declared, "Brother, you do not have any evil spirit residing in you. We can tell as soon as we see a person if he or she is possessed by the evil spirit."

I heaved a sigh of relief and then he asked me, "Brother, why do you ask such a question?" I then narrated to him the verbal pounding against me in my absence in 2008 in a 'Home Group' in Victoria and subsequent developments. I asked that question to at least two more pastors who were being used by the Lord to drive out evil spirits in India and they echoed the same thoughts as Pastor Massey did. Can you now see how much effect the fallacious charges had on me? At times my mind wanders as to what initiated the condemnations, I faced from a believer?

I was then reminded by the Lord not to be judgemental and leave the matter to Him. After our fellowship, we prayed and blessed each other had lunch and I continued my journey to meet another pastor - Pastor Raju. He was thirtyish but looked younger, lean and about 5 feet 6 inches tall.

Pastor Raju inhabited in the same province and district but in a different city called Subathu. It is 20 kilometres northwest of Solan city. It is a little cantonment town and has a Gorkha fort built in the early years of the 19th century. This cantonment town quartered the British soldiers at the time of British rule.

I introduced myself as brother-in-law of Anita and Gerry. He was naturally elated because after a long time he could learn about them. I apprised him about their well-being and their walk in Christ. He was excited.

Later we discussed our testimonies. He shared "Brother James, in the interior of the province people were under the bondage of evil spirits. They were enslaved to alcohol, and the poor were being exploited. Evil spirits had been driven out from many and people were being healed in the name of Jesus Christ. Seeing the miracles and propelled by the Holy Spirit the masses were coming to the Lord and confessing Christ as their Savior." He also expressed his concerns about how the Anti-Conversion Act was being misused by the administration against Christians to harass them. Yet, the Lord's work was progressing! A thought resonated within me:

For the kingdom of God is not a matter of talk but of power.
1 CORINTHIANS 4:20

Listening to him about the works of our Lord, I marveled about His unbiased nature. I came to realize that *Salvation* was for all those who *accepted Jesus Christ as their Savior*, even if they were illiterate villagers or people who lived below the poverty line or some of those who sold their body for money to buy wheat flour or rice to cook food at home to feed their families and if possible to free their land from the clutches of money lenders. It then struck me that Christ too kept the company of the unlettered people and the neglected! Salvation was not only meant for literates and professing intellectual Christians who came to church in crisp well ironed clothing and maintained distance from the lower income and marginalized, but God indeed had come for both the Jews and the gentiles, rich or poor, black, brown or white. Now they all were a part of God's household! I could hear an echo in my mind:

> *Consequently, you are no longer foreigners and strangers, but fellow citizens with God's people and also members of his household, built on the foundation of the apostles and prophets, with Christ Jesus himself as the chief cornerstone.*
> EPHESIANS: 2:19-20

It was there, while listening to these testimonies and works of pastors I understood the most important thing is to have *FAITH*. Even if a person is ignorant of the *Word* because of illiteracy, or the Bible not being available, or simply not being able to understand the Word, but had accepted Jesus Christ as Savior, he or she is saved. Faith in the Word is critical otherwise the Word is merely a blot of ink on a piece of paper. Therefore, those who are illiterate or who are not strong in the Word should rejoice that they have accepted Jesus Christ as their Savior by faith. By faith Salvation is theirs, and by faith Eternal Life is theirs. They must keep on growing in faith and believe in the message of the Cross. Their walk with our God is worth emulating. As I said earlier, the verse which comes best to my mind is:

> *For it is by grace you have been saved, through faith--and this is not from yourselves, it is the gift of God--not by works, so that no one can boast.*
> EPHESIANS 2: 8-9

If possible, we should be strong in the Scripture as well. To do so, we should seek people who are strong in the Word and build bridges to learn the Word. We have to be humble in our endeavor as a wick of a candle can only be lighted if it is bent a little. We should also keep on doing good deeds through the Holy Spirit. About the importance of 'faith' in the Bible, it is well written in Hebrew 11.

'Faith' with 'Deeds' is good. It is written:

> *You see that a person is considered righteous by what they do and not by faith alone.*
> JAMES 2:24

And 'Faith' with 'Works and Knowledge of the Word' is the best weapon, I summarized.

It is while talking to these servants of the Lord, I also comprehended that people who had good knowledge of the Word should not browbeat those who have strong faith but less knowledge of the Scripture, or are in the process of learning the Word. The Scripture makes it crystal clear that even Satan knows the Word! Therefore, people strong in the Word should be gentle, considerate, support and uplift those who are weak in the Word to enable them to be equally strong in the Word as them. This should happen without any pride, prejudice and should be done in all humility. I think this should be our moral duty as believers and I do believe this would please and delight the Lord.

My prayer for all those who are made to feel inferior anywhere in the world because of lack of knowledge of the Word is:

> *I keep asking that the God of our Lord Jesus Christ, the glorious Father, may give you the Spirit of wisdom and revelation, so that you may know him better. I pray that the eyes of your heart may be enlightened in order that you may know the hope to which he has called you, the riches of his glorious inheritance in his holy people, and his incomparably great power for us who believe....*
> EPHESIANS 1:17-19

Pastor Raju does not belong to any denomination. He works independently without any salary from anywhere nor has a second job. How many pastors or Pharisees of today are willing to do this?

Though invited, I did not get any opportunity to speak at Pastor Raju's church as it was mid-week, and I had to return to my own hometown. Perhaps, next time if it is the will of our God.

Hissar in Haryana: By the time I reached Hissar, my hometown, Christmas celebrations were in the air.

One day a young man, Victor David, from the Methodist Church of Hissar, came to visit us. He was about 45 years of age, around 5 feet 9 inches, with big round dark black eyes and his face well supported by a moustache. During our conversation he said, "This year I am planning to have a Christmas Fair on the 25th of December in the Municipal Park just across the St. Thomas Methodist Church."

The last Christmas Fair in Hissar was in 1979, when late Rev. Joel Singh was the pastor. What Victor was planning was a commendable gesture, but unfortunately some factors went against him.

First, he was not a church elder, and perhaps a novice in organizational skills and probably inexperienced to handle such a big proposition. He also did not have his own following and standing in the church. In my opinion there were some Christian stalwarts who did not want to loosen their grip on the church and activities of the church. These stalwarts were a few seniors who did not relish giving younger generation the reins of the church. In fact, they could forge an alliance and engineer a sort of coup and torpedo Victor's plan. How could Victor possibly think of shattering the iron shackles of these stalwarts in the church? It was a typical David and Goliath scenario.

Second, Victor was in the disgruntled faction of the Methodist Church, so it was all the more difficult to hold a successful Christmas Fair as he neither had financial clout nor manpower. Were my fears ill-founded?

Victor, despite the unfavorable winds, was determined to sail his ship to the port he believed he was destined for. He got approval from the civil authorities to hold the Christmas Fair. He was also successful in obtaining signatures of pastors of many denominations in Hissar. These endorsements signified he had their support and they would encourage their congregation to attend the Christmas Fair. The countdown had now begun.

These signs were very encouraging, but the last hurdle left to be cleared was that of finance. Despite the blessings and promises of a few stalwarts and pastors, nobody was coming forward to meet the promised financial support. Victor was in despair, alarmed, and exasperated. This disunity amongst Christians frustrated him and led him to my mother's house. I was pleased to see him.

Victor revealed, "Somebody within the congregation had given a paltry amount of money which I used on the publicity of the Christmas Fair." He inhaled and continued, "Time is running out, since invitations to civil dignitaries had already been distributed, print media and other media had been informed of the fair, but the finances were short to organize the event." Listening to him, I realized he was in for a turbulent time and he was also at the vortex of it.

I felt the urge to help him but first had to ask the Lord. After he had finished pouring his heart to us, I assured him, "As a family we would be surely contributing some money." But did not disclose to him how much it would be. Again he had only an assurance!

"Come and meet me tomorrow," I suggested. "And also bring the written assurances which pastors of various denominations have given you and the permits which civil authorities have issued to you for holding the Christmas Fair 2009."

When he had left our house, my mother advised me, "Be very cautious in financial dealings with one and all." Who could argue with this sagacious advice?

Victor came the following day with all the papers, handed them to me and said, "Brother, have a look at the papers to your heart's content."

I studied the sheaves of papers meticulously. Once satisfied with the veracity of the official documents, I gave him a small amount. Even though it was little, Victor was ecstatic because we were the second family to give him some financial support. In his overjoyed state of mind he announced, "Brother, you will be the main guest speaker in the Christmas Fair 2009."

I let his announcement pass, because I knew all too well it would not happen due to the divergent interests of different factions within the local Christian community. Also, because Pastor Raju had already divulged to

THE LORD MY PROTECTOR

me how the government was misusing the Anti-Conversion Act, I was not very keen on speaking in public. I did not want to end up in jail with my passport impounded while my wife and my two sons were waiting for me in Victoria to celebrate my return and the New Year. I resolved in no way would I want to be seen giving testimonies in public regarding Jesus Christ, His grace, mercy and blessings while some officials lurking in the crowd waiting for any opportunity to use the Anti-Conversion Act against me. After all, the Lord had given me brains to use!

With about a week remaining for Christmas and the Fair, financial progress was still stagnant. To me it appeared Christmas Fair was probably an imminent avalanche of disappointment for Victor. One day the Spirit of his Son woke me up from sleep in the middle of night and revealed, "You will be speaking at the Christmas Fair and you should start preparing for the same." And the Spirit continued, "James, you have to give more money to Victor for the Christmas Fair."

My reply to the financial part of Lord's directive was, "Lord, I do not have money."

The Spirit of truth gently nudged me, "You have, James." Can't hide anything from the Lord!

The next morning, I left a message for Victor on his phone to stop by. He came and collected the money. He had the biggest and brightest smile.

After giving Victor many days of hardship, scare, stress, and sleepless nights, the big day finally arrived. The Municipality Park is about 3-4 acres in which old Indian Blackwood and Neem trees stand majestically. Upon them were crows and other birds sitting and chirping loudly and clear as if announcing, "It is time to start the Christmas Fair, come one and come all." On the edges of the boundary walls were around 15 stalls of different kinds of food and eateries and approximately the same number of games stalls. The loud speaker was playing blaring music which was competing with the decibels emanating from the traffic flow on the road. Near the main entrance gate was a beautiful well decorated stage which had sofas for special guests and speakers to sit on. The back wall of the stage was well decorated with bright colored banners of Christmas supported by pink, blue and white colored cloth, a noticeably high stage. The weather was clear with a game of hide and seek continuing between the sun and the clouds. It was slightly windy and there was a nip in the air.

After the Christmas service was over in the church, the Christmas Fair began. Christmas songs were sung by the choir which came from a different province. The crowd started trickling in slowly. Some came from the church which was just across the street and others came from all corners of the city. While sitting on the sofa on the stage with other people I hoped I wouldn't be the first speaker. The reason was simple, I wanted to follow the lead of other speakers, because of the Anti-Conversion law hovered uppermost in my cerebrum.

But my Lord had other plans. I was indeed the first guest speaker and was given no time limit or a definite topic. I started to speak about my childhood, coming to church from across the road and not spending time in the church but outside. How I lived a life of "An Almost Atheist" and spent my days in wilderness without acknowledging God's presence and the manner in which the Lord called me, and is using me now.

After I finished sharing some of my testimonies, I stepped down from the stage and to my surprise found a line of people waiting for me to pray for them. They wanted prayers for healing, employment, personal, and professional issues. People with abilities and with disabilities formed a line. People of all ages, color, castes, religions and genders were just waiting for me to pray for them. I was stunned.

I was not prepared for this special favour and did what was the best at that moment. I prayed with the people, and interceded on their behalf. Though I prayed, I was also overwhelmed and in awe of the magnitude and intensity of the situation and was shaken by the prince of air and he overplayed with my faith. This happened when a paraplegic man asked me to pray for physical healing. While my mind wilted under the raging storm of doubts, I clung fast to the harness of my faith and kept on praying.

Ironically, while my faith was dwindling and was heading for a catastrophic debacle the crowd to the Christmas Fair and the line of people for prayers was swelling. Despite the diminishing faith, I continued to pray for the people who wanted me to pray for them.

Prayer was my only weapon. And I wielded it despite my doubts. About ninety percent of the prayer seekers were non-believers who honored the church and made frequent visits to it, listening to God's Word and then went back to their own lifestyle.

Seeing the response of the crowd, Victor announced, "Brother James would later come on stage to share his testimonies and will pray for you. Please remain seated."

By the middle of what appeared to me as a marathon session of intercession I felt tired, thirsty and exhausted. I realized it would be wise to go home, revitalize and return again in the evening. In my opinion there was no point overstaying there without any spark left in me. Now I understood why Christ at times left the crowd just to be all alone! Victor, seeing my predicament requested other speakers to take over. I left for home while other speakers started preaching the good news and praying for the people.

That evening when I was resting and recuperating at home and preparing to return to the Christmas Fair, I was asked by one of our neighbors, "James, when was the last time you celebrated Christmas in Hissar?"

"About 15 years ago."

My neighbor challenged me, "Go back to the church at this very moment and see the vast change that had occurred since, and you will see all roads of Hissar lead to the Methodist Church."

I could not believe what our neighbor had stated, because 15 years ago there would be approximately 150 Christians coming to the church for the Christmas service, which lasted about 1½ hours! I took the challenge and hired a rickshaw to take me there, but half a kilometre away from the church I stopped the rickshaw, paid the rickshaw puller and said, "Thanks, you may please go now as I will walk the rest of the way."

Why? Just like all roads led to Rome at some point in history, all roads indeed led to the church that evening. Even though I walked, it took me quite some time to reach the destination. There were traffic jams everywhere! Unbelievable! People of different faiths were coming to the church for two reasons, to pray in the church and to enjoy the Christmas Fair. At 7:00 p.m. I could see an ocean of people in the park and numerous guest speakers on the stage preaching in excitement amongst the crowd of unbelievers.

Victor informed me that about 100,000 people must have come since the start of the service and until midnight of the fair. I could not check the veracity of his statement. God be praised for His work through Victor! May Victor carry the rich legacy forward in a harmonious and honest way.

While 100,000 people must have come to church and the Christmas Fair, many more heard hymns, sermons, and testaments because of loudspeakers which covered a larger area and reached the ears of those who could not come. For the first time I saw the advantages of an open air venue working in our favor.

While loudspeakers played their role that day, local newspapers covered the Christmas service and the Christmas Fair the following day. I do not know about the local TV coverage. For me this by itself was mind-blowing and I was happy and contented seeing our Lord's work being done by the Holy Spirit. It was indeed liberating and spirit lifting.

I was sad too. I saw Christians in the Methodist Church Hissar proclaiming Christ worked miracles in their church as if our Lord heard prayers in Hissar church only and nowhere else! I realized they projected that our God and Christ's sphere of influence and power was just limited to one building! They were merchandizing and marketing our God. Why? So that the pious gullible non-believers come and say their prayers, and give offerings which fill the coffers of the church. Commercialization of Christ! Nonetheless, God did not show favoritism to only the Christians. Many non-believers were also blessed by coming to the church not only on Christmas but also on any other day of the year.

In India, besides Hissar, I covered about 12 different cities in approximately 30 days. It was a satisfying and enjoyable experience. I thanked God for giving me this opportunity and fervently prayed that He gives me more such opportunities to glorify and exalt Him.

Is not our Lord the best protector?

> *Inscribe it in your soul: The Lord, our God is not blindsided, cannot be taken by surprise and is not limited to any building. He does not need commercial marketing as He can look after Himself.*

CHAPTER SEVENTEEN:
Our Home Group

Teach me your way, LORD; lead me in a straight path....

PSALM 27:11

In 2008, when the Lord gifted us a house, we were naturally jubilant. Within one and a half years of coming to Canada and owning a house in Victoria, BC, gave us a great feeling of worldly security.

The Lord transformed our house into a home by leading, weaving, and knitting our family by a common thread of His love. Both Tripta and I believe this gift is to be managed by us to exalt Him and glorify Him by opening the doors of our house to people who want to come and to know Him, to develop an intimate relationship with Him in the company of fellow believers. Perhaps we were seeking partnership with our Lord.

The Spirit of counsel and of might started prompting me to start a Home Group. My reply was, "Who would come? We live in the outskirts of the city and we know few families." One day while visiting us our friend Melony Gilbert suggested, "Why don't we start a Home Group?" My reply to her was the same that I gave to the Lord earlier. Thankfully, she persisted. Eventually it dawned on Tripta and me that perhaps; God was using her to let us know that He was serious about starting a Home Group in our house!

Our Home Group started with just three persons: Melony, Tripta and I. Melony's zeal for the Lord is huge. She is about Tripta's height, fair with blue eyes and shoulder length hair. God has blessed her with a beautiful voice and she uses that golden voice to sing songs that glorify our loving Heavenly Father only. All three of us were just fledglings not embedded in the Word. However, the common factor was the love for our Lord. We wanted to be strong in the Word and took Peter's command with all seriousness:

> *Like new born babies, crave pure spiritual milk, so that by it you may grow up in your salvation, now that you have tasted that the Lord is good.*
> 1 PETER 2:2

On Melony's suggestion we started with just having prayer sessions. We would meet together on Monday evenings and just pray. Few weeks later, we shifted the day from Monday to Friday as it was convenient since on Saturday the schools and offices remained closed.

Then one day what Pastor Mahender had prophesied in Dubai came to happen. I started sharing the Word. For the prophecy to come to be true it took about 11 years, but it happened. Praise be to our Creator! Within a few months I became bolder and tried to cautiously emerge from my self-imposed shell and share the Word. Was the Holy Spirit goading me? In the beginning, the messages were written by the Spirit of wisdom and of understanding on a piece of paper. After few weeks, I would just follow the prompting done by the Spirit of the knowledge and the message would just start rolling from my tongue. The Spirit of Jesus would indicate references from 10-12 books in the Bible. To my surprise those references were always in order and relevant to the theme which the Lord gave. This was indeed precious, pleasing, and also amazing.

Lord had other plans too. Once when conversing with Pastor Mahender on the phone he prophesied, "The Lord is showing me a vision. I can see that a man is sharing the Word of God in your Home Group, and that man is not you." A few weeks later the Lord reconfirmed that to me. The question was how would I know who the man was?

It happened in the summer of 2010. Melinda used to come to our Home Group. Perhaps she convinced her husband Vic to come too! Vic, a former pastor in the Armed Forces of Canada, started coming. After observing us for few Fridays, Vic spoke to us: "Though your intentions are good you lack in the knowledge of the Word." Vic was trying to uplift us and was suggesting that our thrust should be firmly ensconced in the Scripture. I believe Vic wanted us to reach a standing as described in the Bible:

> *Then we will no longer be infants, tossed back and forth by the waves, and blown here and there by every wind of teaching and by the cunning and craftiness of people in their deceitful scheming.*
> EPHESIANS 4:14

Vic brought his brother Ted with him and started sharing the Scripture. He would drive from 15 kilometres from his house, no matter what the weather was-just to share the Word! I was bowled over by that. I could not believe his love for our Lord! Later, Warren also started coming. He led us in praise and worship every Friday for about a year or so.

On September 2010, the Spirit of truth revealed to me "Vic is doing a fine job. You will learn a lot from him for I have sent him!" It was as if lightning had struck me, I was astounded because only then I realized the promise of the Lord about sending a man to share the Word had come true! The Lord had led Vic to make us well versed in Scripture and to be sound in Biblical doctrines. Praise be to God!

In the following years, twice the Spirit of Jesus impressed upon me about Vic's vast contribution amongst us. I just hope our Home Group is moving in the direction the Lord is taking us. We want Him to be the Pilot. I am positive that the direction is:

Preach the word; be prepared in season and out of season; correct, rebuke and encourage —with great patience and careful instruction. For the time will come when people will not put up with sound doctrine. Instead, to suit their own desires, they will gather around them a great number of teachers to say what their itching ears want to hear. They will turn their ears away from the truth and turn aside to myths.
2 TIMOTHY 4: 2-4

Vic is my mentor too. When I do not understand verses of the Scripture, I go to him to understand, digest and assimilate them. He is a man who has walked with our Lord for many years. He is very strong and clear in the Word. Almost every year he goes to Mexico to do God's work. I fondly call Vic 'My Paul'. God bless him and his family, and use him more and more.

Members of our Home Group have visited sick people in their homes, in hospitals, and have prayed for them. Since 2012 we have been doing Christmas Carol singing in our neighborhood. While caroling we collected non-perishable food items for the Langford Community Food Bank. The next day we donated the food and cash donation to the Food Bank on behalf of our sub division. Twice we celebrated 'Resurrection Day' within our subdivision. God willing, He will use us for more of His work in the years to come. The glory be to God!

By the grace of the Lord, since April 2008, the Holy Spirit guided people to our Home Group. We have welcomed people from all walks of life to come and attend our Home Group on Fridays. If they wanted us to pray for them on other days of the week, we have welcomed that too. We have never questioned their religion. People would come and continue coming for few days, few months and years and then some would stop coming. We all have been luxuriating in this spiritual journey.

Unfortunately, there have been times when misunderstandings occurred. Personal verbal assaults and judgments have been pressed by one person. Consequently, the number of people shrank. The walk of Lammie (Emily) Seinen and Elaine Trussler with the Lord is worthy of praise. God bless them and their family too and use them to glorify Him. They have been great captains of their ship at their respective home and church too. At its zenith 17 people used to come. The number fluctuated with the season, averaging about 10-12 and 5-6 at times. Just like in churches, number of people coming for meeting is low in summer. Perhaps summer outdoor activities take preference over God. I sometimes wonder what if the Lord takes off for a few months or a day!

There were times when Tripta and I were very busy between school, work and parenting. We would therefore be really tired and needed a 'reboot' of energy. During these moments of weakness I wanted to hang a 'Stop Sign'. However, better sense prevailed; after all, who was I to close what God had opened? Instead we pray and looked to the Lord to strengthen us. Which other way can anybody suggest for a perfect rejuvenation and robust growth?

The Home Group will run Lord's course of time. I do not worry about the number of people coming, nor the longevity of it. I admit it is not we who run and manage it but 'He'. Since April 2008 there have not been more than 15-20 Fridays when we did not meet. Did we ever imagine it would run so long? No! When it all began, we thought it would all be over in a few months or a year at the most but now it is 2017. The Lord has His plans and His ways.

Periodically, we have invited people to come and share the Word of God with us in our Home Group. God has been kind in sustaining us. Missionaries, pastors, and laymen and women have come to share the great work our Lord is doing in distant lands and in Victoria. Our faith has increased exponentially listening to them. Vic often talked about his experience in Mexico.

Pastor Dan and Susan shared about their struggles when they were planting their church in Victoria and how God helped them. They also testified about the Lord's work in Taiwan. There were some speakers who had a very intimate relationship with the Lord. One such person was Bill Jackson. He is about 5 feet four inches, and is around 58 years of age. We called him to our Home Group in July 2011. His testimonies were very powerful. He talked about his and his wife Judy's role in Alpha group. They were:

- volunteer Alpha advisors for Alpha Canada and represented Alpha in local churches.
- teachers and trainers of Alpha class leadership to many church pastors and volunteers.
- seminar teachers in Alpha conferences across Canada. The courses they developed and taught were prayer training and Alpha instruction in a small church home setting.

Bill disclosed while in an Alpha conference with other believers God had revealed to them that he was a pastor of His church. Bill maintained that our Lord commissioned him for exalting the Heavenly Father and that, he was given the name 'Gladiator' for the Lord. God bless Bill and his family for doing God's work. Our members were thrilled to hear his testimonies. Praise be to the Lord for sending Bill to our home.

In 2010, I attended his Home Group to share my testimonies. In that meeting our family, Gerry and Anita were also present. When Bill prayed for Gerry, the Spirit of the LORD touched Gerry and he fell flat on the ground!

Bill and Judy were good hosts. God bless both of them to be such a wonderful team and servants of God. I also gave testimonies in 2016 to the Men's Group of his present church, the Highway Christian Fellowship in Sidney. I was given unlimited time to speak and I spoke for about an hour exalting the Lord!

Around 2010, Mr. Johnson Samuel and his wife came to our Home Group while they were visiting Victoria. They are members of New Life Fellowship Association in Bombay. He is a trustee of the association. They talked about their ministry in India and also shared from the book of Psalms.

We invited Bob and his lovely wife Pat Newstead to our Home group. They talked about miracles and Bob maintained that the calling of his life was to function as a prophet (Ephesians 4:11), which involved more than the simple gift of prophesy. God bless them.

We also called Douglas and Peggy Scott. They shared awesome testimony of their faith and how the Lord redeemed them from hopeless situations. God bless them both.

We have also welcomed people from our own Home Group to share the Word. In general, a layman cannot do that in a church. Should we therefore not encourage them to share in a safe, secure, and uplifting environment of our Home Groups? I share the Word under Vic's guidance and at times when he is not there. God be glorified for His plan.

Moses's pleading to our Lord is heart rendering: *"If you are pleased with me, teach me your ways so I may know you and continue to find favour with you...."Ex*odus 33:13. I pray our Home Group members have similar prayer in their lips and heart.

Today, I am thankful to the Lord for being persistent and sending Melony to start the Home Group. God bless her and her family. Many people coming in the Home Group have blessed us. Many more have been blessed by us and other Home Group members by coming to the meetings. Many have become strong in the Word and in their walk with our Savior. Still many have seen and heard great testimonies about the Lord. Many have 'Tasted the Lord.'

Have you tasted the Lord?

> *Inscribe it on your soul: It is our moral duty to be strong in the Word. With the Word comes understanding and wisdom. And with that our lives, homes and churches are illuminated.*

CHAPTER EIGHTEEN:
Testimonies of Blessings and Israel Trip

Taste and see that the LORD is good; blessed is the one who takes refuge in him.
PSALM 34:8

When I was far away from the shadow of our Lord I would attribute His blessings to my wisdom, vision, planning, fate, and hardwork but never to our God through Jesus Christ. How vain can humans be? Now when I am being led by my Saviour Jesus Christ, I have realised even when I was "An Almost Atheist", God was working in me. I was not an atheist in His Eyes. Perhaps my parents' prayers were assisting me.

God's blessing on us have been manifold and have been coming without ceassation. Some we prayed for and petitioned, and many blessings He just showered on us. Tripta, often says, "James, since you have come to the Lord, He has blessed you and us abundantly and also used us to bless others." I am sharing few of His choicest blessings which He has showered unconditionally on us and on others for the sole purpose of praising and exalting Him. Why miss an oppurtunity ? Testimonies are important after all:

> *They triumphed over him by the blood of the Lamb and by the word of their testimony;...*
> REVELATION 12:11

I believe there is no testimony which is small or big. I strongly subscribe to the belief that testimonies help us evade a state of apostasy as it shakes us into believing that our God is a living and delivering God.

Some of the testimonies are of restoration of people from situations where they could have been lost because of the stations they found themselves in.

On March 27th, 2011, I received the dreaded phone call which none of us wants. In my case, it came in the night knocking me off from my deep slumber, though momentarily. Madhu di was on the other side of the phone and she was speaking from Sattal. She suggested me to brace myself and then started sobbing and crying inconsolably, "James, … I just got a phone call from Prem. Pa has been admitted to hospital in Kodaikanal. He…(sob)… is on ventilator because he cannot breathe properly. I have suggested Prem to tell the doctor to try to keep him alive until I reach there," she continued, sobbing. "And for all practical purposes he is… no more. Please also inform Mamta about the same as I cannot reach her."

I looked at the watch, the time was 2:00 a.m.

Tripta also got up when the phone rang. While listening intently, she suggested, "Phone Mamta di immediately, and inform her about Pa's condition."

I advised her, "Now nobody can change the situation. Let her sleep, and I will inform her in the morning." I then turned over and tried to sleep but couldn't. Tripta was not satisfied with my line of thought. She got up, went to the other room, phoned Mamta di, and comforted her.

While tossing and turning in bed and still trying to sleep, I asked our Lord a question, "Lord, is my father no more?"

"He is alive and he will live," the Spirit of truth said emphatically.

I did not dare to ask: how long? I turned over and went off to sleep!

After comforting Mamta di, Tripta came back to the other room and settled in bed. Due to the noise of the squeaking bed, I woke up and suggested her to let Mamta di know what had been revealed to me: Pa is alive and he will live. Tripta did that.

After she delievered the message, Mamta di started praying to the Lord giving thanks for showing His mercy on our father and for prolonging his life.

The following Sunday, I gave testimony in our church about the Lord's assurance to us about my father's health.

After about a day and a half Madhu di reached the Hospital in Kodaikanal, and so did Khrist, who at that time was in India for official purposes. I received an email written on 1st April 2012 which Khrist sent to all of us as he was astounded to see the official records of the hospital.In the records it is written:

"...It seems because of chronic bronchitis and infection in his lungs, he could not breathe and therefore his heart stopped beating. At 10:45 a.m., (as the hospital records show) he was treated for respiratory and heart failure. They could not feel his heart beats (pulse) for about 4 hours and also could not record any blood pressure. He was put on a ventilator (a mechanical device to help support his lungs to breathe) and gave his heart a few stimulants to help encourage it to beat again. They were successful in resuscitation but were not sure, what happened and why and therefore the confusion."

Could we call this as resurrection of my father? Resurrection is the pillar of Christian faith and we have to dig our feet in this truth. Paul surmised about resurrection:

> *And if Christ has not been raised, our preaching is useless and so is your faith. More than that, we are then found to be false witnesses about God, for we have testified about God that he raised Christ from the dead. But he did not raise him if in fact the dead are not raised. For if the dead are not raised, then Christ has not been raised either. And if Christ*

has not been raised, your faith is futile; you are still in your sins.

1 CORNITHIANS 15:14-17

My father responded well to the resuscitation efforts. He talked, wrote and drank tea. All of us wanted our father to live at least till July 2012 so he could give Mamta di away in her marriage. We prayed for the same to happen. I even started believing the Lord was sending me the message that my father will live that long, but He didn't. I learnt a very important lesson: under immense emotional pressure we can make mistake of believing our emotional outbursts or desires as God's will. And this has happened to me on several occasions.

Our father lived as per the will of the Lord. I thank my Lord for giving us one important week to reconcile with our father. In this week of His grace and mercy, there was immense spiritual healing. Pa had a few of his beloved ones at his side. My father's condition did fluctuate over a week before he eventually joined 'Jesus's Partnership Company' because of a stroke. There was immense peace with all of us for the Lord had called him in His time. We did not have to remove him from the medical support system. Therefore, there was no feeling of guilt for any of us. God took care of that!

Should we be upset with our Heavenly Father for not extending his life so that he could give away Mamta di's hand in marriage and therefore stop going to church or stop believing in him? No. On the contrary, our faith increased as we saw His hand in all this. We thank our Lord for resurrecting our father for a week and providing a dignified exit and not a demeaning one to the everlasting peace. Our family was overwhelmed with the Lord's compassion, mercy and grace which allowed reconciliation, healing and restoration amongst us all. Praise be to Him!

In July 2009, Warren[α], shared devastating news in the church during prayer request time. He disclosed, "The doctors have diagnosed that I might have cancer, and it is located in the inner part of my cheek." Warren said that the doctor was a very experienced man and just by looking at the tissues which were sent for biopsy had indicated that he might have cancer.

The church prayed for him, so did many families, and Home Groups. One day when I was praying for him in my private 'Relationship Building Time' at home, the Spirit of truth revealed, "Warren does not have cancer."

I gave the message to him.

Later when the result of biopsy came, it indeed was cancer! The diagnosis was announced to him by the doctor. After he heard doctor's verdict, Warren came to meet me in my workplace, at Fairway Market. He was visibly disturbed, and restless. He stated, "Put on your cloak and let me know what God's plan is as the doctor has declared - it is cancer."

I too was shocked when he disclosed the doctor's diagnosis. All types of suspicions crossed my mind. Did I hear it wrong? Did I hear my Shepherd's voice or was it Satan as a ventriloquist imitating our Lord's voice? Was there any chance of interchange of the tissue sample with some other patient?

"Let's pray right now," I earnestly intoned as I arrested my own conflicted emotions,

I prayed with him, there and then in the aisle, and the Spirit of truth spoke: "No cancer."

The two worlds were now colliding- the scientific medical world and the spiritual world. Which to trust? On 13th July, 2009, the Lord commanded me to read Job: 5:8-9, where it is recorded:

"But if I were you, I would appeal to God; I would lay my cause before him. He performs wonders that cannot be fathomed, miracles that cannot be counted."

This was irrefutable and indisputable evidence that Warren's life was redeemed. Reading the scripture I sent him an email stating that he would be healed by God's grace and mercy.

In the meantime, the second biopsy test was undertaken. What was the diagnosis? No cancer! Praise be to our Healer! Our Lord saved Warren from the claws of the terminal disease which obviously has mainly one outcome in most of the cases unless the Lord redeems.

Another revelation occurred in 2008 while we were in the family camp at 'The Cowichan River Bible Camp' in Duncan. Tripta came to me and requested, "I want you to pray for Gordon and Sarah Munro." Gordon and Sarah are members of the same church that we go to and we meet them in the church quite often.

I asked her, "Do they have a special request and have they given you permission for me to come and pray for them?"

Tripta affirmatively answered, "Yes, they have given permission and they do have a special request."

"What is the request?" I responded inquisitively.

Throwing a furtive glance at me but with conviction in her voice Tripta replied, "They want the Lord to bless them with a child and Sarah is not able to conceive."

I went with her to pray in the Chapel at the camp. They were waiting for us. While praying, the Spirit of the knowledge commanded: "Open the book of Ruth: chapter 4 and read from verse 11 onwards."

I gave the Lord's message to them and then we opened the chapter and started reading. Remember, I still did not know a lot about the Bible and all four of us did not know where the book of Ruth was. And what it was all about? We looked through the 'Table of Contents' in the Bible for the book of Ruth, opened it and read the recommmended verses. To our amazement the chapter talked about Ruth marrying Boaz and then conceiving!

On 1st June, 2009, the Lord again declared: "They will have a child in 2010."

When Sarah concevied, Gordon phoned and confided in me about the great news. Glory be to God!

It did not stop here. In the Bible, it is written:

So...and she gave birth to a son.
RUTH 4:13

Sarah gave birth to a baby boy! Sarah and Gordon have named him Zachary. Does it not remind us that before we were conceived He knew us?

What the Spirit of truth told us in 2008, the doctor confirmed in 2010! Thus our Lord resurrected the womb of Sarah. God be praised. Is there a story in the Bible about that?

Another miraculous event occurred in November 2007. One member of our church's 'Praise and Worship Team', Matthew[α], came forward with a request during the prayer request time. He had Sciatica pain and it was at its peak. Many people prayed for his healing. After the church service was over I went to him and prayed. The Spirit of the living God settled over me and gave me a message which I passed to him. Matthew did not come to church for a Sunday or two and that worried me. I wrote an e-mail to the person heading the 'Prayer Chain' to inquire about Matthew. After inquiries we came to know he was healed. God be praised for healing Matthew and therefore his ability to play guitar in the church.

Yet another example of His grace and mercy. While constructing the new extension of our house in 2011, my arms, palms, fingers and back became very sore. Prior to this, I had done little physical work in my life, therefore my body was not conditioned for the kind of heavy physical labour which goes into building a house. Doing this kind of work took its toll on my body. I was also working as a produce clerk in Thrifty Foods in Colwood and there too at times I had to lift heavy boxes.

I went to the family doctor. After doing some tests he diagnoised my problem in my palms and fingers as tendonitis. The doctor prescribed cortisone injections. He also wrote a note suggesting that until further notice I should not return to work at Thrifty Foods. The work which I was doing was physically taxing and could prove to be detrimental to my health.

Our family took the matter to our Saviour Jesus Christ. He acted the way only He could. First, He provided an employment opportunity for me to work which did not involve any kind of lifting of heavy load. My career path took a sudden change and within a week, I got a job as an Education Assistant with Saanich School District 63, Victoria.

He then healed me of tendonitis without any medicine going in my body! Praise be to God! The healing did not happen immediately but over a few months. My hands were healed and I could comfortably work again.

In early 2012 Pastor Bob announced in the church, "There will be a meeting in our house on Monday evening. The purpose of the meeting will be to pray for an important arbitration meeting amongst Penny's (his wife) lawyers, Insurance Corporation of British Columbia(ICBC), and an arbitrator. The meeting is scheduled for coming Tuesday."

Penny was in a car accident in 2006 in which she was injured and ICBC was not willing to pay her the insurance. So much for the insurance premium we pay every month! The matter had already dragged on for several years.

I went to attend the meeting in their house. Many prayed but not me. After the meeting was over, I came back to our house and confided with Tripta, "I could not pray because of headache, and there was no urge within me to do so."

That night around 8:00 p.m., Tripta phoned them. Penny was on the line. Tripta sought Penny's permission to pray for her. While she was praying on the phone the Lord started tugging at me and delivered a message. I interuppted Tripta and whispered, "I would like to pray for Penny over the phone and also convey Lord's message to her."

When Tripta finished praying she gave me the phoneto me. I started praying for Penny. While praying the Lord repeated the same message which He had given me few minutes earlier. I relayed it to her. The next morning, I sent them the same message, but this time by e-mail.

Guess what happened in the court room on Tuesday? Our Lord indeed led the legal tussle in the court room and Penny's lawyer found favour in the eyes of the judge! Penny's case which had been dragging on for some years came to a culmination with a settlement in her favour. Praise and glory be to God!

In 2009 I was unemployed for some months. We had not spoken to anybody about it. During the time of my unemployment, my friend Andy Carrier came to our house one day. I had not met Andy for about two years and it was nice meeting him.

We invited him inside and served him tea. While we were talking and having hot Indian tea-chai, Andy quietly handed me an envelope. I

TESTIMONIES OF BLESSINGS AND ISRAEL TRIP

opened it and to my surprise there was cash inside. Tears flowed down my eyes. There was no condition attached with this generous offer. His left hand knew not what his right hand was doing. Is it not the way we are to do Lord's work as per Matthew 6: 1-4 ? Intrigued, I asked Andy, "How did you come to know that we were under financial strain, especially when we had not spoken about it to anybody ?"

"The Lord had impressed upon me," He humbly replied. We believed in his statement. Tripta recalled our Lord had used a raven to feed Prophet Elijah. It is written:

> *The ravens brought him bread and meat in the morning and bread and meat in the evening, and he drank from the brook.*
> 1 KING:17:6

The same Lord sent Andy twice to us in our moments of financial crisis and the amount Andy gave was enough to pay our monthly house mortgage! Praise be to God for Andy's listening ears and doing heart! I am often mesmerized by the way our Majestic Lord works. Praise be to Him and glory be His forever! Andy has done a lot for many people and has never regretted it. God bless him and his family. He is a wonderful father, husband, friend and disciple of the Lord.

God's benevolence continued. The Westminster School in Dubai used to send students to a program called 'Global Youth Leaders Conference' (GYLC) in Washington, D.C. The students were selected by teachers on the basis of excellence in academics and extra-curricular activities. From here was borne a dream which I cherished and kept in the incubator of my heart. It gave warmth to my dream until the time came for it to bear fruit. My cherished dream was: God willing, one day I will send my children to this particular conference.

The Lord resurrected my dream in Canada about six years later.

When Fazal reached the grade 10, I suggested to him to read about 'GYLC' program. He googled it, liked it and applied. He was selected to participate in this program, but the problem was: finance.

If the problem was the same, so was our ever reliable solution: God through Jesus Christ. As a family we took the matter to our Heavenly Father and prayed. On May 22nd, 2011, the Holy Spirit promised, "Fazal will definitely go to the program, Rahul, your younger son, will also go with him to the United States of America, but not to the program, and I have already made a pathway."

We were concerned about raising finances for our son Fazal's journey and here our Lord disclosed that Rahul too was going! Did He not understand our problem? This however meant doubling our efforts to raise the money in the same time period. After a lot of thought, we decided to do fund raising by selling 'Home Made Indian Food'. Rahul, Fazal, Tripta and I worked as a team to achieve our goal. We sold the food in our church, college where I was studying, to friends in Tripta's office, and in our neighborhood. Tripta rose to the occasion yet again both as a wife and a loving mother. It is written:

> *Houses and wealth are inherited from parents, but a prudent wife is from the LORD.*
> PROVERBS 19:14

In my case this is true. It is also true that Fazal and Rahul are blessed by the Lord to have a mother like her. We were able to raise funds for Fazal but not for Rahul. Poor Rahul! What happened to God's promise?

We failed. But we handed over the baton to the Lord in the final stretch and He gave us a stupendous and resounding success. He sprinted in the race and lunged on the finishing line because He did not forget His promise. It is written:

> *God is not human, that he should lie, not a human being, that he should change his mind. Does he speak and then not act? Does he promise and not fulfill?*
> NUMBERS 23:19

He opened the hearts of our family: my sisters, my cousin Ranjit Chetsingh, Tripta's sisters, and Khrist, all contributed toward's Rahul's trip! Blessed is the man who has kind hearted and understanding relatives! Because of the power of the Almighty the plan which was as good as dead was resurrected by our Heavenly Father and Rahul and Fazal went to the USA and visited Cleveland, Atlanta, New York City and few other places.

Further miracles were apparent. While the Lord arranged a house for us and a free car, He also helped us to add an additional room in our house for the benefit of those who came to our house in His name and for our family too. Victoria is an expensive place to live, and our house is small. I went to the Lord with a prayer. "Lord, I want to add a room to our house. The room will be used temporarily to accomadate visiting evangelists, preachers, pastors should staying be a problem. Lord you know when my mother came to Victoria in 2009, she slept on the floor of our sitting room. She had difficulty climbing the stairs. When my mother comes next time, my desire is that she has a room for herself and not have to sleep on the floor again. Please Lord, bless us to build a room."

In Psalm 127:1 it is written, *"Unless the LORD builds the house, the builders labour in vain...."* The Lord did bless us and it is a beautiful testimony as to how it came to happen.

In 2009, the Advocate whispered in my ear, "Extend your house." I was buoyed by this directive from the Lord, since we had that desire in our heart for some time but were hesistant. In November 2009, in faith, we applied for the building permit. After giving the application, municipality secretary informed me, "You will have to pay license fee, building permit fee, and variance fee. You will also have to get soil load bearing test done and have to have perimeter drainage..." I was disheartened, left the office, and went to our house almost giving up on my dream.

About a week later, I went back to the office. This time a different secretary came. She opened her mouth to speak but even before she could say anything, I said, "Our house is under Affordable House Programme. Therefore, there should be lower fees...." I then realised that she did not have the background knowledge of the history of our application! I apologized and then stated my case from the beginning. Once the secretary verified the veracity of my statement, she gave me an assurance that the fee in that case would definitely be lower.

Hearing the good news I further inquired, "Do you think that we should get the soil load bearing test re-done, keeping in mind that your good office undertook this endeavour a year ago before the main house was built?" The secretary understood my logic, frowned, looked in their official records and then waived even that. We paid only $80.00 for the building permit! In the entire process we must have saved approximately $1000! Since I drew the extension plan myself we saved some money there too. God is great all the time!

Eventually we got the permission to build about 265 sq. feet of area comprising of a master bedroon, a washroom and a closet in late 2009.

The Spirit of the living God kept insisting we begin construction, but I had my doubts about the financial aspect. Where would the money come from ? At times I would think, perhaps it was not the right Shepherd who had spoken to me. I had to be extremely guarded. After all, the matter involved borrowing money or spending the little money that we possesed, or both! We had to be cautious, as I could hear echos of doubts in my mind. 'What if we are not able to settle in Canada, then this expense will be a waste of money? If there is an emergency in the family, where will the cash come from? Who will lend us? Why would they lend?' When faced with these questions I would ask the Advocate, "If indeed you are the Holy Spirit; we want to see an increase in the cash balance in our bank account.If it happens, we woud take it as a sign that indeed this was from the Holy Spirit."

Did it happen that way? Did we get more work which would increase the cash balance? Did we win a lotto ? Did somebody give us cash as gift? Did our Lord redeem us? The Lord resurrected our dreams and the plan that was in limbo because of my doubts was executed by Him.

In the first quarter of 2011, I started getting the same message from our Lord: "Start construction"- albeit at a greater frequency. One day when I received the similar message from the Lord to start construction of the room and I responded, "But you have not increased the cash balance, how can we then do it?"

The Spirit of wisdom and of understanding spoke, "What is your problem? Do you want the extension?"

"Yes."

"Why do you insist it has to be your way and not mine?" The question by the Lord to me left me flabbergasted. Finally, on 22^{nd,} May 2011, the Spirit of counsel and of might commanded, "Build the extension and finish it before November 2011."

With the money we had in our bank we started construction. Our Lord helped us by lowering the cost of construction-His way of doing things and not ours-by increasing our bank balance!

When we wanted to start building, I went to meet a man who was working with an excavator in a subdivision next to our house. I requested him to submit a quote for the excavation for the foundation. He came to our house to have a look at the site of construction and quipped, "Two cases of beer!"

I was stunned. I was expecting a huge amount, and here two cases would cost me about $48.00! From then on, we knew, our Lord would see us through in this endeavour of house extension. After realising that the Lord was at work, we started enjoying the construction of the new room by just stepping back, mentally reclining on a chair and watching how the Lord would bring it to pass.

My friend, Mike Munro, a general foreman in a construction company, and now a businessmen, went beyond ordinary friendship and helped us in construction as if it were his own house. He was there with us right from the planning to the conclusion of the project. He used his contacts, collegues, and sent his friends to build. He kept an eagle's eye on quality of construction.It worked out well. God's hand could not allow shoddy work. God bless him.He loves the Lord. The Lord is using him and his wife Kim mightily and in all humbleness they have opened their house , purse and wallet for His work. They are also very good parents and are teaching their two boys to walk with the Lord.

God helped us in getting cheaper deals just at the moment when we needed them. It was as if companies like Rona, Home Depot, Slegg

Lumber and few others knew what construction materials we wanted next and they would come out with competitive deals as if they wanted to be in the 'good books' of the Lord by pleasing Him. I also got the contractor's price which is lower than the general public price for new materials.

Much later we realised why our Lord wanted to finish the house extension by November 2011. The building permit was expiring in November 2011, and we were not even aware of it! By His grace the Lord enabled and empowered us to finish the house extension in October 2011.

The Lord had not finished showering His blessings on us!

An incident which left me speechless was when we saw how He wove the circuitous ways to fulfill His promise. Incredible are His ways indeed! In the month of October 2011, while reading the Bible, a deep longing arose within me. Without even giving a second thought, I blurted to the Lord, "I want to visit Israel." Preposterous!

Having put this request to the Lord, amnesia regarding this plea took over. About a month later the Spirit of grace revealed, "I have heard your prayer about going to Israel, and you will be going." I was naturally thrilled but also a bit apprehensive as the Lord did not reveal when. I was feeling guilty as in my prayer request I had not included my family accompanying me to Israel. Nevertheless, I got bold and requested the Lord, "Heavenly Father, have mercy and let our family visit Israel as well."

On 10th January, 2012, the Spirit of Christ disclosed, "James, you will go with your family, and I have made all the arrangement for it to happen including your boarding and lodging." Again, there was no definite time set for the visit. We were upbeat that the Lord has opened a way for us to go as a family to be amongst His chosen people and favored country-Israel.

An important and interesting point of recollection at this moment was that we had finished building the house extension in October 2011 and were financially tight. Yet, the Lord promised, "I have heard your prayers and your family would be going to Israel." Yahoo! I became so excited that I went and bought lotto tickets even though our Lord had not recommended me to do so. It appeared; I wanted to go prior to God helping the plan come true!

My enthusiasm and faith on God's promise regarding going to Israel from the date of petitioning to the Lord till mid-March 2012, reached such a crescendo that I recalled a similar situation in Bible which can summarize my thoughts:

> And [prophet] Elijah said to [king] Ahab, "Go, eat and drink, for there is the sound of heavy rain" …. "Go and look toward the sea," he told his servant. And he went up and looked. "There is nothing there," he said. Seven times Elijah said, "Go back." The seventh time the servant reported, "A cloud as small as a man's hand is rising from the Sea."… "Meanwhile, the sky grew black with clouds, wind rose, a heavy rain started falling.…
>
> 1 KINGS 18:41-45

The hand sized cloud that Elijah's servant saw started turning dark and rained. In our lives from the small seed of trust sprouted a seedling and it matured into a heavy laden fruit tree. Though, we had to wait for more than a few months before it happened unlike Elijah's servant who had to go only seven times in a day.

And this is how the Lord worked. He opened a new chapter in Mamta di's life. The new horizon in her life started rather unexpectedly. I was thrilled with the plot and desperately wanted to go to Israel. I increased my prayers and petitions to the Lord at a feverish level. The Lord was not piqued by my eagerness. Probably He was overjoyed to see my dependence on Him.

The harbinger of the wonderful news was Ma. She informed me that Mamta was about to get married and the bridegroom Husam Ghishan was from Jordan. Husam was eager to have the wedding in India and Jordan. Learning that, I gave my word to Ma that all four of us would be there for Mamta di's wedding ceremonies both in India and Jordan in July 2012!

Our tax returns from 2012 enabled us to purchase two return tickets to India. Fazal, was working part time at McDonald's while studying in grade 12 agreed to pay for his air ticket. He also graciously offered to save enough money for one-way air ticket from Canada to India for Rahul's air flight. Fazal worked hard to keep his promise.

The Lord's promise was still only half realized. Husam graciously offered to pay for Tripta's two-way air ticket between India and Jordan. He also benevolently opened his home for our boarding and lodging! Our Lord's blessing overflowed. When we landed at Queen Aliya International Airport, Amman, Khrist gave USD $300.00 to help cover our visa fee in Jordan when we were checking in at the immigration counter. My family gave us some money for going to Israel-Jordan's neighboring country. Lord made our dream a reality. What was unthinkable and impossible, our God made it possible. Is it not true that our God's promises end up with 'yes' and 'amen'?

By the grace of our Lord we visited India, Jordan and Israel in July, 2012. He kept all His promises. Praise be to him.

God's hand was unbelievably seen in all these testimonies. Is it not?

> *Inscribe it in your soul: Step into the Lord's plan and the deliverer will deliver.*

CHAPTER NINETEEN:
Community Involvement

And now these three remain: faith, hope, and love. But the greatest of these is love.
1 CORINTHIANS 13:13

Our Lord has given to all believers an indomitable spirit and not a timid one. With the Holy Spirit in us, Chrisitans should not live a cocooned life in their comfort zones of materialism, Home Groups, and few hours of Sunday service in the church. We should challenge our own potentials, capacities,and talents given by the Lord and walk in the Lord's plan, under His umbrella and direction. We are ambassadors of Christ and therefore should spread His fragrance to the vast spectrum of people and community. Our Lord is the living Lord; His Spirit will guide, transform and enable us to be His wise and bold ministers.

I believe the Lord has laid an open circuit in each of us. We just have to accept our Lord as our Saviour and the circuit is closed, and with that there is energy and light in the dark. Therefore, our rightful place is the community. However, when we venture in the community it is advisable that: *a person's steps are directed by the LORD....*(Proverb 20:24)

When we arrived in Canada, I witnessed community involvement and social inclusion at the fore. In India and Dubai, somehow in my youth my eyes blinked and I missed the magnitude of both, but in particular I missed social inclusion. Ensuring adequate balanced nutrition, and care of people with different and challenging abilites are the core values of the Canadian society. A holistic and sustainable approach is sought and therefore all people are included.

Victoria being a small town, community involvement and social inclusion is often visible. In the Jubilee Chruch too it flowed under the gravitational pull of the society. We were direct beneficiaries of the benevolence of the believers. They were good to us and helped us feel at home with their handshakes and smiles. Our cultural integration was therefore smooth. In retrospection, I can see the hand of the Lord in that too.

With the waxing and waning of every lunar cycle, our Lord led us from position of weakness to a place of strength, and by 2011 we were in a favourable disposition to help our community. Though we were not financially sound, there was a willingness to do whatever we possibly could do. The smaller scale of community service that we planned did not worry, perturb or dislodge us from undertaking those projects. We as a family tried to be in the community too.

Tripta initiated the community work and also saw that each member of our family was a partner in it. Our community work started within the Jubilee Church. In our church some internees use to come to attend the service. She thought the best would be to offer them 'Home Cooked Indian Food'. We sought permission from our pastor and found favour for this venture. Tripta then made delicious, mouth watering and taste bud challenging food. We packed the food and took it in our car along with kitchen cutleries.

Just before the church was to start, we invited the pastor, his wife, the Chaplin who use to come with the internees and the inmates to the small hall adjacent to the church. All of them were touched by the gesture and blessed us. Needless to say they remarked that hopefully there would be more such benevolent and gracious gestures.

Our Lord then wanted us to reach beyond the shores of Victoria. His commandment of 'Loving our Neighbour as Ourselves' took a new dimension for us which I could not have imagined earlier. One day in 2008, the Lord proclaimed, "Organize a medical camp in India." I was mystified.

From my perspective, 'My Neighbour' meant our subdivision, our church or Victoria. But India? We had left India many years ago when we went to Dubai. Later we came to Canada. Then why did God choose India? The Lord knew better than that! To me it was all bizzare and I was bewildered but chose to follow the Lord's will and tried to work on the logistic of it. My strength and my will failed. I opted out-- incorrigible that I am!

I waited for another two years with my back turned towards my Lord in this matter hoping that He would forget the matter or change His mind. It didn't happen. His whisper echoed and reverberated in my mind and amplified after seeping in each cell of my heart and brain. In fact, He repeated the same challenge again in 2010. By now I now realised that our loving Heavenly Father would not change His decision and I could not make Him alter it. So the best was to be obedient and not resist! Thereafter, I stopped being Jonah who ran away from the Lord's directive of going to Nineveh and preach there. I stopped ignoring His plan and went on my knees to seek His blessings.

We started the logistics of it all over again. The looming questions were: where in India ? In which year ? Partnerships, if any? If the answer to partnership was 'yes' then with whom? A person or an organisation? While we were soul searching for the answers, I immediately understood the canvass was too big for us to paint. It dawned on me that it would be impossible for us to do it all alone, and we could not do it in our own strength. I also concluded, as a person, I did not have the foresight to undertake such a massive exercise. So we went to the Lord again. As usual, He made the complex equation into a simple linear equation. He narrowed down to Kodaikanal, where I had spent about eight years of my youth.

In Kodaikanal I had a friend, Jaichandran Nadar. He had opened a rehabilitation centre for children with special needs in partnership with Church of South India and Christopher Blind Mission around 1996. Jaichandran had donated about an acre of his prime land in the downtown area of the city for this project. He was a believer, therefore I could trust him.

I contacted Jaichandran on phone and divulged to him about the Lord's directive for me. He was estatic to know about the Lord's plan of blessing his organization. During our conversation I asked him, "How can we help your organisation?"

He cheerfully suggested, "A laminating machine would be a good idea, since that is what the organisation is looking for."

"Why the laminating machine?"

"Because our children laminate the pictures, photographs, and the table mats which are then sold in the market. This way we are able to sustain ourselves."

Intitutively I asked, "What is the cost of the machine?"

"Give me your e-mail address, James. I will send you a quotation and also send you another information." With gratitude in his voice Jaichandran blessed me and put the phone down.

I received the e-mail with the quotation. Later I realised that our Lord had asked us to organise a medical camp and not supplying a lamination machine! Yet again I bit off more than I could chew because I succumbed to human wisdom and not God's directive.

I sent Jaichandran an e-mail asking him about critical medical needs of his organisation. He suggested, "You can help us in funding a specialist doctor's visit." Elaborating on it he said, "The specialist doctor has to come from Chennai. The funding would include: transportation ticket for a doctor, his boarding and lodging, plus his professional fees."

I enquired about the cost and Jaichandran gave me an approximate amount per trip. Once I had the magical number, I committed to Jaichandran, "Our family would do fund raising for at least one lamination machine and at least one doctor's visit for children." I had faith not in my own abilities but in God, and this hope stemmed from the Bible:

> *For in Scripture...and the one who trusts in him will never be put to shame.*
> 1 PETER 2: 6

COMMUNITY INVOLVEMENT

By God's grace, our family was able to raise money in Victoria and India. I entreated friends and went to some stores to raise money. By now people had seen us fund raising in Victoria for people with special needs on few occasions and therefore they trusted us. Consequently, it became easier to do fund raising. Thrifty Foods where I worked gave generously. When I phoned a few friends in India and requested donations they agreed without any reservations. The money raised was enough for two visits of the specialist and one lamination machine. Once again in 2013 we raised money for them.

My sons Fazal, and Rahul, did some fund raising for Heart and Stroke foundation,Canada in March, 2012. We also organised one day free food distribution in less priveleged neighborhood in Hissar, Haryana in December 2009. They were delighted, and I hope God opens more avenues for us to do His will in His time. What would happen if Christians stop doing the good deeds?

> *Inscribe it in your soul: The Good Samaritan act should be directed by our Lord because it is pleasing to Him rather doing it just to massage our inflated egos.*

CHAPTER TWENTY:
Obedience is What the Lord Desires

※

> But Samuel replied: *"Does the LORD delight in burnt offerings and sacrifices as much as in obeying the LORD? To obey is better than sacrifice, and to heed is better than the fat of rams.*
> 1 SAMUEL 15:22

Umpteen times, I looked the other way because of lack of faith and boldness. On some occasions, I have been obedient to the Lord's commands, directives, albeit hesitatingly. However, Yeshua never recorded any of these against me because of who He is. As my Heavenly Father, He was always patient.

Some of such incidents which required obedience but were challenging for me to undertake are related to Christmas Carol singing and Resurrection Sunday celebration. We initiated their celebration in our subdivision.

Rain lashing and howling winds, low temperatures and occasional snow are characteristics of weather in late fall and winter in Victoria, BC, Canada. Snowfall often reminds Tripta and me of the Christmas cards depicting the Christmas season when our Savior Christ was born and leaves us nostalgic about the Christmas celebration in India. Those beautiful memories of Christmas and Christmas Carol singing, bonding among the carol singers, the hot tea, cake, and other treats offered in the houses we visited in India had to be revisited and shared with our children as they had never participated in Christmas Carol singing. We resolved to have a grand resurgence of the Christmas Carol singing spirit in our family by caroling in our subdivision. We speculated there could be no other better way to bring the good news to our neighborhood.

In my own 'Relationship Building Time', I went to the Lord to seek His approval and blessings. He nodded to both. Then we proposed the plan in our Home Group in November 2012. Since it was the first time everybody was excited and more or less unanimously agreed. In the beginning, some were skeptical about the success of it because of weather conditions and because of the unchartered territory - our neighborhood. I realized that genesis of such an endeavor in high probability might have a tentative start. Nonetheless, we planned regarding the variables which could be controlled by human and left the balance in the hands of the Sovereign Lord and approached His throne with prayers.

When I discussed the idea of Caroling in our neighborhood with my teenaged sons they cautioned me about the reaction of the neighbors and were very apprehensive. Aren't all the teenagers like that?

"Be careful, this is not India; people might just slam the door in your face," Fazal forewarned, with concern in his voice. Coupled with guarded and pragmatic approach, Rahul exhorted, "If you do not take permission from them prior to the program they might shout at you using some abusive colorful language." I was touched by their concern for us.

Tripta and I heeded to the concerns of our sons and initiated the pilot project of taking consent from our neighbors before we would embark on this adventure. Of about hundred houses in our neighborhood, we visited approximately 15 in the first round. Our neighbors, in general, were happy about the idea of having Christmas Carolers coming to their home, singing and wishing them a Merry Christmas. A few had reservations. The responses of our neighbors varied from:

1. "We will miss it this time."
2. "You are welcome, do ring our doorbell when u come so that we know u r there, and if we are here then we will sing with u in our drive way."
3. "We too will join u in the subdivision."
4. "Thank you for organizing it."
5. "Oh! Live carols- I will be waiting for you."

Our pastor encouraged us.

Weather permitting, and when we had time, Tripta and I went to visit other neighbors in our subdivision. By the end of third week of November, we had visited most of the houses, and 31 houses were keen that carolers bring good tidings to their homes and sing Christmas Carols.

The next daunting task was to have musical instruments and good singers. I sent an e-mail to Nola our church member, querying, "Is it possible that the Church lends us some musical instruments for caroling in our neighborhood?"

"Sure we can, you just have to ask Pastor Bob first," Nola responded.

I sent an e-mail to Bob about it and he agreed to lend us some musical instruments.

Now we had to pray to our Lord for good weather so we could go caroling in the evening.

On December 22, 2012, the weather was inclement with high intensity wind and rain. Knowing this weather was harbinger of a bad time, I kept on praying and pleading to our Lord again and again. The swings in my mood and faith were like leaves fluttering in a moderately strong breeze. Nevertheless, I went on my knees many times. On 23rd December, 2012, the day when we had planned Christmas Carols, the dark grey and black low rain clouds started dispersing but only after giving me a scare in the morning because it was drizzling. Once the drizzle stopped my hopes ascended. By the time it was 3 p.m. the sky was clear, I was upbeat, and praised and thanked the Lord.

However one problem still remained: we had few carol singers. Our Home Group consisted of 4-8 persons of whom two were away and we were left with only two good singers in our midst. Tripta was worried about the small number of Carolers. On her suggestion, Tripta and I went on our knees and prayed to the Lord. "Lord we thank you for clearing the sky, for giving us music instruments, and we also thank you for sending us Carol singers!" We had prayed in faith and thanked the Lord for sending singers to us. Is not faith to be like this in unforeseen conditions?

Praise be to God, He heard our prayers! When we stepped out at 6pm from our house for Carol singing we were 20 people in all. Of the twenty people, five people decided to come at the last hour! The carol singers were Christians, atheists, and people from various nationalities and some from churches of different denominations. We also had a Santa Claus who handed cards to all the houses we visited that evening.

When we started singing carols there was glint in the eyes of most, a glimmer of happiness, excitement and great expectations. Our eyes said it all. The giggling teens, serious elders, and leisurely strolling youths blowing the cold air from their mouth as if they were blowing a cigarette smoke were a treat to the eyes. None of us were now worried about musical notes, flat voices or rhythm. It was just plain singing with zest. We sang Christmas songs. Our subdivision resounded with our voices, resonated with our music instruments, and echoed with our clapping hands. We sang till our throats were hoarse and our hands red from clapping.

We visited about 28 houses and by God's grace people welcomed us heartily. Some of them offered us cakes, sweets and candies. A lady who we did not visit heard us singing at her neighbors' house came out of her house and hollered, "You did a great job." A family was in such in awe with the splendor of the group and our valor that the mother vociferously commented, "You have quite a number of carol singers, and some of you are even wearing colorful costumes as well." An elderly couple was sitting outside in their patio and waiting for us since 6 p.m.!

People could not believe that they were witnessing Christmas Carol singing in their neighborhood and at their doorsteps.

It was nice to see young parents picking their 2-3 years old children up from their beds just to meet the carol singers! The elderly people were overjoyed perhaps, because they were reminded of their youth when they did caroling. For the youth of our subdivision, it was something they had only seen in a movie or TV show, and they too were exhilarated. The cats and dogs of the homeowners were probably surprised to see deer horns on human beings! It was beyond their comprehension and they responded with meowing and barking.

It was quite an eye opener for the teenagers of our church as they were actively participating in singing carols perhaps for the first time. Caroling was over in 90 minutes, and then come carolers came to our house. We thanked our Lord for a good time and enjoyed tea and snacks.

A day after the carol singing, a mother came from our subdivision to our house and thanked us for organizing it. She shared with us how happy her child was when he had received a card from Santa Claus! Praise be to our God for clearing the sky and hearing our prayer. Tripta commented, "It was as if the Lord was saying, you just step out in faith and I will do the rest."

> *Who has the wisdom to count the clouds? Who can tip over water jars of the heavens…?*
> JOB 38:37

The above verse reverberated in my mind. By stretching it a little, I deducted who can withhold rain except God?

As if defrosting the permafrost of psychological and social conditions was not enough, the Lord did one more incredible, stunning and mountain-like faith building incident in our lives. He withheld the rainclouds thus carrying the momentum that he had built forward. He indeed was tracking our faith!

After the Lord had shown to our Home Group, friends, and our neighborhood, that He is the Sovereign Lord who controls everything, including the weather, the Lord spoke again in His own ways declaring

OBEDIENCE IS WHAT THE LORD DESIRES

His Sovereignty in January 2013. Reveling in the grand success of caroling, our Home Group and I were itching to take another quantum leap of faith…probably, our very own great commission in our neighborhood without preaching. The hope was to create a remote possibility of opening doors for communication about our loving God, Jesus Christ.

Yet again, I prayed to our Heavenly Father to seek His blessings and approval regarding the plan. Once again He gave His sanction and blessings. In January 2013, I proposed in our Home Group, "We should have an outreach program in our neighborhood on Resurrection weekend, the theme being 'Resurrection of Jesus Christ'". On the Resurrection day (Easter), Christ was raised from the dead on the third day after his death on the cross.

After long animated deliberations, we came to the conclusion that the Resurrection weekend being a long weekend, people would probably opt to go to camping or other outdoor family activities. Therefore, we decided to celebrate resurrection of Jesus Christ on Saturday, April 6th at 12 noon. Our Home Group decided to have barbecue (BBQ). The members decided to give free hot dogs, potato chips, and cold drinks. We allocated corners for drawing, coloring, and craft for small children, for games, and for music. We also decided to have a short skit on 'Resurrection'. Several members and teens from our church volunteered to co-ordinate with us in 'Resurrection' program.

Discussion started about the 'Resurrection' program in the month of January and continued until the event took place. The exchange of ideas resulted in breaking insulation of our thoughts and streamlining the planning. In one of the meetings in February 2013, one of the Home Group member asked, "What if it rains?" This was a genuine concern because it was rainy season and in all possibilities it could rain. "It is not going to rain," I responded.

Was I confident of the statement which I had made? Yes, I was, because I had addressed this question to our Lord in my 'Relationship Building Time' and He had given me assurance of taking care of the weather.

From this point on we clearly saw the Lord's hand in directing our program. Even before we asked for help, people gave food items, and volunteered their services to support the event. Friends who were connected to businesses got us concessions in food products. We were just in the planning stage and donations started pouring in! Praise be to our God.

Our faith naturally increased more and more with each donation coming in or being promised. We were able to get insurance for 250 people at a cheaper rate and got permission from the Langford Municipality to hold the function in our neighborhood park.

The weather though was still not abating, and wherever we discussed the event people would ask me or Tripta, "What if it rains?" Our stoic answer to all was the same: "It will not rain." We could not let a dent be made in our faith.

The invitations were printed and I went door to door to invite our neighborhood for the function. People in our subdivision were happy with yet one more event in the neighborhood but still the looming question in everybody's mind was, "What if it rains?"

As we entered the middle of March, I started looking into the weather reports in meteorological websites. I found the reports encouraging. Meteorologists predicted - almost no rain and bright sunshine until March end. What else could we ask for? Our spirits were spiraling skywards.

While we were in the last week of March, I studied the weather report of next fifteen days on a website. My jaws dropped, the pupil of my brown eyes broadened and I gulped pockets of air with a loud noise down my throat. The meteorological department in their website showed weather would be intemperate for next 15 days! In disbelief and shock, I checked another website. There was no change in the images: almost no sunshine - rather clouds and rain for next 15 days!

For one whole day my confidence shook and the trajectory of my conviction and faith plummeted from northbound to southbound at a rocketing speed. In my desperation and crisis of faith, I sent e-mails to many believers requesting them to pray for the event, especially good weather without rain! I became more like Peter who instead of focusing on Christ started looking at the tempest and thus was drowning until Christ took his hand as inscribed:

> *Shortly before dawn Jesus went out to them, walking on the lake. When the disciples saw him walking on the lake, they were terrified. "It's a ghost," they said, and cried out in fear. But Jesus immediately said to them: "Take courage! It is I. Don't be afraid." "Lord, if it's you," Peter replied, "tell me to come to you on the water." "Come," he said. Then Peter got down out of the boat, walked on the water and came toward Jesus. But when he saw the wind, he was afraid and, beginning to sink, cried out, "Lord, save me!" Immediately Jesus reached out his hand and caught him. "You of little faith," he said, "why did you doubt?" And when they climbed into the boat, the wind died down. Then those who were in the boat worshiped him, saying, "Truly you are the Son of God."*
> MATTHEW 14: 25- 32

While my certitude started wobbling like a drunkard, I started counting innumerable times when our God had reclaimed the lost ground and uplifted me. I recalled the time when He had stopped precipitation while we were carol singing on 23rd December, 2012. I also started voraciously reading and devouring from the Scriptures about Abraham, Moses, Joshua, David, and a few others. While reading about them I developed respect for the disciples' faith in Yeshua. I tried to inculcate faith by focusing on Christ. My fluctuating faith slowly started finding anchor in our Lord. As my faith wavered less in intensity and frequency I also talked aloud to myself. "The Lord cannot change, He will take us out of this situation that we find ourselves in."

In my solitude, I would go to the Lord frequently to give me assurance and reassurance regarding good weather! The Lord would always be gentle but stood firm: "It will be bright and sunny; also there will be no rain or snow." For sure, there was no flossing of memory required there!

Our Lord however had just one condition. "Walk in obedience and faith and give a testimony about fulfilment of my promises regarding this event." Once He even said, "It will not rain during the event but will rain thereafter and that my protection is there for the event."

On 5th April, the Canadian weather website showed that it would rain, but there might also be sunshine. However, the newspaper weather report still did not show any sunshine. On the same date my friends Sofie and Neil Heinrichs asked, "James, do you have 'Plan B'? Plan 'B' referred to have an alternate plan in case it rained.

"None," I retorted with confidence.

I did not want to forfeit my faith in our Heavenly Father. I believed in the promise of our Lord, therefore I knew it would be a clear day. My motto of the day was, if I could not believe in my Lord and my God, then I could not believe in anything or anyone. While talking to my brother on the phone on 5th April and sharing the newspaper report about rain, he recommended having 'Plan B' ready.' Ashu also sent me an e-mail and suggested, "Be ready with 'Plan B'". To both the above suggestions I responded, "There is no plan B." By now our enthusiastic and vibrant Home Group was confident that the sky would be bright and clear.

On 5th April, around 4 p.m. a day before the event, the moment of reckoning had come. In the evening the sky was heavily overcast and the rain was pounding the man-made and natural landscape. I was standing outside our house in front of the main door with my son Rahul and was praying it would stop. I had the invitations in my hand and knew very well that that was my last chance to cancel the event or postpone it or at least go for 'Plan B'. This way, I could save my face in my neighborhood comprising of about 100 families, people from our church and Home Group. I was now standing on the precipice of my faith. Was I willing to trust God?

I recalled how the Lord had spoken to me about this event and guided me to read:

> *Trust in the LORD with all your heart and lean not on your own understanding; in all your ways submit him, and he will make your paths straight.*
>
> PROVERB 3:5-6

OBEDIENCE IS WHAT THE LORD DESIRES

I remembered the faith of Moses and marveled if any reservations were running through his mind when he was standing in front of the Red Sea with the Israelites and the mighty army of Pharaoh was pursuing them, as mentioned in Exodus 14 in the Bible.

In my turbulent state of mind, the Lord spoke to me:

> *He says, "Be still, and know that I am God; I will be exalted among the nations, I will be exalted in the earth."*
> PSALMS 46:10

I knew that by extension of the above verse, our Lord will be exalted in our neighborhood. With prayers on my trembling lips and anxiety waning, I gave marching orders to myself and my son. "Let's go in the rain and distribute the invitations to our neighbors."

We walked with the invitations in our hands and went for the last time in our neighborhood to remind them that despite the anticipated downpour we were still going ahead with the plan of having a free BBQ the next day. What was possibly going through my son's mind? I did not have an answer to that. What I knew was this could be a key moment of faith building in his life.

It rained all night. While asleep my sub-conscious state of mind was constantly praying to the Lord and imploring to stop the deluge as He had promised me. I was beseeching Him. I recalled Genesis 32 in the Bible where Jacob physically fought with the Lord until dawn. In Victoria, I was pleading with the Lord for a clear sky and reminding Him again and again about His promise to me.

In our neighborhood the rain stopped around 7 a.m. and in some other areas it stopped around 8 a.m. None of the volunteers and Home Group members were sure if the function would be held. In fact, one of the volunteers asked the group leader of the 'Serve Team', "It is 8 a.m., and it is still raining, will the function be held?"

The group leader responded, "We know it is raining, but we are packing our truck and will be leaving soon for the venue."

At 11 a.m. Ashu came to our house for the program and proclaimed, "What other proof do we need about our God's faithfulness?"

He said this because it was just as the Lord had promised: "It will be bright and sunny; also there will be no rain or snow." When the event started, many of us were on tenterhooks as to how the neighbors would respond.

When the BBQ was on and the air was full of the fragrance of fresh barbecued sausages, our neighbors started trickling in and our smiles became brighter and broader. Vic and I were constantly praying in our respective homes and thanking the Lord for the clear sky and keeping His promise. Vic, was praying in his house as he was sick, and could not come to attend the program. I was praising and thanking the Lord at my house for being true to His promise. Later, I joined the event. While I was there, one of our neighbors said, "Aren't you lucky that it did not rain and it is bright and sunny?"

"We had been praying for it," I replied gently. For a believer what has luck got to do with Lord's work? But yes, I loved basking at Lord's work of deliverance from a lose-lose situation.

The event was from noon until 2 p.m. Many people came from our neighborhood to enjoy the fellowship of each other, but some did not come. At about 1:15 p.m., Ashu came to me and while looking at the sky commented, "James, the rain clouds are drifting in." I shrugged my shoulders and smiled.

At 1:45 p.m., we mentioned to the gathering that since we had insurance till 2 p.m. we would now pack up. Whereas our neighbors were enthralled by our initiative of bringing the community together, we were happy because our faith had escalated seeing the redemptive work of our Lord. By the time we cleared the park it was 3 p.m. The 'Serve Team' from our church and many others left. Only a few of us went back to our house to have tea, and to give thanks to our Lord for the wonderful time and for keeping His promise. While we were praising the Lord one of us looked outside the window and commented, "It has started raining again!" The time was 3:15 p.m. It was surreal; the Lord had done it again! The rain continued until the following morning, with one exception this time: I was not supplicating to the Lord in my subconscious state to stop it as I was sound asleep.

Pastor Bob Greene of our church put the following news in the newsletter of our church, which covered the event.

A) Saturday was Amazing!!!
GOD PARTED THE WATERS!!!

A week of rain—19 hours of sun—now a week of rain, because we prayed. When I asked James several weeks ago if they had planned for rain, all he said was; "It won't rain."

Thank you to the Home Group that meets at James' for obedience and grace and hospitality. They organized a neighborhood barbeque, let the whole neighborhood know, and included Jubilee in the event.

What a joy to be the ones who helped build community in this neighborhood. Most people didn't know their neighbors, now they do, they met them while Jubilee, the Serve team and the Roy Home Group cooked hot dogs, supervised play, did craft and connected people with each other.

B) For the encouragement of the neighbourhood event. The Lord, our mighty God stopped rain for 6 hours during the 'Neighbourhood Event'

At a personal level, I learnt a lot from this episode. The crucial one was this: no matter where I was aligned, our God, being who He is - is a gracious, loving and merciful Heavenly Father. He will forgive our sins, shortcomings and deliver us. I conclude this because from somewhere in the middle of January 2013, to April 5, 2013, I had moved slightly away from God. I had become judgmental and the lure of the world was much within me. Yet, my loving Heavenly Father overlooked it all because, He is who He is. He looked in my heart, which was still stubbornly anchored in His Word. My heart still loved Him with all my might, all my strength, and still acknowledged Him as the only truth.

I also learnt it is nice to be on the windward* and not leeward* side of God's blessing and this situational position could be attained by rooting deep in the Word and faith. Later in the week during my evening walks in my neighborhood at times I met my neighbors they often remarked, "Weren't you lucky, it did not rain during the event?"

"That is what we had prayed for," I commented with a beaming and radiant smile.

The Lord had spoken not only to me, my family, our Home Group, our church but also to our neighborhood. We did not have to speak to our neighbors about our Lord. He did that by stopping rain.

As a Home Group we had decided that we would not push our faith on anyone. But God spoke in a very different way to about 100 people who were there. Many more in our neighborhood who heard, saw, and read on Facebook about the 'miracle'-"It will be bright and sunny; also there will be no rain or snow." The initial comments and the photos uploaded on Facebook were from our neighbors and not from the people in the Home Group. Later some of our Home Group people too uploaded some photos to Facebook. I hope the mutation[*] of heart and mind has taken place in the lives of some people. We just walked in faith and obedience.

Isn't obedience to the Lord of paramount importance?

> *Inscribe it in your soul: Metamorphosis in the unbelievers can take place by watching the lives of the believers. Therefore, it becomes imperative for believers to walk upright in the eyes of our Lord.*

CHAPTER TWENTY-ONE:
In God's Rest

~~~~~

Teach me to do your will, for you are my God;...
Psalm 143:10

I called myself "An Almost Atheist" until the age of 46. By that I meant I was 99 % an atheist, and did not acknowledge existence of God. However, somewhere in my memory only 1% of the Biblical bedrock still existed though in a recessive mode.

This Christian foundation was laid by our parents because they saw the hand of God through Jesus Christ in their lives. They had strong Christian doctrines and were deeply entrenched in it. In my youth, I was swayed away from this bedrock, became spiritually dead but was not annihilated by the deceiver. By the blessings and plans of the Lord coupled with blessings and prayers of my parents, I came closer to the Creator. My parents adhered to their role in all seriousness of bringing their children to the Lord. They were not merely biological parents; both believed children were precious gifts, the wealth and trust of the Lord given to them by Him. They managed their responsibiltiy in partnership with the Lord. Every evening before going to bed as a family we spent time together which we fondly called "Relationship Building Time". During this time we read the Bible, sang hymns and prayed together.

Reminiscing about it today, I am sure in their own private prayer time they interceded for us and probably their role model in the Bible was Job. He used to regularly sacrifice a burnt offering to the Lord thinking that perhaps his sons and daughters committed some sin and cursed the Lord (Job 1: 4-5) while engaging with outsiders.

After my parents separated, my siblings and I migrated to Hisar with Ma. She was a strict discplinarian and took us to the Methodist Church every Sunday. When in the church, within few minutes I would leave the service and wander in the church complex and later outside just to be in the market area to do window shopping. While in college, I was discontent and frustated. I did not want to be ridiculed, mocked, or isolated by my fellow students for being a Christian. The worldly, circumstances forced me to become of the world. There was no point spending my youth searching for a kind of life which had promises of the future life at the expense of sacrificing dreams in the present. It was all weird to me. Therefore, I ditched Christianity and became a renegade child. Clearly that was my myopic vision of life.

After graduation from University, I started looking for work. I was not selected as a lecturer in a college despite having the qualifications and merit. Finally, I got a job as a school teacher and also drifted further away from the foundation of Christian doctrines laid by my parents. I stopped being in the company of believers and my close friends were from different faiths. Some were atheist just like in my school and college days. Living in the Hindu country of India, I witnessed the Hindu way of Life. A few of my friends were Sikhs and some were Muslims. Later when selected as a teacher to work in Dubai, I saw the Muslim culture.

Looking at the shadows of my walk in the world, perhaps my parents suspected that I had drifted from the Biblical foundation they had laid. However, my parents did not stop praying for me. They knew very well since the foundation was strong the ship would soon come back to the haven after facing the realities of the ruthless world.

The tug of war between my parent's prayers and my dreams for my future continued for a few decades. I was enticed and lured by the 'Babylonia of the World': a cesspool of power, opulence and greed.

The traps of deceit, flattery, bribes, betrayals, debauchery, treachery, and naked passion entrapped me. The games people played to reach the top echelon of society in a short time. It was all a matter of convenience. Lucifer was ruling under names of different brands or labels. He has not changed his way even in 21st century. The deciever's ways were concealed, and at times salacious crafty designs were luring gullible people like me. He was always seeking pervious and porous minds which were invigilant or ignoraant of the Word or who had no faith in the Lord or did not know the Lord. He wanted to saturate their minds with a maze of appealing treasures of his design that possessed a seducing effect. The accuser wanted them to be redirected to him, to take custody of their soul and become their surrogate guardian. He hoped eventually the bird's soul and spirit would suffocate and die in the designer's golden cage.

Each day the Mammon attracted me. I was more than willing to calibrate my bearings of this world and succeed. This fatal attraction took me further away from the foundation laid by my parents.

My quaint days and years in wilderness came to an end when the Lord in His time, grace and mercy slowly started revealing Himself to me in a series of intriguing ways. It was not the way Christ revealed Himself to Saul (Acts 9) but it was a way. Just one photon of the true Light (Jesus Christ) was enough to illuminate my spiritually dark world and send me scurrying to the archived section of my life and dig out the Bible to know Him. I could not see the complete picture at once but could not ignore the partial picture and revelation of His multifaceted nature any further. These revelations happened over many years. Even when the Lord revealed Himself to me, my science degree and logical thinking dominated and obfuscated my way. My heart had hardened over the years, and my mind was wrestling with these new revelations. But Light was eclipsing darkness because the Lord persisted and His perseverance bore fruit. Slowly, layered mountains of excuses, reasoning by mind, stubborness of heart, and blindness towards the Word denuded and peeled away. Layer by layer it eroded, and I stood naked without any defence.

From this place of nakedness I realised the truth of the futility and irrationality of Mammon ways. Minor and false gods in the form of human hierarchial order in the workplace, government, money, and power had to be removed from the higher podium that I had given to them. It was just a mirage.

When I had hyperthyroidism the fear of death had settled in, though it did not have any medical reasoning. The utter helplessness of just being an observer when my heart palpitation increased made me look towards a hand which could take me out of that situation, a hand I could depend on for the rest of my life. In this state of weakness and despair a stronger hand was required. A hand I found- a strong hand!

The Lord's hand took me out not only from the spiritually deserted ravine I had chosen to but also out of many other desperate situations. I also saw Him working in lives of many other believers. The Lord's hand first promised the deliverance and then delivered me. I realised I could depend on His hand. He was willing to resuscitate me in His own ways and time. How many incidents could I dismiss and deny as quirk of fate or coincidencee? 100? 200? 300? More? Why could I not accept this new data? What was preventing me to give myself unconditionally rather than submitting with terms and conditions written in fine print?

I could no longer take refuge in the policy that 'ignorance is bliss'. I embraced the truth and accepted Christ as my Saviour, my Jehova-Elohay and became His 'Adopted Son'. He took away my ambivalent nature of living in the world of darkness and light and turned the equation from 99 % of a dormant Biblical foundation to 100% active Biblical foundation. He changed me from 'An Almost –Aethist' to 'His Servant'. I was now like a ship which had just left the port when the anchor is pulled-the mighty waters of the ocean gave way and the sea birds flew away. I was free and airborne. This was my resurrection in this life while still alive. My parents exulted, and also my Creator. He became my cornerstone.

Once I repented and submitted to Him without any terms or conditions He was exuberant and rejoiced in my homecoming and to my heritage in Him. With the peace which comes through Him only, I was further convinced I was on the right path by accepting Christ as my

Saviour. The veil now was totally lifted and instead of a partial view I had clear and complete vision.

The bright part was from my state of apostasy I did not bow down to any man-made image or idol but to our Heavenly Father through Jesus Christ, the Messiah. I observed the impromptu ways of the Spirit and the works He cajoled, suggested, directed, goaded, and commanded me to undertake. The Spirit always asked me to open the Bible and never any other Holy Book of any other religion. This was surprising because in today's world every book is available. I could have read any other Holy Book but it never happened. There had to be a reason for that. The reconfirmation, healing, prophesy all were happening at the name of Jesus Christ. The episode of crucifixion (chapter 7) testing of the Spirit (chapter 9), my baptism (chapter 11) convinced me that the Holy Spirit had to be somehow related to Jesus Christ. None of the work was illegal, wrong, immoral or against the Bible.

The transformation into a new life had to be done not by me as it would not penetrate deep within me and therefore would not be permanent. It would bleed when the rain came. It had to be done by the Holy Spirit. I stopped chasing illusions. With the Lord taking over the cleansing of my spirit in me I slowly metamorphosed into a new person and the old died . Now the Lord navigates and supervises so that I do not waste time and energy in cutting the arms of the octopus. They are too many and rejuvenate.

Under the tutelage of the Holy Spirit, I had already started reading the Bible in December 2006. While reading it, I started connecting the miraculous events in my life since late 2006 to the events recorded in the Bible. To my amazement, some miracles in my life and also in the lives of believers I walked with proved to me that the miracles recorded in the Bible were similar, and therefore the Bible was a reflection of the Lord also working in 21st century. I was healed when people prayed for me; the Lord used me to heal people with prayers. Similarly, our Lord used many to heal the sick in the Bible and the Lord Himself healed all diseasess. The Lord used me to prophecy and it came to pass; many prophesied over me and their prophecy too came to pass. In the Bible too people prophesied which stood the test of time. Many other incidents happened in my personal life. The monochromatice[*] photon of light dispersed[*] and I realized there were many colours to it; He was indeed omnipresent, omniscient and omnipotent, Jehova-Elohay, Jehova-Jireh, Jehova-Rapha, Jehova-Shammah, Jehova-El Shaddai, Jehova-Roi, Jehova-Raah in the past and also in the present. After submitting to the Lord my faith was thus buttressed.

I also read foot notes of NIV study Bible and other study Bibles which related historical records about Christ. When the Spirit of the Soverign Lord revealed Himself to me, I could not deny the existence of Christ, the Messiah and through Him our Heavenly Father. During the trip to Israel in 2012 I saw archaeological evidence. The walk of believers and testimonies of many convinced me further. Now there were many rays pointing towards Christ's existence. Each evidence acted as a strong brace for my faith. I was now akin to the sunflower plant always seeking the Light for my spiritual growth and meditating upon it. While in this state, I often envied and admired the apostles for being with Jesus Christ on this earth and any day I would have willingly traded my educational degrees and wordly trappings to be with them.

Today, when time has withered my physical body, my soul and Spirit belong to the Lord-I look back and wonder why I ever sidelined God. There is no satisfactory answer. Possibly because my college friends vocalised their views which were not similar to mine! Or because I could not play sports on the Sabbath I became angry with God ? That would be obnoxious and childish. Yet it happened. This only proved that I was a weakling who was finding a scapegoat for my own bankrupt moral strength. I wanted justice but ignored God.

I am aware that I might fall but I do pray not to fall. Adam knew God well. He used to walk with the Lord daily. Yet Adam fell. It is because I read the Bible, know the Word, and have a relationship with our Heavenly Father through Jesus Christ who interceds for us that I have been able to avoid many camouflaged traps of Satan. When weak, I asked Him for help, and He lovingly extended His hand and took me out of the dark deep jungles like the dense tropical rain forest where I could have been lost.

God's unflinching, unfailing, unending and consuming power of love is there for us even today. The rich of this world do not, in general, share their riches; the powerful people of this planet do not share their power. But our Heanenly Father went much beyond.

> *For God so loved the world that he gave his one and only Son, that whoever believes in him shall not perish but have eternal life.*
> JOHN 3:16

The verse still stands true and will stand true till the end of the world.

It was not infatutation on His part that would last for a little while and then wither away. It was God's love-*AGAPE*. Eternal life is for all only if we are willing to have faith and believe in Jesus. Jesus Christ of Nazareth did not come for a few people; He came for all. God loves us all equally. He rejoices when the lost sheep return. With this love also comes peace which none can give, sell or buy. We do not have to propitiate anything to Him; instead we just repent and acknowledge Christ as our Saviour and Lord by taking His name.

Therefore, I pray to my Heavenly Father, "O Soverign Lord, my God, creator of heaven and earth, who never forgets nor forsakes those who love you, who is merciful, compassionate, gracious, and forgiving, whose love endures for ever, hold the little fingers of our family tight in your palm while we walk with you. I pray that you reveal yourself to my generation, and generations after, people we know, and to people we do not know, that we do not put you in a box and not interpret your Word through our wisdom but from wisdom that comes from you. That we remain humble in your sight. Humble not as people perceive us to be, but as we should be in your sight, not ours. Not to judge people in the quietness of our thoughts during stillness of the night or during our evening walks. I plead with you to teach us your ways, that you give us many opportunities to exalt your name as a river nourishes many plains and we too bring to people the richness of your Word. That you give us wisdom and increase our faith, and that we remain firm in the Word. Also, that we do not consider grace as not earned but as a gift from you.

We not consider your righteousness as ours and take latitude with your mercies and grace and commit sins. That Tripta and I bring our children and grandchildren to you just the way our parents did. We cannot be everywhere, but you are. That we may serve you just as Joshua wanted and said:

> But if….But for me and my household, we will serve the LORD.
> JOSHUA 24:15

And we remain in your rest, Amen.

[*Inscribe it in your soul: Let not the high tide of the mammon snatch or drift us away from our Saviour.*]

Isaiah 66:9

"Do I bring to the moment of birth and not give delivery?" says the LORD.

"Do I close up the womb when I bring to delivery?" says your God.

GLOSSARY

Abaya: A traditionally long black robe or dress which women in UAE wore. In general, Muslim women wear it.

Affordable Housing Program: Since 2004, the City of Langford's Affordable Housing Program has provided families with lower-income housing in Langford's many new housing developments. The affordable houses are priced at 60% of market value. Successful applicants to the program are chosen on a points system, based upon pre-selected criteria.

Bhula: Younger brother in the dialect of the Tarai (Hill) region in Uttarakhand province /state (formerly Uttar Pradesh).

CARE: It is one of the largest poverty-fighting organizations in the world. It provides relief to people hit by disasters and emergencies, and contributes to economic empowerment that strengthens livelihood over the long term, starting with women and girls who are often marginalized and among the world's poorest. It operates in more than 90 countries.

Centrifugal Force: Force which draws the object outwards when it is in circular motion.

Centripetal Force: Force which draws the object inwards when it is in circular motion.

Di: Elder sister in the dialect of the Tarai (Hill) region in Uttarakhand province /state (formerly Uttar Pradesh).

Dish-Dasha: Long white robe .UAE men traditionally wear the dish-dash also referred as dish-dasha.

Dispersion: The separation of light into colors by refraction or diffraction with formation of a spectrum.

Diwali: A Hindu festival. It is celebrated to mark the occasion of god Rama's triumphant return from his battle and victory over an evil giant, Ravana who had abducted Rama's wife, Sita to Sri Lanka. Rama and his army fought a battle against him and succeeded in killing Ravana and in bringing back Sita.

Eid: a) Bakra (Goat) or Eid ul-Zuha or Eid –al –Adha: The Muslims around the world believe that Allah (God) commanded Ibrahim (Abraham) to sacrifice his son Ishmael. Ibrahim followed Allah's orders. At the last moment Allah provided a goat and on his directive Ibrahim replaced his son with the goat and sacrificed it to Allah. Many Muslims wear new clothes and attend an open-air prayer meeting during Eid-ul-Zuha. They may sacrifice a sheep or goat and share the meat with members of their family, neighbors and the poor. In the Bible the incident is the same but instead of Ishamel, it is recorded in the name of Issac.

b) Meethi (Sweet) Eid also called Eid-al-Fitr: The Muslims worldwide observe this as a month of fasting. It is called Ramadan month. The month lasts 29–30 days based on the visual sightings of the crescent moon. Fasting is obligatory for adult Muslims, except those who are suffering from an illness, travelling, pregnant, breast feeding, diabetic or going through menstrual bleeding.

Fruit of the Holy Spirit: Galatians 5: 22-25: Love, peace, forbearance, kindness, goodness, faithfulness, gentleness and self-control....Not conceited, not provoking, not envying.

Gifts of the Holy Spirit: The following are the work of one spirit (1 Corinthians 12:7-10). Message of wisdom, message of knowledge, faith, gifts of healing, miraculous powers, prophecy, distinguishing between spirits, speaking in different kinds of tongues, interpretation of tongues.

HAU: It is now called Chaudhary Charan Singh University

GLOSSARY

Harijans: Also refereed as untouchables, Dalits, Scheduled Caste, Harijan. They were formed the lower most section of Hindu social society. Mahatma Gandhi called untouchables as Harijans- "Children of God". Common work for them was: 1) killing or disposing of dead cattle or working with their hides for a living, (2) pursuing activities that brought the participant into contact with emissions of the human body, such as feces, urine.

Hijab: The head-scarf which covers the neck and part of the head. Worn by Muslim women in UAE and in general by Muslim women all over the world.

Hijri Calendar: It is a lunar calendar. It consists of 12 months of 354 or 355 days. As it is a lunar calendar, there is an annual drift of 10 days, which means that it is not synchronised with the seasons, with the dates being repeated every 33 years.

Holi: Festival of Hindus. It celebrates the victory of good over evil and also the triumph of devotion. It occurs usually towards the end of spring.

Janeu: A sacred thread which is slung diagonally across ones chest and back, from shoulder to waist. It is supported on the left shoulder and wrapped around the body, falling underneath the right arm. This sacred thread is worn by Brahmin (highest caste of the Hindus) males during the thread-ceremony. It is traditionally performed on Hindu boys to mark the point when they begin their formal education. Not all the Hindus in India wear the Janeu.

Keffiyeh: Traditional head scarf worn by UAE men.

Kohinoor Diamond: The Kohinoor is the famous jewel which the British took away illegally (from India's perspective) from India while they were ruling India between 1858 to August 1947. It is still in their possession.

Leeward Side: As the wind blows across a mountain range, air rises and cools and rain clouds can form on the windward side. This is why windward sides of mountain ranges tend to get heavy precipitation. When the air sinks on the leeward side of the mountain range, it is usually much drier and warmer therefore it gets less rain. Therefore, vegetation is different on two sides of mountains.

Ma: Mother

Mahabharata: The battle was between the royal rival cousins: The Kauravas and The Pandavas, their armies and their allies. Just before the Mahabharata was to begin, Arjun of the Pandavas did not want to fight his cousins. It is at this moment Hindu bhagwan (god) Krishan and an ally of the Pandavas gave a sermon to Arjun and reminded him of his duties (Dharam) and work (Karamas) on the land of Kurukshetra – hence the battle of Kurukshetra .This entire message has been written in the Holy Book –the Gita. The fifth century Indian Mathematician, Aryabhatta, calculated the date of the Mahabharat battle to be approximately 3100 B.C. from the planetary positions recorded in the Mahabharat.

Makar Sankranti: A Hindu Festival. Unlike other Hindu festivals which follow the lunar motion; Makar Sankranti follows the movement of the sun. It marks the beginning of the sun's movement from Tropic of Capricorn to Tropic of Cancer. In India, this is the day winter officially ends and spring begins. Crowded rooftops, fun-loving rivalry to outdo each other in kite flying skills and delicious traditional feast of hosts are the hallmarks of the day. The excitement continues even after dark. In some provinces, the nights see the arrival of the illuminated box kites, often in a series strung on one line, to be launched into the sky. Known as 'Tukkals', these kites add a touch of splendor to the dark sky.

Meandering: A meander, in general, is a bend in a river and is formed in the old stage of the river when moving water in a stream erodes the outer

GLOSSARY

banks and widens its valley, and the inner part of the river has less energy and deposits silt. The process is called meandering.

Mirage: An optical illusion caused by atmospheric conditions, especially the appearance of a sheet of water in a desert or on a hot road caused by the refraction of light from the sky by heated air.

Monochromatic: Light of one color. In scientific terms, it means light of a single wavelength.

Mughals: Muslim dynasty of Turkic-Mongol origin that ruled most of northern India from the early 16th to the mid-18th century (1526-1761). After that time it continued to exist as a considerably reduced and increasingly powerless entity until the mid-19th century.

Mutation: A sudden change in the gene.

Navaratri: A Hindu festival. In Navaratri festival, Durga's /Kali Mata's nine forms are worshiped, each in a different day. She is a Hindu goddess and the believers think she is a Creator and Preserver of the entire world. The festival represents victory of good over evil.

Niqab: Worn by women in UAE and in general by Muslim women. It covers the mouth and nose and only leaves the eyes exposed. Alternatively, some women pull their hijab over their faces so no part of their face is visible.

Ox Bow Lake: A U shaped lake formed during the old stage of the river when it is meandering. It is cut off from the main river and therefore is not fed by water from its river.

Pa or Papa: Father.

Pooja: Worship to appease god and seek his blessings.

Protection Money: Money offered to gangs to protect the businessmen and not harm the business and also the property.

Shalwar Kameez: The shalwar are loose pajama like trousers. The legs are wide at the top, and narrow at the ankle. The kameez is a long shirt or tunic, often seen with a Western-style collar or can be collarless. The kameez is generally worn with pajamas.

Windward Side: As the wind blows across a mountain range, air rises and cools and rain clouds can form on the windward side. This is why windward sides of mountain ranges tend to get heavy precipitation. When the air sinks on the leeward side of the mountain range, it is usually much drier and warmer therefore it gets less rain. Therefore, vegetation is different on two sides of mountains.

FOR THE ALBUM

A "Thank You" card from C.S.I. Rehabilitation Centre in Kodaikanal, Tamil Nad-India (chapter19)

Ma and Khrist in Hissar distrubuting food in our neighbourhood. December 2009 (Chapter 19)

People of all faith in Hissar church, India, for Christmas December 2009-(morning) Chapter 16

The crowd is still there at night in Hissar church, India, celebrating Christmas December 2009 (Chapter 16)

Sharing my testimony in the Christmas fair in Hissar, India–December 2009 (Chapter 16)

The church that was burnt by fundamentalist in Kasauli, India; later God used the fundamentalist to rebuild it (Chapter 16)

Celebration of Resurrection of Jesus Christ BBQ party at our sub division (Chapter 20)

Theological College in Uttarakhand, India where I shared my testimonies (Chapter 16)

Rahul and Fazal in Bethlehem where Christ was born (Chapter18)

Place where Christ was Baptised-Jordan (Chapter18)

Golgotha (Skull Hill): Where Christ was crucified-Israel. Tripta, Rahul and I (Chapter18)

Outside Christ's Tomb also called Garden Tomb-Israel. Many believe it could be the garden of Joseph of Arimathea (Chapter18)

NAME: Roy James A AGE: 46 DOB. COMPLETE EXAM DATE: Jan 19, 2009	PHN: CHIEF COMPLAINT: follow up Thyroiditis
PAST MEDICAL HISTORY: 2006 moved here from United Arab Emirates and India. Immigration physical done 2006 diagnosed Hyperlipidemia Hepatitis B vaccine series completed in 2007 High myopia followed by Dr. Jones He is overweight, BMI 26.3 ideal weight 155 lbs. Right inguinal strain WCB 2008 resolved Hyperthyroidism July 2008 reviewed by Dr. Phillips diagnoses Thyroiditis, TSH has returned to base line Anxiety and palpitations improving Impaired glucose homeostasis	**FAMILY HISTORY:** Father still alive hypertension and diabetes age 75 Mother alive with hypertension age 71 Paternal uncles died in there 60's all of them lived in India, 1 had stomach cancer and died age 65 in India He has an uncle with diabetes WORK: Fairway market SMOKING: neg ALCOHOL: neg EXERCISE: currently not active encouraged to start walking ALLERGIES: NIL **MEDICATIONS:** Currently none

REVIEW OF SYSTEM:

1. He had palpitations in the fall October and November was reviewed by Dr. Eby at St. Anthony's clinic, ECG was normal, diagnosis was anxiety. He has had several ECG's done all of which has been normal. He had been treated with Metoprolol for palpitations during his Thyroiditis with improvement however he does not wish to continue on with this at this time. He condition is improving.
2. He has gained 13 lbs in the last month.
3. Recent lab work CBC normal, TSH normal at 5.0, glucose fasting 5.9, GFR 73, Cholesterol 7.02, Triglycerides 20.37, LDL 4.83 cardiac risk calculation 8%. Over all this is low risk.
4. No other new complaints today.

Doctor's Report about hyperthyroidism (Chapter 11)

PHYSICAL EXAM: Roy James A

HT: 5'7   WT: 168 lbs   BP: 110/70   P: 70 regular

BS: 5.3

HEENT: High myopia 9 diopter correction in the right eye 8 diopter in the L otherwise eye exam is unremarkable. Good dentition, neck exam no obvious goiter today.	PELVIS/RECTUM: Prostrate 1+ benign
CHEST: clear	EXTREMITIES: Peripheral pulse present, vibration sense intact
CARDIAC: S1 S2 Normal no murmurs	NEURO: grossly normal
ABDOMEN: soft non tender no masses mild abdominal obesity	SKIN: no worrisome lesions

ASSESSMENT AND PLAN:

1. Mildly over weight
2. Hyperlipidemia with over all low cardiac risk encouraged diet and exercise. Palpitations previously investigated no worrisome cause thought to be related to anxiety.
3. Thyroiditis now resolved follow up lab work in 6 months

SOME IMPORTANT EMAILS

e-mail which I wrote to Warren: (Chapter 18)

Hi,
 sometime now u will be going to see the specialist. We will pray and are praying for u .
 God is going to heal u that is His word, and He keeps his word. I pray that, this is what u will hear (that u have ben healed and your visit to him was futile) from the specialist.

James

e-mail which I wrote to Penny (Chapter 18)

Hi,
 Go in peace knowing that the Lord is with you . Do not ask the Lord for favor's, but go in faith that the Lord has already granted peace to you and is with u today .His promises ends with Yes and Amen and therefore say thanks to the Lord . It is not, "if the Lord is with you who can be against you. "But read this passage as, "The Lord is with you so who can be against you."

James
7:50 a.m.

e-mail which the Jubilee prayer group got from Matthew (Chapter 18)

Dear Jubilee,
 Thank you so much for your prayers (that I covet). I thought that I'd give you an update on my sciatica. Up to last Friday, it was quite debilitating; very painful and very difficult to sleep. On Saturday

morning, I went for a long walk (which helps to pump out the inflammation) and afterwards, I felt extraordinarily well. Between then and Monday, I improved dramatically such that the pain level was reduced by about 90%. So now I sleep nights and am quite ambulatory with just a little numbness in the toes. Having had a few bouts of sciatica in the past, I know that what usually takes two months or longer has happened in three days! So I am very thankful to the Lord for His mercy and healing. I also thank God for all of you and your prayers. May all glory, honour and praise go to our heavenly Father for what He has done for me.

Love in Christ,
Matthew